Homophobia
in the Black Church

Homophobia in the Black Church

How Faith, Politics, and Fear Divide the Black Community

Anthony Stanford

Foreword by Dr. Khalil Gibran Muhammad

 PRAEGER

AN IMPRINT OF ABC-CLIO, LLC
Santa Barbara, California • Denver, Colorado • Oxford, England

Library of Congress Cataloging-in-Publication Data

Stanford, Anthony.
  Homophobia in the Black church : how faith, politics, and fear divide the Black community / Anthony Stanford ; foreword by Dr. Khalil Gibran Muhammad.
      pages cm
  Includes bibliographical references and index.
  ISBN 978–0–313–39868–1 (hardcopy : alk. paper) — ISBN 978–0–313–39869–8 (ebook)
1. African American gays. 2. Homophobia—United States. 3. Gay rights—United States. 4. African American churches. 5. African Americans—Religion. 6. African Americans—Attitudes. 7. Homosexuality—Religious aspects—Christianity. I. Title.
HQ76.3.U5S752   2013
306.76′608996073—dc23   2012049360

ISBN: 978–0–313–39868–1
EISBN: 978–0–313–39869–8

17 16 15 14 13   1 2 3 4 5

This book is also available on the World Wide Web as an eBook.
Visit www.abc-clio.com for details.

Praeger
An Imprint of ABC-CLIO, LLC

ABC-CLIO, LLC
130 Cremona Drive, P.O. Box 1911
Santa Barbara, California 93116-1911

This book is printed on acid-free paper (∞)

Manufactured in the United States of America

*No one knows better the sacrifices made to complete
this book than my family, Felicia, Robert, Christopher, and Lauren.
To all those champions of equality, and to my sister Angel,
who knows that the Ice Man Cometh.*

Contents

Foreword

In one of the most surprising twists of the 2012 presidential race, Vice President Joe Biden announced his unconditional support for same-sex marriage. "I am absolutely comfortable" with it, he told David Gregory of *Meet the Press* on May 6, just days before North Carolina voters passed a state constitution banning all rights for gay couples. This wasn't just a typical Biden gaffe. This was an unscripted game changing moment for President Barack Obama, who had no choice now but to follow Biden's lead. In a tight race where a crucial swing state had just joined 29 other states with constitutional bans and 40 states overall with various prohibitive laws, the president stepped into history by announcing his support for gay marriage. *Newsweek* captured the moment with a cover shot of President Obama, looking contemplative, his eyes toward the heavens and a glowing rainbow halo atop his head. Headline: "The First Gay President."

As gay rights activists hailed President Obama for being the first sitting president to support marriage equality, controversy erupted from the pulpits and broadcast mics of conservative black pastors. Overnight, a man who had been viewed by legions of black ministers as ordained by God to be the second coming of black redemption in the United States—a messiah figure fulfilling Martin Luther King, Jr.'s, dream—was now under attack for threatening to destroy the institution of marriage, the black family, and the legacy of the civil rights movement. Reverend Bill Owens, a leader on the black Religious Right and the founder of the nearly 4,000-strong Coalition of African American Pastors, repudiated the president during a National Press Club appearance in late July. "Mr. President, I'm not going to stand with you," Owens said, "and there are thousands of others across this country that are not going to stand with you with this foolishness." Calling the president "Judas," Owens charged him with betrayal and selling out to gay Hollywood.

In a nation where black Christians all sing from the same hymnbook on the set of a Tyler Perry play or T. D. Jakes movie and vote for black candidates only because they are "black," the marriage equality debate throws in sharp relief how diverse blacks really are in post–civil rights America—for better or for worse.

Where did the vitriol come from? How deeply rooted and widespread is homophobia among black Christians and African Americans writ large? With same-sex marriage, are white evangelicals and black Christian conservatives becoming one and the same? For some African Americans, has sexuality replaced the color line as the defining problem of the twenty-first century? Will the much-touted Rainbow Coalition of African Americans, Latinos, Asians, single white women, young voters, and gay rights activists—who reelected President Obama—dissolve behind the dark clouds of a postracial, antigay backlash? And who is responsible for the rising rates of suicide among young black LGBTs? Or the tragic violence directed at them?

In *Homophobia in the Black Church*, journalist Anthony Stanford answers these questions and many more. He peels back the thick layers of bigotry among black Christian conservatives, revealing how today they define King's beloved community "For Straights Only." What happened in the 2012 marriage equality debate was not just high stakes electoral politics. It was also high stakes sexual politics tied to deep commitments to forms of religious fundamentalism among black preachers.

Black churches have long been sanctuaries from the demons of racism and white supremacy, and have often been critical sites of resistance and radicalism that have given birth to black liberation theology and black freedom movements. But as *Homophobia in the Black Church* makes clear, they have also been spaces of discrimination, stigma, and shame. "In a society where African Americans have been victims of racial oppression, it is difficult for many of the same people to be self-critical and view themselves as victimizers, treating others in ways that they deemed oppressive to themselves," writes Stanford.

Family values defined by patriarchy, heterosexual norms, woman-as-helpmate, and hypernotions of black masculinity embodied in the figure of the virulent black male pastor—the symbolic race man—are nothing new to black churches.

What is new, according to Stanford, is the insidious impact of money and the Religious Right's attack on abortion and LGBT rights. Through President George W. Bush's faith-based initiatives, surrogates of the Christian Right courted the most conservative, Bible-thumping, homophobic black ministers with millions of dollars in social service grants. Many of these pastors led congregations of the black working poor. These were communities in desperate need of support to address poverty, hunger, early childhood education, counseling and a range of other social problems. Whereas an unstated policy of "don't ask, don't tell" had shaped the culture of many black churches for decades, everything changed with the coupling of social service grants to political mobilization against gay rights.

Homophobia in the Black Church details how as the money flowed in, antigay pastors of the prosperity gospel such as Creflo Dollar and Bishop Eddie Long intensified their advocacy against LGBT saints. Long, a supporter of President Bush who was later accused of multiple counts of sexual abuse by several young men in his congregation, received a $1 million grant from the U.S. Administration for Children and Families. Although billions of federal funds were distributed to churches with ties to the Religious Right and the Republican Party, black churches received only a small fraction. There was also notable dissent among well-known progressive black ministers. Reverend Jeremiah Wright, pastor emeritus of Trinity Church in Chicago, was a vocal opponent of antigay movements under Bush.

Still, recent surveys of black attitudes toward same-sex marriage are trending in the wrong direction, with evidence of sustained intolerance. Will Reverend Bill Owens and the Coalition of African American Pastors find renewed favor in the Republican Party in time for the next presidential election? Will the 2012 Rainbow Coalition hold when a majority of Americans still oppose universal gay rights? *Homophobia in the Black Church* argues that if change is to be truly embraced by African Americans in general and black Christians in particular, it must first start in the churches. The legacy of the civil rights movement demands nothing less.

Dr. Khalil Gibran Muhammad
Director of the Schomburg Center for Research in Black Culture
New York, New York

Introduction

As governor of Texas, George Bush gained a heap of experience learning the pros and cons of using taxpayer dollars in secular and spiritual endeavors. It also didn't hurt that the openly religious Bush remained true to his political base by first promising to alter and then radically changing the way that religious organizations and government interact. Bush's motivation and commitment were steadfast, and were attributes that his supporters and political foes saw as confirmation of his strong personal faith. As a presidential candidate, George W. Bush had made faith-based funding a key feature in his domestic policy. It was something that Bush said would level the playing field for faith-based providers, making it easier for them to compete for federal funding on an equitable basis with others.

However, political adversaries of the newly elected president's faith-based program alleged that there was a political strategy at play, which prompted a groundswell of controversy. Faith-based initiative opponents from the left and right claimed that the Republican Party (GOP) and Christian Conservatives were using the federal funding to target African American churches, ministers, and religious organizations. They alleged that the GOP was willing to do this to gain black voter support and a foothold in the Black Church. Some faith-based funding antagonists were adamant when leveling this powerful charge that struck some as very credible.

From the start, similar accusations had been made by challengers of Bush's domestic agenda, preventing bipartisan support for the president's key domestic plan. Opponents were gaining momentum by asserting that the creation of the White House Office of Faith-Based and Community Initiatives (OFBCI)—and plans to drastically change the relationship between the federal government, churches, and other religious organizations—might compromise the separation of church and state. They bolstered their position by saying that faith-based initiatives would likely erode established safeguards aimed at preventing a blurring of the line.[1] By putting the Constitution in play, faith-based foes were able to slow support for the recently elected president's domestic plan. However, in the end, the expansion and sweeping reforms related to federal funding for religious and charitable organizations would eventually prevail under the Bush administration.

Whatever Bush's motivations were, it turns out that faith-based initiatives were a mix of good and bad that garnered strong support and stout opposition from their inception. Yet over a decade later, the lasting effects of Bush-era faith-based initiatives on the lesbian, gay, bisexual and transgender (LGBT) community are not entirely known. There is however, convincing proof that faith-based competition and a dependency on federal funding may have exacerbated an already strained relationship between the black LGBT community and the traditional Black Church. It's also possible that those who opposed Bush's domestic philosophy, believing that it had a quid pro quo feel that favored the conservatism of people like Grover Norquist, Karl Rove, John Dilulio, and evangelical conservatives—all architects of faith-based initiatives—were likely onto something.

FAITH-BASED INITIATIVES AND THE BUSH ADMINISTRATION

It turns out that speculation about federal funding and the tax-exemption status of churches and other religious organizations was on the mind of Iowa Republican senator Charles E. Grassley (R-IA). Senator Grassley, a devout Baptist, announced in 2007 that his office would look into the spending practices of some of the nation's wealthiest megachurch ministers. Grassley was particularly interested in the so-called Prosperity Preachers, who use a prosperity theology focused on the premise that God provides material wealth for those he favors. Among those investigated were two prominent members of the black clergy, one of whom had been a recipient of faith-based federal funding during the Bush administration. A black megachurch minister from Atlanta, Bishop Eddie Long, captured Senator Grassley's attention. Bishop Long had also caught the attention of the Southern Poverty Law Center, which named him "One of the most homophobic black ministers in America."[2]

Bishop Long is one of the Bible-toting black religious extremists whose fierce inflammatory rhetoric against black LGBTs is well documented and central to an increasingly intolerant homophobic black culture. So it is not surprising that Long, along with other black ministers who espouse hateful preaching against black LGBTs, was one of the earliest supporters and recipients of Bush-era faith-based funding. It is also what prompted some to believe that the competition for faith-based funding, and the expectation of ongoing federal financial support, had helped to encourage a campaign of animosity against black Christian LGBTs. The possibility that faith-based funding had facilitated and amplified discrimination against black homosexuals, by an already unsympathetic black community, seems entirely plausible.

Homophobia in the Black Church lays bare the long drawn-out struggle between the Black Church and black Christian LGBTs. It lifts the veil on the secretive and vicious homophobic black culture that punishes and exiles many black homosexuals to live their lives in the shadows. Going further, it examines the ways that black Christian LGBTs, who are often already victims of their families and communities, are scorned by black religious leaders and made to suffer what is tantamount to a social crucifixion that some believe was amplified by competition for federal funding.

The consequential discussion about the legislative maneuvering that made it possible to fund openly religious organizations in a whole new way is necessary. However, great care was taken when writing this book to avoid a wonkish and technical reporting of the political gamesmanship involved in fulfilling President's George W. Bush's commitment to compassionate conservatism. Members of the black clergy who publicly proselytize against the LGBT community are identified in this book to show how the exploitation of the Black Church by Christian evangelical conservatives was instrumental in subverting the Black Church and promoting the ideology of Christian evangelical conservatism. Now, over a decade since the dawning of Bush-era faith-based initiatives, and as "Don't ask, don't tell" (DADT) has been rescinded, it seems an appropriate time to discuss the predilection to homophobia and longing of some black clergy to feed at the trough of federal funding. It's also a fitting opportunity to reveal how they were handily co-opted and used by GOP conservatives and religious extremists to create a nightmarish state of affairs for black LGBTs.

Advancement of the key domestic agenda of the Bush presidency represents the fulfillment of a promise made by candidate Bush to the conservative wing of the Republican Party and Religious Right. By putting into practice faith-based programs that were aimed at resolving the country's social problems, the newly elected president's viewpoint of compassionate conservatism would be realized. In furtherance of this, Bush's action to establish the OFBCI, coming only nine days after his swearing in, was seen as proof of his allegiance to the most conservative wing of the Republican Party and Christian Coalition loyalists. To evangelicals, family-values supporters, and Christian Conservatives like Ralph Reed, the former executive director of the Christian Coalition, the president's campaign of compassionate conservatism had gone from a presidential hopeful's political vision to a reality that was coming to fruition in the Bush White House.

It was an enormous step in that the president had fulfilled a campaign promise to go forward with a national agenda that was in harmony with that of key supporters who had boosted his candidacy among Christian Conservatives and party traditionalists. However, a number of things prevented the smooth ratification of the president's plan, among them vocal opponents of the domestic agenda who contested its legality. Organizations like Americans United for Separation of Church and State, and the American Civil Liberties Union (ACLU), resisted the advancement of H.R. 7, known as the Community Solutions Act of 2001, on the basis that it violated the First Amendment. They and others raised concerns about the increased possibility of religious and sexual discrimination that faith-based programs proposed by the president might present. The authorization of the Republican domestic plan ultimately came down to Bush's use of his presidential executive powers to initiate an historic transformation in the way that churches and other religious organizations would be treated by the federal government and Bush White House.

Black political leaders and clergy had either not yet recognized the possibility for increased intraracial discrimination that the Bush domestic programs presented for black LGBTs, or chose not to speak out. Prominent leaders like the Reverend Jesse L. Jackson, for example, seemed preoccupied with the idea that the Bush administration was conspiring to exclude him, and other black leaders, from planning and policymaking related to faith-based initiatives. Reverend Jackson said, "I know the subplot: This is an attempt to play one group against the other."[3]

Elsewhere, the political squabbling that was expected following proposal of the president's domestic agenda came to pass. However, its duration and intensity were not entirely anticipated. In fact, someone unfamiliar with the practice of the federal government funding religious-based organizations might have assumed that it had never been done before. However, federal funding of religious-based organizations has in one form or another existed for years. For example, the Salvation Army has been a recipient of federal funding since the nation's creation.

There were a series of fits and starts, some prompted by growing opposition to the president's domestic agenda and others unrelated, for example, the nation's shifted focus in the aftermath of the September 11, 2001, terrorist attacks. One objection that hindered implementation was launched by the ACLU, which implied that faith-based funding was likely to cause discrimination based on religion. Others protested, saying that faith-based initiatives programs were a violation of the separation between church and state. Eventually, President Bush took steps to unilaterally put his agenda into action with two executive orders that addressed faith-based funding on December 12, 2002. Bush's Executive Order 13280 created two additional executive departments to augment the five agencies already participating in the administration of faith-based initiative programs. But it was the issuance of Executive Order 13279, which required equal protection for faith-based and community organizations, that triggered immediate controversy.[4]

It was this controversy, in part, that compelled me to contemplate writing a book about homophobia in the Black Church. However, it was also a need to understand the reasons for widespread homophobia in the black community, and what (if any) role politics, faith-based funding, and religious extremism played in growing homophobic attitudes in black culture. My yearning to understand the rampant homophobia mindset would eventually include a personal challenge to overcome the foreboding feeling that by exploring these questions, I was doing something wrong, even violating a code of cultural ethics. In time, I'd come to understand that this feeling of telling tales out of school that I somehow instinctively felt was shared by other African Americans.

It was the troubling intuitive feeling that bothered me most and caused me to question why I or anyone should feel guilty for wanting to explore an issue so important to the black community. In fact, the more I thought about it, the more a sense of obligation developed to understand why the subject of homosexuality prompted such a visceral reaction in the black community. It also contributed to a need to know if federal faith-based funding had been employed by the Bush administration and religious extremists with the intended purpose of taking advantage of a homophobic black community to advance a campaign against gays and same-sex marriage. To my way of thinking, this was central to understanding what had occurred during the Bush era, and whether faith-based initiatives had enticed black ministers, bringing them under the control of GOP conservatives and religious extremists.

When I announced a sabbatical from my newspaper column to write this book, word spread quickly that the subject of the book was homophobia in the Black Church. In the beginning, I thought it was just my imagination and even conceded the possibility that I had become a bit paranoid. However, over time, I concluded that the discernible change in the way some people interacted with me was real. Some would, for example, ask, "What makes you want to write about that?" They would then sarcastically add, "Why do you want to open that can of worms?" These and other instances made me feel that not only were my motivations being questioned, but my own sexual identification. Several members of traditional black congregations, whose approach bordered on confrontational, asked, "Just who and what do you intend to write about?" Undeterred, my interest was stimulated and in a way, such encounters became the impetus for understanding and enlightening others about the paralyzing homophobia that exists within black culture. However, as an African American Catholic, I was exceedingly aware that my own religion had failed miserably on every level to deal with homosexuality. As a Catholic, I had been embarrassed by the scandal and cover-up of pedophilia that had been permitted to continue for years inside the American Catholic Church. I confess that my critique of the harsh preaching toward black LGBTs that was springing from the pulpit of some black churches made me feel like a hypocrite. I could also understand how it opened me to criticism as an intruder. Yet I felt that this was no reason to negate or diminish the need for answers related to the Black Church and the powerful homophobic position taken by many blacks. Or my desire to know if religious and political conservatism had been influential in ramping up antigay sentiment and opposition to same-sex marriage in the black community.

A variety of sources, including black LGBTs who were raised in the traditional Black Church, would eventually share their personal experiences, helping me to understand what I had not previously comprehended. As a result, I came to appreciate the awesome power wielded by the Black Church and to see more clearly the role it played in shaping the black cultural perspective toward homosexuality. Through this exploration, the reasons that black LGBTs were being ostracized by their own families, friends, and faith community were less ambiguous. It was not difficult to see that the maltreatment of black Christian LGBTs by some black ministers was and continues to be central to the deepening divide, and a contributing factor to the breakdown of an already fragile black family structure.

When working on a story related to the sudden spike in suicides among young LGBTs, I reached out to members of the black clergy. In doing so, I naively admitted that my knowledge about the virulent homophobia within the Black Church was limited. I was shocked by some of their responses. In retrospect, should I have surmised that since homosexuality is considered culturally taboo by the black community, the same viewpoint would be shared by black clergy? Maybe. Yet it is clear that blacks have not dealt with the issue of homosexuality very effectively. Though difficult for the black community to accept, the reality is that the contagious scorn and repudiation toward homosexuals emanates from the community's cornerstone, the Black Church. This highlights an enormous failure, and as if to corroborate this exceptionally disheartening observation, the response I received when reaching out to members of the black clergy was mostly venomous, condemnatory, and disturbing. In almost every instance, it seemed the clergy member was attempting to justify the unfair treatment of homosexuals by using biblical scripture to support the abuse. Of course, I realize that this is not the genesis of the problem, nor does it reflect the position of the entirety of black ministers. However, it is difficult to refute that this continues to be the position taken by many black ministers. As difficult as this is to accept, what most affects me well over a century since the end of slavery is the extent to which the stain of human bondage continues to affect the collective psyche of blacks. This is an essential point because to comprehend slavery's lasting legacy, it is necessary to understand its pathology and diabolical genius.

The subject of the attitude of blacks as it relates to homosexuality prompted me to think about something that had not entered my mind for many years. It came from what some might consider an odd source, and some might even wonder what this person could possibly have to do with the subject of homophobia in the Black Church. However, as it turns out, the celebrated U.S. humorist Richard Pryor, who had a lot to say about many subjects, made a pointed observation about the importance of masculinity in the black community. It was during the 1970s, when people were more familiar with the sometime vulgar and profane comedian from Peoria, Illinois, for his talent as a standup comic. The masses didn't yet think about this very funny man as someone with a social conscience and an interminable connection to the black diaspora. Yet Pryor helped blacks to better understand themselves, the origin of social ills that affect their community, and the insidious impact that racism has on their lives. However, Pryor would go on to receive the inaugural Kennedy Center Mark Twain Prize in 1998.[5] When the country finally realized his exceptional awareness of race and politics, and Pryor's distinctive ability to translate for mainstream America the essence of the black experience, his persona was transformed. Pryor achieved this remarkable feat by using humor to talk about the strained relationship between blacks and whites. For example, he would explain how it was possible that more than a century since the end of slavery, blacks still perceived themselves as struggling under a racist society.

Race, war, politics, and yes, black sexuality, were Pryor's areas of expertise. He used his standup routine to skillfully illustrate nuances of the black experience. What Pryor was doing was creating an opportunity for dialogue. One way he accomplished this was by mastering the black cultural tradition of talking or joking about another person or a person's family members. In black culture, this is known as playing the dozen, or signifying. Pryor frequently used this comedic technique to discuss sensitive issues like race relations and cultural differences between whites and blacks. In time, it became Pryor's trademark and a basis of his celebrity. Unfortunately, Pryor's astute observations were never fully acknowledged or seen for their potential to dissect America's race problem.

More than three decades ago, during a comedy routine dealing with race, Pryor offered the audience what he described as the most important question ever debated by white people. Speaking in the exaggerated vernacular of a white man as only Pryor could, he posed a question whose answer he inferred was of the utmost importance to the entire Caucasian race. Referring to the way that some black men hold their crotches, similar to the way pop star Michael Jackson did, Pryor said this: "White people go: 'Why you guys hold your things?' to which a black man responds, 'Cause you done took everything else . . .' "[6] Pryor's comedic genius is a double entendre that strikes at the core of the homophobic mind-set that is common in black communities throughout the United States. Pryor's observation comes as close to describing the pathology and neurosis toward homosexuality that has plagued the black community for generations. Pryor's insight begs the question: Had he identified the source of black homophobia, yet not fully connected it to the homophobic psychosis permeating black culture? It certainly sounds like an extremely acceptable conclusion.

There is no doubt that Pryor linked the fact that some whites are paralyzed with fear of the stereotypical sexual prowess of the black male, who has been since slavery considered dangerous and at the center of America's racial discord. It is too bad that Pryor's profound observation regarding the importance of masculinity in black culture was not seriously analyzed by sociologists and scholars, or regarded as a revelation by blacks, helping them to understand the genesis of the pervasive homophobia that has for generations consumed black culture. It's impossible to know what effect, if any, Pryor's observations would have had on the black community's stance toward homosexuality if they had been taken seriously. However, it seems that if nothing else, they would have opened a dialogue that may have had some effect on the strident homophobic attitudes that continue to prevail throughout black culture.

There is no doubt that Pryor opened wide the door for blacks and whites to engage in a meaningful discussion. However, neither was ready or willing for the kind of race relations that would force them to deal with the issue that is central to the relationship between blacks and whites, as was pointed out by Pryor. As a result, not much has been done to preclude the spread of homophobia or the tormenting of black LGBTs. The consequence has been an unremitting wrath that black homosexuals have had to endure. As scapegoats, they are routinely humiliated in their communities and churches, and bear the brunt for our failure to confront the problem head on. Already primed and with little standing in the way, it now seems inevitable that some black ministers would participate in a united campaign initiated by religious extremists against LGBTs and their fight for equality. By the time George W. Bush took the presidential oath and the era of faith-based initiatives began, some black religious leaders could be counted on to support not only the newly elected president's domestic agenda, but a crusade against homosexuals and same-sex marriage spearheaded by evangelical Christians.

The theory that the Black Church and religious organizations were used during the Bush administration to carry out a campaign against homosexuality and same-sex marriage is partly demonstrated by the unconventional relationship that formed between white evangelical Christians and some black clergy. It appears conceivable that the lure of faith-based funding contributed to forming these uncommon relationships and as a result significantly affected the stance of some black ministers.

In retrospect, the likelihood of increased discrimination now seems inevitable, especially given the dire financial position of many Black Churches during the Bush era. The desperate need for funding to battle a host of social ills plaguing the black community was instrumental in opening the door to religious extremism. Given the intense effort of the Christian Right to defeat LGBT advocates who were fighting for equality, expansion of antigay forces to include black clergy may have become a logical necessity. Not only that, but by including powerful black megachuch ministers, resistance to gay rights could be propagated by a formidable multiracial religious and political front. What better way to capitalize on the divide between the Black Church and the black LGBT community than by making federal funding available, while at the same time mounting a united force against gay rights?

With little to prevent it, or to alter the course of events, some black ministers were willing to deliver their congregations to the evangelical effort against homosexuals and advocates of same-sex marriage. Not only was this devastating for the Black Church, it was also a crushing blow for black Christian LGBTs who were caught up in a religious and political struggle to which they had no recourse or real means of defense.

January 29, 2001, when the Executive Order establishing the White House Office of Faith-Based and Community Initiatives (OFBCI) was signed by President Bush, began the formal rollout of his key domestic policy. A blitz to get faith-based initiatives was underway. It was also the start of a financially driven and intensified intraracial bias carried out by members of the black clergy against members of the black LGBT community, something that might have been unfathomable, even to Richard Pryor.[7]

In the chapters that follow, the likelihood that faith-based funding was used by right wing conservatives and the Religious Right to advance their political and moral agenda are explored. In addition, the connection between federal funding funneled through the White House OFBCI and an increase in proselytizing against black LGBTs by black clergy is looked at. Answering the crucial question related to whether President Bush's faith-based "armies of compassion" under the control of the Republican Right and heavily armed with federal funding were inducements and used to encourage participation in an escalation of retribution against the black LGBT community is also explored.

NOTES

1. http://www.in.gov/ofbci/. Accessed May 1, 2010.

2. Southern Poverty Law Center, "Face Right," *Intelligence Report*, Spring, 2007, 24.

3. Jo Renee Formicola, Mary C. Segers, and Paul J. Weber, *The Good the Bad and the Ugly: Faith-Based Initiatives and the Bush Administration* (Lanham, MD: Rowman & Littlefield Publishers, 2003).

4. Union, Because Freedom Can't Protect Itself, 2001.

5. http://www.kennedy-center.org/programs/specialevents/marktwain/. Accessed May 1, 2010.

6. http://www.brown.edu/Departments/MCM/people/cokes/Pryor.html. Accessed May 1, 2010.

7. Refers to Executive Orders 13198 and 13199, which established the White House Office of Faith-Based and Community Initiatives (OFBCI) and delineated responsibility to the federal agencies to carry out specific actions.

ONE

The Faith-Based Solution

But we know that the law is good, if a man uses it lawfully.[1]

It is likely that the impact of President George W. Bush's domestic programs will be studied by scholars and social scientists for years to come. The fact that President Bush's successor, Barack Obama, the nation's first black president, continued and even expanded the Bush-era Faith-Based Initiative program that provides federal social service dollars to churches and religiously based organizations guarantees that the debate over the controversial program will continue into the foreseeable future is certain.

This comes as no surprise when one bears in mind that the perception of governmental action often differs from one segment of society to another, and that programs and policies frequently accommodate certain groups, resolve specific problems, and achieve a particular result. That said, to conclude that Bush's faith-based initiatives did not serve a need and produce positive results would appear a difficult position to defend. It is similarly hard to refute that clergy, churchgoers, religious organizations, and members of the lesbian, gay, bisexual and transgender (LGBT) community may have been pawns and victims of discrimination as a result of what were believed to be a well-intended Bush domestic policy. However, David Kuo, who was a high-ranking member in Bush's Office of Faith-Based Initiatives (OFBI) from 2001 to 2003, after leaving his post revealed that the faith-based initiatives were mostly used to garner political support with both evangelical Christians and traditionally Democratic minorities. "Kuo alleges that then–White House political affairs director

Ken Mehlman knowingly participated in a scheme to use the office, and taxpayer funds, to mount ostensibly 'nonpartisan' events that were, in reality, designed with the intent of mobilizing religious voters in 20 targeted races."[2]

The larger question, of course, is whether Bush's "compassionate conservative" philosophy was effective and is best measured by the churches, religious and social organizations, and people served. At issue here is whether Bush-era domestic policies, specifically faith-based initiatives, produced adverse consequences for specific segments of U.S. society.

This book examines that question on two fronts: (1) Did Christian evangelical fundamentalists use their political might to influence the Bush White House, to entice black ministers to support their domestic agenda focused on family values, in order to defeat gay marriage and ultimately encourage a climate of discrimination against black LGBT Christians? (2) and Did the Republican Right use federal funding to boost voter support among blacks?

Few dispute that the politically and religiously charged environment that existed during the last decade spurred a heated debate, widening the divide between proponents and opponents of LGBT rights. Same-sex marriage, the U.S. military's "Don't ask, don't tell" policy, and a host of related moral issues contributed to the colossal societal chasm that frequently breaks along party lines.

It also appears obvious over a decade since Bush's domestic agenda was implemented that if not for its potential to spawn intraracial, sexual, and religious discrimination, the Bush-era domestic programs had the potential to serve some of the needs of low-income minority communities. However, it is not yet entirely clear what effect Bush's faith-based initiatives have had on the center of the black community, the Black Church.

Ironically, as faith-based initiatives were moving into areas targeted for social reform, soaring hateful rhetoric from the evangelical Christian Right was reaching a fever pitch. The extremist views espoused by some white clerics like Reverend Louis Sheldon, founder of the Traditional Values Coalition were also advocated by some black clerics who identified with the fire and brimstone method of shaming members of the LGBT community. Sheldon and his organization were praised by former U.S. attorney general John Ashcroft, who touted organizations like Sheldon's saying, "A strong voice of the traditional values that have been the foundation of America's greatness is essential if we are to have good government policy. We need to have these values expressed and no organization does that better in Congress than Traditional Values Coalition."[3]

The outspoken Sheldon's feelings about homosexuals are clear from statements he has made, for example, "As Christians, we view homosexuality not only as an unhealthy lifestyle, but the Bible views homosexuality as a sinful behavior." Sheldon even once suggested that people with AIDS be quarantined like lepers.[4] And further:

> As Homosexuals continue to make inroads into public schools, more children will be molested and indoctrinated into the world of homosexuality. Many of them will die in that world. ... Americans should understand that their attitudes about homosexuality have been deliberately and deceitfully changed by a masterful propaganda/marketing campaign that rivals that of Adolph Hitler. In fact, many of the strategies used by homosexuals to bring about cultural change in America are taken from Hitler's writings and propaganda welfare manuals.[5]

Was it the construct of Bush's faith-based funding, the climate of extreme religion and politics, and the need for federal funding that exacerbated the relationship between the Black Church and black Christian LGBTs? Or was the already tenuous environment primed to explode with intraracial discrimination and repudiation against black LGBTs? It is not possible to answer this question without an understanding of Bush's ideology and devotion to his faith. Here and throughout this book, an attempt is made to do so. Going back to Bush's days as Texas governor and specifically, the now legendary meeting between Bush and evangelist Billy Graham over a quarter of a century ago is a good place to start. Bush, who is known for his remarkable redemptive potential, has said that after the meeting with the illustrious Graham, devotion to his faith became more focused:

> I also recognize that a walk is a walk, I mean, it's a never-ending journey. And I've got a lot of imperfections like anybody else. And the more I got into the Bible, the more that admonition "Don't try to take a speck out of your neighbor's eye when you've got a log in your own" becomes more and more true, particularly for those of us in public life. And so my style, my focus and many of the issues that I talk about, you know are reinforced by my religion.[6]

However, to say that Bush's refocused faith was the sole reason for his action to broaden the government's role in funding opportunities for faith-based organizations is purely speculative and highly unlikely. It is far more likely that the presidential Executive Orders—official documents, numbered consecutively, by which the president of the United States manages the operations of the federal government,issued by Bush and key to the expansion of procedures for allocating federal funding—were instead influenced by a number of factors, including politics. To detractors and political adversaries, Bush's perspective and plan conflicted with the Constitution's First Amendment as it relates to the separation between church and state, which says, "Congress shall make no law respecting an establishment of religion, or prohibiting the free exercise thereof; or abridging the freedom of speech, or of the press; or the right of the people peaceably to assemble, and to petition the Government for a redress of grievances."[7] Based on what they viewed as a violation of the First Amendment, opponents of faith-based funding launched a vigorous challenge of the president's plan, which became the impetus for the obstruction that prevented bipartisan support for Bush's domestic agenda.

Try to envision what the strategy sessions must have been like during Bush's 2000 campaign. Imagine the contemplation and coordination that went into integrating Bush's conservative position and strong religious beliefs to satisfy GOP traditionalists and religious fundamentalists, all while avoiding alienating the rest of the country. Such a feat seems unattainable. But was accomplished by cleverly sidestepping and combining Bush's well-known religious ideology and political vision into a domestic strategy that spoke to the average person. It was still an arduous challenge, especially Bush's plan to revamp the way religious organizations receive and use federal funding, something that had been a longtime Bush concern.

Looking back to Bush's time as Texas governor, the Texas Penal Code in effect during his tenure, and the relentless charge he led to deregulate faith-based initiatives and oppose efforts to repeal the criminal prohibition on "homosexual conduct" clearly signaled the strength of his conviction to conservatism. For example, on the issue of homosexuality, the Texas Penal Code was clear, stating:

HOMOSEXUAL CONDUCT. (a) A person commits an offense if he engages in deviate sexual intercourse with another individual of the same sex. (b) An offense under this section is a Class C misdemeanor.
. . .

PUBLIC LEWDNESS. (a) A person commits an offense if he knowingly engages in any of the following acts in a public place or, if not in a public place, he is reckless about whether another is present who will be offended or alarmed by his: (1) act of sexual intercourse; (2) act of deviate sexual intercourse; (3) act of sexual contact; or

(4) act involving contact between the person's mouth or genitals and the anus or genitals of an animal or fowl.[8]

While Bush professed tolerance for gays, his views related to homosexuality remained consistent during the 2000 presidential campaign; if anyone doubted his position on the issue of homosexuality, it was confirmed when he was unwavering by not supporting gay rights.[9] Once he won the presidency, Bush wanted to do what he had done in Texas and give religious groups that delivered social services and received federal grants the right to display religious symbols, scripture, and icons. While this may not sound like a big deal, the notion of allowing churches and religious organizations the openness that was central to Bush's domestic strategy was met with stiff opposition and came precariously close to running afoul of the Constitution's First Amendment by crossing the line of demarcation between church and state.

Bush also ran the risk of igniting a political firestorm and increasing trepidation among an emerging gaggle of antagonists indifferent to his ambitious domestic agenda. Bush believed that the restrictions placed on churches and faith-based organizations that receive federal funding were onerous. Since his days as Texas governor, Bush had believed that religious organizations were better-suited and more capable than government of delivering social services to communities and individuals in need. As it turns out, Bush's logic proved difficult to counter, especially considering the experience and skills that organizations like the Salvation Army had acquired from their many years of serving low-income and minority communities.

Under Bush, The Lone Star State had gained a reputation as a frontrunner in developing effective faith community partnerships. Governor Bush had used the charitable choice provisions of the 1996 Welfare Reform Act to allow churches and religious organizations to compete for government contracts to deliver social services,[10] The 1996 Temporary Assistance for Needy Families (TANF) legislation replaced Aid to Families with Dependent Children (AFDC) and brought to an end entitlement to federal assistance. TANF gave Bush an opportunity to appoint the Faith-Based Task Force, which he wisely used to pinpoint barriers to faith-based groups.[11] Bush went further, doing something that had not been done on a state level. He asked the task force to recommend ways that Texas could create an environment in which faith-based groups could succeed and in which regulations did not lessen their faith mission. The task force was comprised of 16 clergy and volunteers from across Texas and submitted its recommendations in a report titled "Faith in Action" to Governor Bush on December 17, 1996.

Some might conclude that it is nothing more than a coincidence that Bush's inner circle of advisors when he was a presidential candidate and president of the United States shared his view of the domestic strategy that the country should pursue. Yet on the other side, adversaries of his domestic plan, among them the American Civil Liberties Union (ACLU), which singled out faith-based initiatives for a number of reasons (foremost of which was their potential for religious discrimination), were apt to disagree, and did. Many believed that the president's domestic agenda had been shaped by the right wing of the Republican Party and Christian fundamentalists.

Of course, there were powerful religious leaders like the 700 Club's Reverend Pat Robertson, who expressed his concern about the potential consequence of religious organizations accepting federal funding (though Robertson and other religious fundamentalists seemed more concerned about government interference than they did about the potential for religious or sexual discrimination that might occur). Like others, in the end, "The payoff was significant. Pat Robertson's controversy-plagued Operation Blessing, for example, was awarded $1.5 million in federal faith-based subsidies."[12]

Just as he had in Texas, Bush either surrounded himself or consorted with members of the conservative wing of his party and evangelical Christians. These impassioned religious traditionalists believed that the constraints associated with allocating federal funds to faith-based groups should be lessened and that the religious fundamentalist effort should be involved in matters related to the body politic. People like Myron Magnet, who in February 2000 wrote the book *The Dream and the Nightmare: The Sixties' Legacy to the Underclass*, related to how the sweeping changes between the privileged and mainstream changed society and increased the underclass. "President George W. Bush told the *Wall Street Journal* that it was the most important book he'd ever read after the Bible, and Bush strategist Karl Rove calls *The Dream and the Nightmare* a roadmap to the president's 'compassionate conservatism.' "[13] Given Magnet's conservative viewpoint regarding governmental intervention, social reforms, and the end goal of the domestic agenda, it made sense that he would be preferred by Bush:

Here again the power of compassionate conservatism's message is its truth, augmented by the deep sincerity of George W. Bush's concern for blacks and his belief that they can succeed in the American mainstream—without depending on destructive racial quotas—and rise to the heights to which he has elevated Colin Powell and Condoleezza

Rice. Certainly the resentful and paranoia-filled message that such black spokesmen as Jesse Jackson and Al Sharpton have retailed can only lead blacks to a dead end, especially since not even the Democratic Party can embrace such extremism for long. Over time, compassionate conservatism's optimistic message will win some black adherents—though when New York City minority schoolchildren assure their teacher that George W. Bush is a card-carrying member of the Ku Klux Klan, that process will take time.[14]

Stephen Goldsmith, the controversial former Indianapolis mayor who became a Bush advisor, was recognized as the point person for the president's domestic agenda and one of the architects of faith-based funding. Goldsmith was also known for his expertise in privatization and budget cuts. He agreed that the impediments that prevented religious organizations from receiving and directly administering social programs should be removed. His viewpoint fit Bush's vision of compassionate conservatism, which sought to remove the harsh edge of conservative ideology while streamlining government's role and encouraging personal accountability. Goldsmith's efforts to "invigorate faith-based institutions, invigorate little armies to help neighborhoods in need"[15] by encouraging churches and synagogues to work directly with schools, police, and social service agencies to solve community problems were extolled by Bush and in keeping with Bush's doctrine and domestic agenda. When speaking about the conservative former mayor, Bush said this about Goldsmith, "He and I share a conservative philosophy . . . I think both of us understand the need to empower and uplift the individual. We understand that there is a role for government."[16]

James Dobson, Ph.D., the controversial founder and former chair of Focus on the Family, was another who battled for Bush during the 2000 campaign and was given credit for several Bush electoral victories. Seen as a watchdog of moral standards, Dobson was a warrior for the Christian Right, whose conservative stance on issues ranging from abortion rights to gay marriage, is no stranger to controversy and does not retreat on conservative issues. Dobson, who is a religious fundamentalist, vehemently opposes homosexuality. According to columnist Michael Crowley, "It was the gay-marriage debate that finally hurled Dobson into politics wholeheartedly. The subject of homosexuality seems to exert a special power over him, and he has devoted much idiosyncratic thought to it. When discussing gays he spares no detail, no matter how prurient."[17]

Also in the Bush camp was former Republican Missouri senator John Ashcroft, who was the controversial choice to become the seventy-ninth attorney general of the United States. It was Ashcroft who, during the drafting of the 1996 Welfare Reform Act, advanced the idea of charitable choice. Ashcroft's concept was a precursor to and in step with Bush's faith-based idea in that it allowed churches to receive taxpayer funds for providing social services. According to Political Research Associates, a group that monitors and analyzes the organizations, leaders, ideas, and activities of the U.S political right, Ashcroft was "An evangelical who does not smoke, drink, or dance, Ashcroft alarmed advocates of church-state separation—of which he has been a vocal foe—when he began conducting daily prayer sessions with Justice Department employees."[18] In January 2001, civil rights activist Judith Schaefer said this about Ashcroft: "John Ashcroft is an extremist; he has a record of insensitivity, if not outright hostility towards women and minorities . . . "[19] When the charitable choice provisions were eventually signed into law, the Clinton administration, realizing the potential for discrimination, advised that it would not permit governmental funding of religious organizations that do not or cannot separate their religious activities from federally funded program activities, stressing that such funding would violate the Constitution.

Appointed in January 2001, political scientist and criminologist John Dilulio, Jr. was tapped to serve as the first director of the White House Office of Faith-Based and Community Initiatives (OFBCI). Dilulio came to fame in the 1990s for developing and propagating the theory that young black men, "superpredators" who grow up in an environment of criminals and without family structure, are likely to become ruthless criminals. Many believed that Dilulio's theory played on the racist fears of white America. Ironically, Dilulio was also the first of Bush's senior team members to resign.[20]

There were also black clergy who during Bush's presidential candidacy, and even going back to his days as governor of Texas, publicly supported the domestic agenda being proposed. For example, Bishop Eugene F. Rivers, a Boston Pentecostal minister and founder of the National Ten Point Leadership Coalition, was one of the black clerics who sought a meeting with president-elect Bush to discuss his domestic programs. Bishop Rivers, an avowed antigay spokesperson, told the *Boston Globe*, "The gay community is pimping the civil rights movement."[21] Another was the Atlanta' controversial Bishop Eddie Long, who in 2007 was named by the Southern Poverty Law Center (SPLC) "As one of the most homophobic black ministers in America." Long openly hyped Bush's proposed federal amendment banning gay marriage.[22] There were politicians, pastors, and an assortment of players who participated in advancing Bush's domestic agenda to varying degrees and for a variety of reasons. Some were actually attempting to transform the way that the federal government interacts with churches and religious organizations. However, the motives of some may have been purely political or more associated with their viewpoint as it relates to the LGBT community.

Long before the issue heated up for Bush the candidate, there had been controversy over the comingling of federal funding and religious organizations. Concern over the issue of the partnership between church and state was increasing. In fact, it had been simmering in the caldron of Christian Right organizations like James Dobson's Focus on the Family and in a number of Texas faith-based programs.[23] In December 1996, Governor Bush issued Executive Order 96-10, directing state agencies to implement the landmark charitable choice provision of the federal welfare law, inviting private and religious charities to deliver welfare services—while at the same time guarding the religious integrity of participating groups and religious freedom of beneficiaries.

The Texas Workforce Commission, along with local workforce development boards, executed the provisions of this Executive Order through partnerships with faith- and community-based organizations. In its December 1996 "Faith in Action Report," prepared by members of the governor's advisory task force on faith-based community service groups, Governor George W. Bush said:

> Government can hand out money, but it cannot put hope in our hearts or a sense of purpose in our lives. It cannot bring us peace of mind. It cannot fill the spiritual well from which we draw strength day to day. Only faith can do that.
>
> One person alone cannot do everything. But one person alone can do something. We must all—each and every one of us—be that one person, doing that something. As I travel Texas, I sense we are ready. People are seizing the moment. They are not waiting for a government committee to meet. They are helping each other, finding their own solutions to the problems plaguing [their] communities.[24]

Riding a wave of firebrand conservatism, evangelicals and Christian fundamentalists were encouraged by the strength of the 1995 Republican movement and the way that the Contract with America had politicized their attempt to participate in the political process.[25] To an extent, Bush's policies and the people who embraced his perspective popularized and politicized the concept of Dominionism, which is said to have been based on the Bible's text in Genesis 1:26: "And God said, let us make man in our image, after our likeness: and let them have dominion over the fish of the sea, and over the fowl of the air, and over the cattle, and over all the earth, and over every creeping thing that creepeth upon the earth."[26]

Sara Diamond, one of the people who made the term "Dominionism" popular, explains the view held by some Christians "That Christians alone are Biblically mandated to occupy all secular institutions until Christ returns."[27] According to Diamond, the theory and interpretation of Dominionism has resulted in a vast majority of Christians concluding that they are anointed by God as caretakers of Earth.

As if they needed emboldening, Christian fundamentalists believed that Bush was referring to Dominionism when he said this about the creation of the OFBCI: "When we see social needs in America, my administration will look first to faith-based programs and community groups . . ."[28]

Bush first made this promise as a presidential candidate on July 22, 1999. However, for pious extremists, it opened the door wider to the notion that theirs was a mandate from God to define for everyone else the meaning of family values and how people should live their lives. In fact, in their effort to introduce their definition of morality onto the political stage, the Religious Right would use the term "family values" to drive home the importance of education, oppose LGBT rights, and regulate morality.[29] Needless to say, when Bush used his presidential powers to advance faith-based initiatives, conservative Christians took advantage of the opportunity to move forward on a broad range of social and moral issues, like fortifying their pro-family position and cementing their stand against abortion, stem-cell research, and same-sex marriage.

There are those who believe that it was evangelicals and religious extremists who caused bipartisan support for the president's domestic programs to fade because of their very radical religious views. Lawmakers who may have given their support were thwarted by overly zealous and sometimes fanatical protagonists who used Bush's statements and faith-based funding policies as a rallying cry for their cause, even flaunting their clout with the administration and consequentially hindering Bush's ability to advance his domestic agenda.

Then there were people like Ralph Reed, who *Time* magazine referred to as "The right hand of God."[30] Cerebral and soft-spoken, Reed is the former executive director of the Christian Coalition, and his skills at presenting Bush's domestic programs in a nonthreatening way were unmatched. In a 2001 *Washington Post* interview, "Reed noted that the religious conservative movement 'no longer plays the institutional role it once did,' in part because it succeeded in electing Bush and other friendly leaders. 'You're no longer throwing rocks at the building; you're in the building.' "[31] As a result, some saw Bush caving to religious fundamentalism and used it to deride his domestic agenda.

Reed was not overreaching. Bush's Executive Order 13199, which created the White House Office of Faith-Based and Community Initiatives, and Executive Order 13198, which formed the five Centers for Faith-Based and Community Initiatives and delineated federal agency responsibilities with respect to Faith-Based and Community Initiatives, was more than symbolic for religious extremists and some members of the Christian Coalition. For some holier-than-thou members of the Christian Coalition, it would take on biblical meaning.[32]

EXECUTIVE ORDER 13198

"By the authority vested in me as President by the Constitution and the laws of the United States of America, and in order to help the Federal Government coordinate a national effort to expand opportunities for faith-based and other community organizations and to strengthen their capacity to better meet social needs in America's communities, it is hereby ordered as follows . . ."[33]

Not two weeks after taking office, Bush used his presidential powers to make his intentions clear by placing at the top of his domestic agenda the expansion of funding opportunities for faith-based and community organizations. As the nation's forty-third president, he created the OFBCI and authorized participating agencies to implement his domestic programs, sending a message of solidarity with the Conservative Right and fundamentalist Christians. Striking what had become a familiar theme, Bush rallied the "armies of compassion," saying:

Government has a solemn responsibility to help meet the needs of poor Americans and distressed neighborhoods, but it does not have the monopoly on compassion. America is richly blessed by the diversity and vigor of neighborhood healers: civic, social, charitable, and religious groups.

These quiet heroes lift people's lives in ways that are beyond government's know-how, usually on shoestring budgets, and they heal our Nation's ills one heart and one act of kindness at a time.[34]

Still, Bush acolytes, GOP conservatives, evangelical Christians, and those who would benefit from implementation of the president's domestic agenda would have to wait a while longer because it was hampered by delays stemming from mounting political opposition. It was all but halted as the country's focus was suddenly changed by the events of September 11, 2001.

It is difficult to think of the OFBCI and not have a sense that it was tailor-made for Bush's philosophy of compassionate conservatism. According to journalist Jacob Weisberg, this is a term that Bush first picked up from historian and presidential advisor Doug Wead in 1987.[35] Long before Bush took the presidential oath, he had become a fairly good politician who had a knack for collecting catchy phrases that in a few words succinctly summed up his political philosophy. By most accounts, he had made good use of his days at the Texas Statehouse, where some believe he was laying the groundwork for a presidential run and an opportunity to implement the domestic policies that he would propose as commander in chief.

Bush's execution of Executive Orders 13198 and 13199 gave opponents something to complain about, and they wasted no time in asserting that these orders blurred the longstanding protections of the First Amendment. However, there is no doubt that the more controversial of the two Executive Orders was 13198. Bush had not only assigned specific functions of the Executive Department Centers for Faith-Based Initiatives (CFBI), but delineated specific responsibilities to agency heads, making them responsible for "Coordinating efforts to eliminate regulatory, contracting and other programmatic obstacles to the participation of faith-based and other community organization in the provision of social services."[36] Executive Order 13198 also gave the CFBIs sweeping power to implement revolutionary change that was viewed as edging dangerously close to the precipice of breaching the constitutional separation between church and state.

This was a disconcerting proposition to some, yet others literally viewed it as a godsend. As for the debate regarding the use of presidential executive powers to implement programs, it centered on whether doing so was in keeping with the founding fathers' intended purpose, or a way for a sitting president to ramrod his agenda through without congressional approval.

However, the truth is that Bush had history on his side, as Executive Orders have been used to help shape the course of the nation's history dating back to its infancy. On June 8, 1789, President George Washington issued the very first Executive Order, instructing heads of departments within the federal government to make a "clear account" of matters in their departments. Exactly what the Executive Order referred to is open to speculation. What makes Executive Orders so effective, notwithstanding the potential for controversy, is that their execution is not complicated.

They do not require the exactitudes of congressional approval and are a very effective way of expediting policy while dodging drawn out public debate. Ironically, it is the simplicity of the Executive Order that can create controversy.

One example of a president's authority can be seen in President Harry Truman's use of presidential powers to carry out an Executive Order in 1948 to end racial segregation in the armed forces. Another historic use of presidential authority occurred during the tumultuous 1960s, when President Lyndon Baines Johnson invoked his influence and used Executive Order 11246 on September 24, 1965 to prohibit discrimination in federal employment. Johnson's order asserted that

It is the policy of the Government of the United States to provide equal opportunity in Federal employment for all qualified persons, to prohibit discrimination in employment because of race, creed, color, or national origin, and to promote the full realization of equal employment opportunity through a positive, continuing program in each executive department and agency. The policy of equal opportunity applies to every aspect of Federal employment policy and practice.[37]

Incredibly, Johnson's directive brought to an end two centuries of injustice. That said, what commander in chief would not find practicality in the occasional use of the Executive Order? The correct answer is none, and to prove it, the Executive Order has been used thousands of times and by every president. Executive Orders have been used since the beginning of the republic to effect important policy change and implement mundane minutia. Needless to say, there are also examples of presidential overreaching. One such incident occurred when the Supreme Court rebuked President Truman for overstepping the bounds of presidential authority when he used an Executive Order to seize control of the nation's steel mills after World War II.[38]

Fast-forward to 2001, when a resolute President George W. Bush used his presidential powers to transform the way that religious and charitable groups interact with the federal government. Like Truman and Johnson, Bush used his executive power to mandate a significant social change, one that prompted detractors to immediately label his action as political, even suggesting that he had used the Executive Order to jump-start his domestic agenda as well as to please the Religious Right and conservative members of his party.

Claims that presidential Executive Orders have been used to advance specific political agendas are not entirely baseless. One of the clearest examples is seen when a newly elected president invokes the power of the office to reverse Executive Orders issued by a predecessor, particularly one of the opposing party.

For instance, in preparation for the Obama presidency, it was reported that

> Transition advisers to President-elect Barack Obama have compiled a list of about 200 Bush administration actions and executive orders that could be swiftly undone to reverse White House policies on climate change, stem cell research, reproductive rights and other issues, according to congressional Democrats, campaign aides and experts working with the transition team.
>
> A team of four dozen advisers, working for months in virtual solitude, set out to identify regulatory and policy changes Obama could implement soon after his inauguration.[39]

Dan Mendelson, a Democratic operative and former associate administrator for health in the Clinton administration's Office of Management and Budget, is quoted as saying, "'The kind of regulations they are looking at' are those imposed by Bush for 'overtly political' reasons, in pursuit of what Democrats say was a partisan Republican agenda."[40]

When the Obama transition team targeted for reversal initiatives issued by his predecessor, these decisions gave the appearance of partisan politics in the same way that President William Jefferson Clinton's Executive Orders were reversed by incoming president George W. Bush.

Heading toward an obvious confrontation with political and religious opponents who were prepared to utilize the First Amendment as a basis to challenge Bush's faith-based funding initiative, the controversy relating to the "establishment of religion" question was central. It immediately roused a mostly partisan debate with regard to the intent of the establishment clause and whether the founding fathers' prohibition was being misinterpreted.[41]

President Bush's beliefs on the separation of church and state were to some extent alluded to in a letter to an American Buddhist leader in which he said:

> As citizens recite the words of the Pledge of Allegiance . . . we affirm our form of government, our belief in human dignity, our unity as a people, and our reliance on God. . . . When we pledge allegiance to One Nation under God, our citizens participate in an important American tradition of humbly seeking the wisdom and blessing of Divine Providence.[42]
>
> President George W. Bush

However, regardless of what Bush and his supporters believed about the separation between church and state, opponents of faith-based initiatives maintained that the changes being proposed by the Bush administration in funding churches and religiously based organizations represented an encroachment of the establishment clause and presented a threat to the separation intended by the founding fathers. While not totally unexpected, it was something that the Bush administration would have to contend with as it rallied support for the president's domestic agenda.

As far as Supreme Court rulings were concerned, some believed that existing court opinions with respect to the separation issue were not necessarily relevant to the president's proposed faith-based funding initiative. For example, in the view of former chief justice William Rehnquist, the term "establishment of religion" was intended to prohibit only the establishment of a single national church or the preference of one religious sect over another. In 1947 the Supreme Court held in *Everson v. Board of Education* that the establishment clause is one of the "liberties" protected by the due-process clause. The Supreme Court ruling elaborated further, by saying that all government action—whether at the federal, state, or local level—must abide by the restrictions of the establishment clause.

> The establishment of religion clause means at least this: Neither a state nor the federal government may set up a church. Neither can pass laws that aid one religion, aid all religions, or prefer one religion over another. Neither can force a person to go to or to remain away from church against his will or force him to profess a belief or disbelief in any religion . . .
>
> Neither a state or the federal government may, openly or secretly, participate in the affairs of any religious organizations or groups and vice versa. In the words of Jefferson, the clause against establishment of religion by law was intended to erect a wall of separation between church and state.[43]

President Thomas Jefferson defended the demarcation between the functions and operations of the institutions of religion and government in our society, stating that "Congress shall make no law respecting an establishment of religion, or prohibiting the free exercise thereof; or abridging the freedom of speech, or of the press; or the right of the people peaceably to assemble, and to petition the government for a redress of grievances."[44]

Regarding the question of separation between church and state, the First Amendment recognizes that intertwining government and religion increases the possibility of conflict and tyranny as articulated here:

For the first 150 years of our nation's history, there were very few occasions for the courts to interpret the establishment clause because the First Amendment had not yet been applied to the states. As written, the First Amendment applied only to Congress and the federal government. In the wake of the Civil War, however, the 14th Amendment was adopted. It reads in part that "no state shall . . . deprive any person of life, liberty or property without due process of law . . ."

Nonetheless, modern relevant precedents can show how the courts might decide the issue of preferring some religious social service providers to others and the problem of coercion.[45]

There appears to be no ambiguity in the language regarding intent, or that the First Amendment makes the clear point that no law forbidding more than the establishment of religion by the government, but even laws respecting an establishment of religion are acceptable. Nonetheless, a test of the establishment clause came in 1971 with *Lemon v. Kurtzman*, which is sometimes referred to as the Lemon Test. In this U.S. Supreme Court case, a state program providing aid to religious elementary and secondary schools was struck down by the court.[46] Challenges like *Lemon v. Kurtzman* provided the structure for the establishment clause.

In Lemon Chief Justice Warren Burger articulated three "prongs," all of which had to be met for a program of aid to a parochial school to survive constitutionally. First, the program in question required a secular purpose; second, its principal or primary effect could be neither to advance nor to inhibit religion; finally, the government aid was not to foster an excessive government entanglement with religion. A violation of any one prong would make a program unconstitutional.[47]

Utilizing the Lemon Test, a court must make an initial determination of whether the law or government action in question has a secular purpose. The aim is to ensure that the government is not involved in matters of religion. Next, the court must determine if the state action would promote or restrict religion. Finally, a decision must be made regarding how any action taken by the court might impact or comingle religion and government, and result in blurring the line between government and religion.[48]

In a test of the court's ruling of *Lemon v. Kurtzman* (1971), *Grand Rapids School District v. Ball* (1985), taxpayers challenged the constitutionality of using public funds for programs offered within religious schools. When the Sixth Circuit Court of Appeals agreed that the First Amendment had been violated, the Grand Rapids School District took the case to the U.S. Supreme Court.

The court eventually ruled 5–4 that the Community Education program was in violation of the First Amendment. Justice Brennan wrote the majority opinion, which included a ban against similar programs. Justice Brennan referenced *Lemon v. Kurtzman* (1971), discussing the three-prong test. Brennan believed that the city of Grand Rapids had passed the first part of the Lemon Test, that is, whether the law or government action in question has a secular purpose. However, Brennan felt that with respect to the second part of the Lemon Test, whether the state action had caused to promote or restrict religion, even if the school district had not intended, the law had been violated.

Justice Brennan asserted that:

We do not question that the religious school teachers employed by the Community Education program will attempt in good faith to perform their secular mission conscientiously. Nonetheless, there is a substantial risk that the religious message they are expected to convey during the regular school day will infuse the supposedly secular classes ... Shared Time instructors are teaching academic subjects in religious schools in courses virtually indistinguishable from the other courses offered during the regular religious day. Teachers in such an atmosphere may well subtly (or overtly) conform their instruction to the environment in which they teach, while students will perceive the instruction in the context of the dominantly religious message of the institution.[49]

A case that tested coercion—that is, the government does not violate the establishment clause unless it (1) provides direct aid to religion in a way that would tend to establish a state church or (2) coerces people to support or participate in religion against their will—was *Lee v. Weisman* (1992):

The case centered on the psychological coercive effect of clergy-led prayer at graduation ceremonies. Principals of public middle and high schools in Providence, Rhode Island, are permitted to invite members of the clergy to give invocations and benedictions at their schools' graduation ceremonies. Petitioner Lee, a middle school principal, invited a rabbi to offer such prayers at the graduation ceremony for Deborah Weisman's class, gave the rabbi a pamphlet containing guidelines for the composition of public prayers at civic ceremonies, and advised him that the prayers should be nonsectarian. Shortly before the ceremony, the District Court denied the motion of respondent Weisman, Deborah's father, for a temporary restraining order to prohibit school officials from including the prayers in the ceremony. Deborah and her family attended the ceremony, and the prayers were recited.Subsequently, Weisman sought a permanent injunction barring Lee and other petitioners, various Providence public school officials, from inviting clergy to deliver invocations and benedictions at future graduations.[50]

The district court enjoined petitioners from continuing the practice on the grounds that it violated the establishment clause of the First Amendment. The Court of Appeals affirmed and found that "The school district's supervision and control of a high school graduation ceremony places subtle and indirect public and peer pressure on attending students to stand as a group or maintain respectful silence during the invocation and benediction." The court stated in its decision, "... at a minimum, the Constitution guarantees that government may not coerce anyone to support or participate in religion or its exercise."[51] In the majority opinion, the court held that the establishment clause forbids clergy to offer prayers as part of an official public school graduation ceremony.

Justice Antonin Scalia offered a powerful dissenting opinion, stating:

> From our Nation's origin, prayer has been a prominent part of governmental ceremonies and proclamations. The Declaration of Independence, the document marking our birth as a separate people, "appeal[ed] to the Supreme Judge of the world for the rectitude of our intentions" and avowed "a firm reliance on the protection of divine Providence." In his first inaugural address, after swearing his oath of office on a Bible, George Washington deliberately made a prayer a part of his first official act as President ... Most recently, President George Herbert Walker Bush, continuing the tradition established by President Washington, asked those attending his inauguration to bow their heads, and made a prayer his first official act as President.[52]

In the 1984 case of *Lynch v. Donnelly*, the question of whether specific government action equates to an endorsement of religion was tested by the court. Justice Sandra Day O'Connor, expressing her interpretation of the establishment clause, forcefully stated, "The Establishment Clause prohibits government from making adherence to a religion relevant in any way to a person's standing in the political community." O'Connor was concerned about whether a particular action taken by government sends "a message to non-adherents that they are outsiders, not full members of the political community, and an accompanying message to adherents that they are insiders, favored members of the political community."[53]

The endorsement test seems especially germane to Bush's faith-based federal funding initiative plan because it deals with how the government can participate in expressive activities, such as religious symbols, graduation prayers, and religion in the curriculum. Most important was the issue of endorsement to the Bush domestic agenda was to ensure that adherents or nonadherents to a religion felt treated equally by the government, while the issue of neutrality was similarly significant. While it may sound rather straightforward, neutrality in treatment means that the government's treatment of religious groups and other similarly situated groups is the same. However, it turns out that the neutrality component was a major constitutional hurdle for Bush's faith-based initiatives.

As Bush saw it, faith-based initiatives would create parity, or level the playing field, between religious and nonreligious social service providers. However, the uniformity that he hoped for would be challenged by some who said that it ran counter to the establishment clause.

The expansion of faith-based initiatives to religious organizations that had not previously participated would require eradicating obstacles that had formerly prevented their involvement. It was therefore paramount that "The barriers to participation of faith-based groups are essentially the four basic parameters within which they must function, namely (1) refrain from direct or indirect proselytizing; (2) provide service to their clients without respect to religious affiliation; (3) keep religious and government grant funds separate, with the latter spent only according to government mandated procedures and subject to audit; and (4) compliance with other generally applicable laws against discrimination in hiring or service based on race, religion, color, age, gender or national origin."[54]

On June 25, 2007, though late in his second term, a victory for the Bush administration came in *Hein v. Freedom from Religion Foundation* wherein the U.S. Supreme Court limited the freedom of ordinary citizens, and their organizations, to sue the executive branch of the government for infractions of the establishment clause of the First Amendment, which states that "Congress shall make no law respecting an establishment of religion."[55] Legal analysts explain:

The original case was *Freedom From Religion v. Towney*. It was filed in 2004-Jun and involved the sponsorship by *the White House Office of Faith-Based and Community Initiatives'* (OFBCI) of a series of regional conferences on federal aid to religious groups. The *Freedom from Religion Foundation* (FFRF) is a group of about 10,000 members, most of whom would describe themselves as Agnostics, Atheists, Humanists, non-theists, freethinkers, and/or secularists. They accused officials of nine federal agencies and the OFBCI of sending " . . . messages to non-adherents of religious belief that they are outsiders, and the defendants send an accompanying message to adherents . . . that they are insiders, favored members of the political community."[56]

In the matter of HEIN, DIRECTOR, WHITE HOUSE OFFICE OF FAITH-BASED AND COMMUNITY INITIATIVES, et al. v. FREEDOM FROM RELIGION FOUNDATION, INC., et al, decided on June 25, 2007 the United States Supreme said, Justice Alito announced the judgment of the Court and delivered an opinion in which The Chief Justice and Justice Kennedy join.

This is a lawsuit in which it was claimed that conferences held as part of the President's Faith-Based and Community Initiatives program violated the Establishment Clause of the First Amendment because, among other things, President Bush and former Secretary of Education Paige gave speeches that used "religious imagery" and praised the efficacy of faith-based programs in delivering social services. The plaintiffs contend that they meet the standing requirements of Article III of the Constitution because they pay federal taxes.

It has long been established, however, that the payment of taxes is generally not enough to establish standing to challenge an action taken by the Federal Government. In light of the size of the federal budget, it is a complete fiction to argue that an unconstitutional federal expenditure causes an individual federal taxpayer any measurable economic harm. And if every federal taxpayer could sue to challenge any Government expenditure, the federal courts would cease to function as courts of law and would be cast in the role of general complaint bureaus.[57]

To carry the faith-based ball, the GOP selected the only black Republican in Congress, Representative J. C. Watts, Jr. (R-OK). Watts, a former starting quarterback, who led the University of Oklahoma to two Orange Bowl victories before playing professionally in Canada. He was elected to the House of Representatives in 1994 in a majority-white district of Oklahoma and was picked to advance the president's ambitious domestic agenda.[58]

Watts's rise to prominence came in a series of GOP responses where he gave the 1997 reply to President Clinton's State of the Union Address.

Seen as a steadfast supporter of family values Watts's stock was on the rise with the GOP. In a 2000 interview with writer Michael Fletcher, Watts provided insight into his thinking:

> He is a strong advocate of "family values" (a conservative favorite) but also supports affirmative action. He has been an outspoken supporter of historically Black colleges and universities (HBCUs) and was vocal in his support of Black farmers who faced discrimination in the federal government's loan programs.[59]

During the interview, Fletcher asked Congressman Watts several questions related to faith-based initiatives and his role in the Republican Party:

Fletcher: Do you foresee a larger role for churches in providing technical training for African-American communities through the faith-based programs supported by President Bush?

Watts: Faith-based community development has been a major force in America for years and will continue to grow. But we shouldn't just be concerned about feeding the hungry, housing the homeless, and clothing the naked. We have to have a technology piece as well ...

Fletcher: Many in the media identify you as the point man for a new Republican outreach to minorities, particularly African Americans. Is this an accurate description? Do you resent it? Has this been a difficult role for you politically, given the demographics of your mostly White congressional district?

Watts: One thing that I always remember is that I should never get used to having the word "congressman" in front of my name. That way, I can always speak my mind. I don't like to use labels like conservative, liberal, or whatever. I don't ever want to be afraid to look at new solutions to old problems. The press, they have to cordon you off in a corner. "He's a Black Republican." Through the years, I've been attacked by the Left. But I've been attacked as much from the Right. People say, "You're not conservative enough." Others say, "You're not Black enough." I've been criticized by the NAACP, but I've also been criticized by the John Birch Society. I don't consult the John Birch Society before I vote. I don't consult the NAACP when I vote either. Despite the

> fact that my district is 82 percent White, 9 percent Black, and
> the rest other, I'm willing to defend the fact that the most
> comprehensive community development legislation in recent
> years was authored by J. C. Watts . . .[60]

Watts wanted to create an environment conducive to faith-based groups seeking government contracts and as a enthusiastic supporter of the president's domestic policies, he became the main sponsor of the president's domestic agenda. As the lone black Republican in the 107th Congress from 2001 to 2002, Watts perspicaciously resisted being saddled with and designated as the spokesperson for black issues, a void that the GOP was desperate to fill. It was a formidable task and huge risk for Watts to sponsor a faith-based bill that would provide expansion of charitable choice and promote religious groups applying for and receiving federal funds to deliver social services. Nonetheless, he supported the bill in the 107th Congress, which included charitable giving incentives for individuals and business, and individual development accounts for the poor.[61]

The GOP hoped that faith-based initiatives would help attract African American voters. "With the GOP at the forefront of a drive to channel more aid to faith-based ministries—frequently inner-city groups operated by and serving African Americans—a slight shift of black voters toward Republicans seemed at least plausible."[62] Bush's faith-based funding initiative was seen as a way of satisfying evangelical Christians and the Conservative Right for their support, and was also a clever method of appealing to black voters who would otherwise in larger numbers distance themselves from the GOP. But Watts wanted to do more. His goal was for the GOP to adopt a comprehensive strategy for black America, but for the time being, he had to settle on leading the charge of the president's domestic agenda. However, even with bipartisan support and Watts pushing the faith-based bill H.R. 7 through the House, given the poisoned political atmosphere after the 2000 presidential election and the way faith-based legislation was wrapped up in both race and religion, it would prove to be a dubious task.[63]

Initially, the Executive Orders issued by President Bush were related to five federal agencies: the Department of Justice, the Department of Education, the Department of Labor, the Department of Health and Human Services, and the Department of Housing and Urban Development. The heads or these agencies were instructed to establish within their respective departments a Faith-Based and Community Initiatives (Center). Later, the U.S. Agency for International Development and Agriculture were added. What the Executive Orders did almost immediately was bring sweeping changes, charging the heads of the departments with eliminating regulatory and contracting obstacles for religious and community organizations. For example, Executive Order 13198 required that appropriate staffing and resources be appropriated with a mere 45 days to begin operations. Then just as suddenly, as the country reeled from the events of September 11, 2001, like other legislative efforts, faith-based initiatives was delayed. Another hard-hitting consequence was that only $30 million in compassion capital funds had been attached to a larger spending bill in late 2001. It was not until early 2002, when former Senator Rick Santorum (R-PA) and then Democratic senator Joseph Lieberman (D-CT) introduced the Charity Aid, Recovery and Empowerment 2002 (CARE) Act that the ball on religious-based funding would move forward again.[64]

There were significant differences between the CARE Act and H.R. 7, one being that the CARE Act was more generous with respect to tax provisions and compassion capital funds. However, the CARE Act did little to expand choice, only making mention of religious nondiscrimination and narrowly explaining how faith-based groups could apply for federal funds. During the fall of 2002, civil libertarians, interest groups and several opposing senators prevented the bill's passage, and it eventually died in the lame-duck Senate. Bush, seeing that the bill woefully lacked congressional support and watching as his key domestic agenda languished and was pummeled by adversaries, on December 12, 2002 issued two additional Executive Orders that addressed his faith-based initiatives.

Executive Order 13280 added two more executive departments to participate in the faith-based initiative domestic policy. However, seen as the more controversial, Executive Order 13279 required equal protection for faith-based and community organizations, and unilaterally implemented the religious nondiscrimination provisions contained in the CARE Act.[65]

According to the American Civil Liberties Union:

Executive Order 13279 had been the broadest of President Bush's mandates in carrying out his domestic agenda. President Bush issued the order ostensibly to provide "equal protection for faith-based and community organizations." But the true aim of this executive order was to circumvent Congress's refusal to permit religious discrimination, coercion and proselytizing in government-funded programs . . .[66]

Obviously, a number of factors led to Bush's use of executive powers to mandate his domestic agenda. Yet in the end, faith-based initiatives would come to mean different things to different people. Few doubted that

Americans might actually benefit from the president's domestic programs. While some promoted the idea that GOP conservatives and the Religious Right had used faith-based initiatives to further their political and religious interests, and in the process, had breached the separation between church and state. It would ultimately lead to accusations that competition for faith-based funding had triggered discrimination against members of the LGBT community, and especially black Christian LGBTs. In spite of this, Bush's vision for the OFBCI to allow churches and faith-based organizations to address the country's social ills continued throughout his administration, eventually spreading to every state in the union.

NOTES

1. Timothy 1:8 Holy Bible King James Version.

2. http://prince.org/msg/105/205231. Accessed February 15, 2012.

3. http://www.theoakinitiative.org/lou-sheldon#.UL-Ls4U4yoQ. Accessed December 5, 2012.

4. Rev. Louis P. Sheldon, http://www.au.org/resources/brochures/the-religious-rights-war-on-lgbt-americans/. Accessed February 15, 2012.

5. Rev. Louis P. Sheldon, http://www.rightwigwatch.org/content/traditional-values-coalition. Accessed February 15, 2012.

6. Interview by Steven Waldman, editor-in-chief of Beliefnet.com, with George W. Bush, October 2000. www.beliefnet.com. Accessed February 15, 2012.

7. http://www.firstamendmentcenter.org/about.aspx?item=about_firstamd. Accessed February 15, 2012.

8. http://www.statutes.legis.state.tx.us/docs/pe/htm/pe.21.htm. Accessed February 15, 2012.

9. http://www.issues2000.org/george_w__bush.htm. Accessed February 15, 2012.

10. http://www.hhsc.state.tx.us/help/financial/temporary_assistance.html. Accessed February 15, 2012.

11. http://www.hhsc.state.tx.us/help/financial/temporary_assistance.html. Accessed February 15, 2012.

12. http://www.au.org/resources/publications/the-religious-rights-war-on-lgbt-americans. Accessed February 15, 2012.

13. http://www.manhattan-institute.org/html/magnet.htm. Accessed February 15, 2012.

14. http://www.city-journal.org/html/11_1_solving_president_bushs.html. Accessed February 15, 2012.

15. http://www.washingtonpost.com/wp-srv/politics/campaigns/wh2000/stories/goldsmith060599.htm. Accessed February 15, 2012.

16. http://nymag.com/daily/intel/2010/04/bloomberg_hires_compassionate.html. Accessed February 15, 2012.

17. Michael Crowley, "James Dobson: The religious right's new king-maker," *Slate.com*, posted Friday, Nov. 12, 2004, http://www.slate.com/id/2109621/. Accessed February 15, 2012.

18. http://www.defendingjustice.org/resources/profiles.html. Accessed February 15, 2012.

19. Judith Schaefer, http://news.bbc.co.uk/2/hi/americas/1120440.stm. Accessed February 15, 2012.

20. http://www.publiceye.org/magazine/v16n2/Berkowitz.html. Accessed February 15, 2012.

21. http://www.bookerrising.net/2007/04/face-right-black-religious-opposition.html. Accessed February 15, 2012.

22. Southern Poverty Law Center (SPLC) Intelligence Report Spring Edition Issue No. 125.

23. http://www.focusonthefamily.com/about_us/james-dobson.aspx. James Dobson Focus on the Family a conservative religious and political action group.

24. "Faith in Action: 1996," George W. Bush, http://www.twc.state.tx.us/svcs/charchoice/faithful.pdf. Accessed February 15, 2012.

25. "Contract with America," http://www.britannica.com/EBchecked/topic/135331/Contract-with-America. Accessed February 15, 2012.

26. Genesis 1:26. Holy Bible.

27. Sara Diamond, http://www.theocracywatch.org/. Accessed February 15, 2012.

28. George W. Bush, http://www.cpjustice.org/stories/storyreader$. Accessed February 15, 2012.

29. http://are.as.wvu.edu/jhicks.htm. Accessed February 15, 2012.

30. Ralph Reed, Reed first executive director of the Christian Coalition, appeared on the cover of *Time* on May 15, 1995, under the title "The Right Hand of God: Ralph Reed of the Christian Coalition."

31. Dana Millbank, "Ralph Reed," WashingtonPost.com. December 24, 2011. Accessed February 12, 2012.

32. For the full text of Executive Orders 13198, 13199, 13279, and 13280, please see the appendices of this book.

33. http://www.archives.gov/federal-register/executive-orders/2001-wbush.html. Accessed February 15, 2012.

34. George W. Bush, http://georgewbush-whitehouse.archives.gov/government/fbci/qr1.html. Accessed February 15, 2012.

35. *The Bush Tragedy*, Jacob Weisberg reprint ed. (New York: Random House Trade Paperbacks, 2008.

36. http://frwebgate.access.gpo.gov/cgi-bin/getdoc.cgi?dbname=2001 _register&docid=fr31ja01-115.pdf. Accessed February 15, 2012.

37. http://www.eeoc.gov/eeoc/history/35th/thelaw/eo-11246.html. Accessed December 4, 2012.

38. http://www.answers.com/topic/executive-order-1. Accessed February 15, 2012.

39. Ceci Connolly and R. Jeffrey Smith, "Obama targets 200 Bush executive actions for reversal," November 10, 2008.

40. http://obsidianwings.blogs.com/obsidian_wings/2008/11/change-we -can-b.html. Accessed February 15, 2012.

41. "Establishment Clause" "Establishment of Religion."

42. Letter from President George W. Bush to Mitsuo Murashige, President of the Hawaii State Federation November 13, 2002, http://www .bc.edu/content/dam/files/centers/boisi/pdf/Kao-Copulsky-Pledge_JAAR .pdf. (Accessed February 15, 2012.)

43. http://www.firstamendmentcenter.org/rel_liberty/establishment/ index.aspx.

44. Thomas Jefferson, http://www.religioustolerance.org/amend_1.htm. Accessed February 15, 2012.

45. Establishment Law, Religion Research, September 16, 2011, http://www.firstamendmentcenter.org/rel_liberty/establishment/index.aspx. Accessed February 15, 2012.

46. 1971 *Lemon v. Kurtzman.*

47. Amy E. Black, Douglas L. Koopman, and David K. Ryden, *Of Little Faith: The Politics of George W. Bush's Faith-Based Initiatives* (Washington, DC: Georgetown University Press, 2004), 44.

48. http://thisnation.com/textbook/billofrights-religion.html. Accessed February 15, 2012.

49. Justice Brennan, http://law.jrank.org/pages/22932/Grand-Rapids -School-District-v-Ball-Taking-Lemon-Test.html. Accessed February 15, 2012.

50. http://religiousfreedom.lib.virginia.edu/court/lee_v_weis.html. Accessed February 15, 2012.

51. http://www.freedomforum.org/packages/first/curricula/education forfreedom/supportpages/L09-SupremeCourtTests.htm. Accessed February 15, 2012.

52. http://www.freedomforum.org/packages/first/curricula/education forfreedom/supportpages/L09-SupremeCourtTests.htm. Accessed February 15, 2012.

53. http://atheism.about.com/library/decisions/holydays/bldec_Lynch Donnelly.htm. Supreme Court Justice, Sandra Day O'Connor. Accessed February 15, 2012.

54. Formicola, Mary C. Segers, and Paul J. Weber, *Faith-Based Initiatives and the Bush Administration.*

55. http://www.law.cornell.edu/supct/html/06-157.ZS.html. Accessed February 15, 2012.

56. http://www.religioustolerance.org/char_choi6.htm. Accessed February 15, 2012.

57. U.S. Supreme Court decision http://caselaw.lp.findlaw.com/scripts/getcase.pl?court=us&vol=000&invol=06-157#opinion1, January 31, 2011.

58. Congressman (R-OK) J. C. Watts. Career Communications Group Inc. http://www.blackengineer.com/people/jcwatts.shtml. Accessed December 6, 2012.

59. Clear Communications Group Inc. http://www.blackengineer .com/people/jcwatts.shtml Michael Fletcher. Accessed December 6, 2012.

60. "I Michael Fletcher 2000 in search of 'new solutions,'" interview with former (R-OK) Congressman J.C. Watts http://www.blackengineer .com/people/jcwatts.shtml. Accessed December 4, 2012.

61. 107th Congress 2001–2002.

62. http://press.georgetown.edu/pdfs/1589010132_Intro.pdf. Accessed February 15, 2012.

63. H.R.7 Community Solutions Act of 2001, sponsored by J. C. Watts (R-OK) and Tony Hall (D-OH).

64. http://www.publiceye.org/magazine/v16n2/v16n2.pdf. Accessed February 15, 2012.

65. Executive Order 13280, December 12, 2002.

66. http://www.aclu.org/transition/transitionplan.html. Accessed February 15, 2012.

TWO

Sexuality: The Weapon of Choice

> For whosoever shall commit any of these abominations, even the souls that commit them shall be cut off from among their people.[1]

For years, the GOP was criticized for its exclusionary reputation toward minorities and perceived indifference to issues affecting inner-city blacks. It desperately needed someone like Oklahoma Republican conservative congressional representative J. C. Watts to prominently place and strategically use in the party's efforts to transform its image and lure black voters.

Actually, Watts began his political career as a Democrat but switched parties in 1989. As a neophyte, Watts was supported by former National Football League (NFL) quarterback and U.S. representative Jack Kemp as well as actor and National Rifle Association (NRA) president Charlton Heston. Watts won a Republican House seat with 82 percent of the vote in a white-majority district of Oklahoma. A "family values" conservative, Watts was seen as a nonthreat by dyed-in-the-wool traditionalists, and his moderate stance on key Republican issues suited their purpose. Above all, the GOP needed someone to illuminate its platform in a way that blacks could relate to, and Watts was seen as the perfect choice. Republican heavyweights like Speaker of the House Dennis Hastert (R-IL) and Republican whip Tom DeLay (R-TX) saw Watts as the perfect envoy for the GOP domestic agenda.

Bush's Faith-Based Initiative program was controversial, and political opponents as well as some religious organizations were taking potshots asserting that it encroached on the First Amendment and was potentially discriminatory. Even Stephen Goldsmith, one of the president's choices to lead the OFBI conceded inherent difficulties related to faith-based initiatives. Marc Stern, an attorney for the American Jewish Congress, said, "If faith is that important, then you have to provide everybody with the services that correspond to their own particular faith."[2] So for Watts, the lone African American Republican in the 107th Congress, to take on the role of advancing the GOP's domestic agenda was extremely risky.

While he would publicly claim that labels were not important, it is a safe bet that Watts was no different from any other minority and didn't relish the perceived role as a token black GOP member. Certainly the last thing Watts wanted in his budding political career was to be defined as the congressional representative for black issues. However, as an ordained minister and the only black Republican in Congress, the role would prove difficult if not impossible to escape. Besides, Watts seemed most passionate about issues affecting minorities and the downtrodden, and as a black man, he was aware of the challenges faced by minorities and recognized the enormous need for social change in America's inner cities. Still, Watts must have also known that while the GOP wanted change, it was not quite ready to welcome everyone with open arms. For instance, the Republican Party was perceived by blacks as wanting to roll back many of the gains made as a result of the civil rights movement. To blacks, the GOP appeared particularly disinterested in programs implemented under Democratic president Franklin D. Roosevelt that had proven beneficial to the black community. Watts must have known that in the black community, the GOP's reputation was one of narrow-mindedness and elitism.

With the Republican leadership solidly convinced that Watts was suited to the task, it was seen as a win-win situation for the GOP. With a black man leading the charge to advance the president's domestic agenda, the GOP had an opportunity to renew its image within the black community. So as Watts worked to finesse the Community Solutions Act of 2001, otherwise known as H.R. 7, to House passage, and while he served as frontman for the president's domestic agenda, he was simultaneously helping to bridge the divide between the black community and the Republican Party while softening his party's exclusionary reputation. Relativity new to politics but remarkably shrewd, Watts realized that if he could successfully shepherd the president's domestic policies through the House, the likelihood of persuading the GOP to launch a comprehensive legislative agenda for blacks and the underclass would be greatly improved. As author of H.R. 7 which contained key elements of the President's agenda to expand charitable giving, Watts worked as hard advancing the legislation as he had gaining yardage as an Oklahoma Sooner football great.[3]

On July 19, 2001, the bill sponsored by Watts and Tony Hall (D-OH) passed in the House of Representatives by a vote of 233 to 198.[4]

In spite of attempts by the White House and Congress to gain bipartisan support and despite Watts's hard work, the push for H.R. 7 had been mostly a partisan effort. However, given a grueling 2000 presidential campaign and the way that faith-based funding comingled religion and race, it was tough going from the start. To further complicate matters, during the summer of 2001, citing family and health concerns, John Dilulio, the first director of the White House OFBCI, resigned due to what some saw as a conflict with the Bush administration. After only seven months on the job, Dilulio was succeeded by Jim Towey, who had been employed as the U.S. legal counsel to Mother Teresa of Calcutta, an organized missionary of charities working around the world. Yet it was the aftermath of the September 11, 2001, terrorist attacks that would dramatically change the country's focus and alter priorities on nearly every front, including the administration's domestic agenda.

When political leaders and the rest of the country finally returned their focus to domestic issues in 2002, Senators Rick Santorum (R-PA) and Joseph Lieberman (D-CT) jointly introduced the Charity Aid, Relief and Empowerment Act (CARE), which was substantially different from Watts's H.R. 7. One of the major differences was that CARE was more generous with respect to tax incentives and making it easier for people to give to charitable organizations. However, another enormously critical change was that it did not expand charitable choice. In the end, the legislation sponsored by Santorum and Lieberman languished in the final days of the lame-duck Senate.

Possibly realizing that his main domestic program was stalled, Bush acted to launch the concept that was central to his presidency. Using his executive powers, Bush cleared the way for faith-based initiatives to get underway and to form relationships between churches, other religious organizations, and the federal government. His action delighted and empowered conservative Republicans and the Christian Right. It also prompted a swift response from a rapidly growing opposition and onlookers like Christopher Anders, legislative counsel for the ACLU, who called Bush's move a "tremendous rollback to civil-rights protections."[5]

Perhaps as a forewarning of the challenges ahead, Reverend C. Mackey Daniels, president of the National Baptist Convention, was tough on the president's domestic program. Daniels issued a press release in early 2001 condemning faith-based initiatives for targeting Black Churches, calling the initiatives "an effort to muffle the prophetic voices of the African American Church." Daniels also used a biblical reference to infer that supporting

Bush's initiative was equivalent to accepting "Thirty pieces of silver."[6] Others shared Daniel's view, but only a few made their feelings immediately known. National black leaders like Reverend Jesse Jackson seemed to hedge their bets on Bush's faith-based policies, telling an African Methodist Episcopal Church on February 4, 2001 this about the federal government, "I'm all for faith-based programs, after-school programs, senior citizen programs transportation ministries. But I fear federally funded, faith-based initiatives. Don't let them get into your books, because they are wolves in sheep's clothing. Money is seductive; the church needs money, but it needs independence even more!"[7]

Lack of widespread public criticism of the president's domestic agenda in the black community and no unified outcry from black leadership didn't necessarily equate to widespread support of faith-based initiatives. Some believed that the GOP and predominately white Christian Coalition were attempting to divide the Black Church against itself, which would eventually speak out regarding the president's domestic program. However, suspicion of the odd partnership forming between the white Christian Right and Black Church was insignificant and had little impact during the start-up of the Bush administration's faith-based funding program.

Surely the GOP did not expect that blacks would abandon the Democratic Party in droves, but it was reasonable to believe that the enticement of programs like faith-based funding would win the support of homophobic Black religious leaders who were desperate for a cash infusion. It is difficult to believe that black pastors and civic leaders didn't understand that the GOP and Christian Coalition wanted something in return for giving them access to federal funding as well as lifting the restrictions that had previously deterred their participation.

Indeed, Black clerics who fit the persona of someone willing to demonize LGBTs and were already in sync with the self-righteous white evangelical extremists could be counted on to use their religious influence to persuade their congregants and other members of the black community to go along with the strategy of social exclusion and sexual bias against LGBTs. Eventually, dissenters would emerge from the black political and religious leadership.

When the White House issued a statement saying that religious groups "would be allowed to maintain their individual identity through hiring," thus allowing religiously funded groups to use public funds while hiring only members of a certain religion, the late senator Edward Kennedy (D-MA) spoke out. Obviously recognizing the inherent possibility for discrimination and that the president's concept may have been intrinsically flawed, Kennedy roared, "Under the new rule, organizations can accept public funds and then refuse to employ persons because they are Jewish, Catholic, unmarried, gay, or lesbian."[8] U.S. representative Barney Frank (D-MA), who publicly said he was gay in 1987, argued in Congress against the faith-based initiatives, stressing that the proposal could easily lead to government-sponsored racism as well as discrimination on the grounds of sexual orientation. Referring to faith-based funding, Stephen Silberfarb, executive director of the Jewish Community Relations Council of Minnesota, said that it "Opens the door for hate groups to receive tax-payers' dollars to support their racist and extreme views."[9] Warnings about the potential for religious and sexual discrimination as a result of faith-based funding became increasingly common. However, black ministers had not yet united or spoken out in a significant way regarding the potential for black-on-black discrimination, especially toward black Christian LGBTs.

As the potentially harmful effects of religious organizations being funded under Bush's faith-based programs slowly came to light, Watts (having spearheaded the Republican Party's domestic agenda) was in the unenviable position of having to defend the president's domestic program and quell growing concerns. However, Watts's relative silence on the issue and failure to address it early on helped to fuel speculation that the Republican blitz and courtship to designate him as spokesperson for faith-based initiatives had chiefly been to achieve the conservative Republican Right and evangelical right's ulterior motive, which was to use Watts and the Black Church to broaden its base and promote compulsory heterosexuality.

This is not to suggest that Watts wasn't onboard and ready to do the bidding of his party and that of the Christian Right because his position on issues of morality, including the family-first policy, which supported a marriage between one man and one woman, were taken as solid confirmation that he was in lockstep on key conservative issues. However, his taciturnity was crucial because he was familiar with the plight of the oppressed and the radicalized Dominionist's view shared by some politically active conservative Christians who through political action are believed to seek influence or control over secular civil government. Watts (by his inaction) gave the appearance of having gone entirely to the side of the white Christian Right coalition.

There is a remote possibility that black clergy and political leaders did not realize that faith-based initiatives would adversely impact the black community and black LGBTs in particular. However, given the history of rampant homophobia in black culture, it is difficult to believe that the possibility for victimization of black LGBTs did not enter their minds.

It also is hard for some people to accept the failure of these black religious and political leaders to speak out in a meaningful way against the perils of faith-based funding. Harder still to fathom is that after knowing of the intensification of hostility toward members of the black LGBT community resulting from competition for faith-based funding, some black ministers continued to assist the GOP and Christian Right. In the end, the limited debate over the pros and cons of faith-based funding to black churches and other religious organizations appears to have ended with the realization that churches and community organizations desperately needed money, and the Bush administration had it to give. While this was the prevailing logic it was denied by some who participated and supported the president's initiative. Still, it at least helps to explain how the disastrous effect on members of the black LGBT community evolved.

Bishop Eugene Rivers, one the first black clerics to support Bush, was also a confederate of Dilulio. Rivers openly criticized black leaders and those members of the Congressional Black Caucus who refused to interact with the Bush administration. Referring to the black community when discussing Al Gore's bid for the presidency, Rivers said, "We stuck all of our political eggs in one basket, the basket got knocked off the table, and then we didn't know how to respond."[10]

As the mad dash for federal funds began, so did the intensity of proselytizing against African American LGBTs. Still, there were only a few black leaders who connected the surging disdain of LGBTs and same-sex marriage to the intense competition for faith-based dollars. As reports surfaced that some religious groups who had received faith-based funding were refusing to offer services to certain individuals based on sexual orientation, and incidents of racial and sexual bias by churches and faith-based organizations began to trickle in, some opponents of faith-based funding began to take note:

> In one instance, in Anoka County, Minnesota, clergy at a publicly funded social service program run by a Missouri-Synod Lutheran church refused to help a transsexual, citing an alleged conflict with church doctrine. . . . In another, in Kentucky, a lesbian who had excellent performance reviews was fired from a Baptist-run but publicly funded home for troubled youngsters after she was photographed taking part in an AIDS walk. . . . And in Georgia, a lesbian was denied a promotion and then fired from her position at a children's home after her sexual orientation came to light.[11]

The Interfaith Alliance and several national religious leaders called on the president to dismantle faith-based initiatives. The leaders feared the

OFBCI was being used as a political football to gain favor with certain groups.[12] Yet from the perspective of white evangelical fundamentalists, the crusade to promote moral decency—standing against same sex-marriage, abortion, and LGBT rights—was uncompromising. While touting Bush's domestic programs, they appealed to certain black pastors to join them in the fight against "evildoers." Black ministers who identified with their views, among them some who had forgotten or were too young to remember the sting of segregation and racial politics employed against generations of blacks, went along.

In some cases, it seems that the collaboration may have been based entirely on getting a shot at faith-based funding. Some black pastors had no problem joining the bigoted white religious zealots in attacking LGBTs and same-sex marriage or in identifying with the fanatics whose ancestors had used racial supremacy to oppress and treat their black forebears as innately inferior. There were, of course, black religious homophobes joining the fray who could teach the most venomous and fanatical white extremist homophobe a thing or two about being intolerant and maligning the LGBT community. They were the firebrand variety whose use of the Bible to oppress others is practiced in churches across America. Their penchant for point fingers at others, along with the enticement of faith-based funding, sealed the deal and guaranteed their participation in a multiracial and religious crusade against LGBTs.

One black evangelical fanatic, Reverend Gregory Daniels, told the *New York Times* in February 2004: "If the KKK opposes gay marriage, I would ride with them."[13] Week after week, the rhetoric grew more hostile. Muslim leader Louis Farrakhan contributed to the animosity toward LGBTs during a Savior's Day celebration in 2003, saying, "But all of a sudden in the night clubs, they started having transvestite shows, drag queens . . . Scripture say no liar, no adulterer, no effeminate will get in the Kingdom."[14]

There were preachers from the white Christian Right coalition and black clergy who were closeted homosexuals and who represented a particularly venomous breed of homophobe. Spiteful and inciting cruelty against openly gay LGBTs, these hypocrites held themselves out as straight-as-an-arrow puritans while concealing their homosexuality and pedophilia. Considered the most reprehensible are those who—keep their homosexuality and deviance hidden, but go out of their way to publicly humiliate and vilify LGBTs as immoral sexual deviants. Their moral depravity allows them to justify using their spiritual leadership to perpetrate lecherous acts against others. On a personal note, this is the sort of immoral degeneracy that caused me to question my association with Catholicism and to publicly discuss the issue in a *Chicago Tribune* perspective, confessing that "Foremost, I was haunted by the duplicity and what I believed was a climate of conspiratorial behavior by the church in dealing with clergy who had preyed on innocent victims . . ."[15]

Jim Swilley, pastor for the Church in the Now, who after a wave of teenage suicides related to their homosexuality and mental torment, revealed to his congregation that he is gay. Swilley, told CNN reporter Don Lemon, "There comes a point in your life where you say 'How much time do we have left in our lives? Are we going to be authentic or not?' "[16] Unlike African American Bishop Eddie Long, there is no record of Swilley using the pulpit to denigrate gay members of his congregation. On the other hand, Long frequently used biblical scripture to slander and incite anger against members of the black LGBT community.

Long's alleged closeted homosexuality, personal torment, rage, and insatiable desire for homoeroticism resulted in accusations by four former male congregants that he used his spiritual leadership to seduce them when they were teenagers. Long eventually opted to settle out of court with his accusers.

Even the staunchest opponents of faith-based funding find it difficult to oppose black ministers who take up strong positions aimed at strengthening the black family structure. The fact that one of the key arguments against homosexuality by black clergy is its effect on the black family does not bode well for the struggle for equality by LGBTs in black culture. It is, after all, a spiritual leader's duty to shepherd his or her congregation to a morally right lifestyle. Still, most people understand that this is far different from what some black clergy are accused of doing from the pulpit.

As an African American who acknowledges that there is substantial proof that homophobia, social marginalization, and the mistreatment of black LGBTs is generated—and in some cases encouraged—by the Black Church, it is difficult to reconcile. This is compounded by the fact that the rebuke of LGBTs routinely occurs on the hallowed ground of Black Churches where homosexuality is considered by some as sacrilegious. The notion that the very place where the civil rights struggle occurred and generations of subjugated people united to rise up against their oppressors is now being used to humiliate black churchgoing LGBTs is, to many, blasphemous.

However, it is necessary to consider that the condemnation of homosexuality is a remnant of slavery, and that the modern-day spiritual castration of homosexuals demonstrates slavery's powerful legacy. The fact that it occurs in a consecrated place where refuge from suffering and judgment should be the rule, and is often carried out by spiritual leaders sworn by the tenets of faith to protect their flock is inexcusable. But the question is, why?

In her book *Sexuality and the Black Church: A Womanist Perspective*, Kelly Brown Douglas talks about the use of biblical scripture to justify the cruel vilification of LGBTs by the Black Church, observing that "While there is certainly no excuse for placing a sacred canopy over any type of injustice or human misery Black people's utilization of the Bible to damn homosexuality is somewhat understandable in light of their history of oppression. It is not simply a matter of bigoted refusal to be 'enlightened' by biblical scholarship or of a narrow-minded literalism."[17]

Author and gay African American Episcopal priest Horace L. Griffin talks about the paradoxical quandary in his trailblazing book *Their Own Receive Them Not: African American Lesbians and Gays in Black Churches*. Here Griffin discusses the unspeakable taboo of homosexuality in a way that few have dared to. While there is no one accepted theory of why blacks tend to be more fervently homophobic, Griffin contributes a sound rationalization:

> There will be those who will welcome this book with joy and celebration, relieved that finally black gay Christians whose experience has been diminished or ignored in black churches can now speak for themselves. Yet there will be others for whom this book will awaken dormant rage and hostility toward homosexuality. Some will decry this book as polemical, untrue, and a diabolical betrayal of the black church. In a society where African Americans have been victims of racial oppression, it is difficult for many of the same people to be self-critical and view themselves as victimizers, treating others in ways that they deemed oppressive to themselves . . . [18]

The predisposition within black culture to commit acts of discrimination against black LGBTs was bad enough without being amplified during the Republican drive to recruit black voters. But at the beginning of the twenty-first century as the need for faith-based dollars increased, so did homophobic attitudes within the Black Church. The precipitous rise of blacks discriminating against LGBTs was augmented by a variant type of homophobia, unique to the black community, that fostered a partnership between white and black religious extremists whose common aim was to defeat the drive for equality being waged by the LGBT community. Faith-based funding was at play, and it offered a powerful example of how money, religious extremism, and self-righteousness can bring together groups that are otherwise diametrically opposed on nearly every issue.

This is the perfect storm that occurred when the Black Church and white evangelicals coalesced around a common theme of hatred and contempt toward a shared enemy, the LGBT community.

In Eric Michael Dyson's soul-stirring essay "The Black Church and Sexuality," he writes:

> One of the most painful scenarios of black church life is repeated Sunday after Sunday with little notice or collective outrage. A black minister will preach a sermon railing against sexual ills, especially homosexuality. At the close of the sermon, a soloist, who everybody knows is gay, will rise to perform a moving number, as the preacher extends an invitation to visitors to join the church. The soloist is, in effect, being asked to sign his theological death sentence. His presence at the end of such a sermon symbolizes a silent endorsement of the preacher's message. Ironically, the presence of his gay Christian body at the highest moment of worship also negates the preacher's attempt to censure his presence, to erase his body, to deny his legitimacy as a child of God. . . .
>
> The black church, an institution that has been at the heart of black emancipation, refuses to unlock the oppressive closet for gays and lesbians. . . . Black Christians, who have been despised and oppressed for much of our existence, should be wary of extending that oppression to our lesbian sisters and our gay brothers.[19]

Both Dyson and Griffin speak forcefully to what became a pervasive mindset within black culture, one so entrenched that for black boys, the indoctrination begins as early as when they learn to speak. Some parents teach the words "sissy" and "faggot," which are used to shun any boy perceived as weak or effeminate. This ethnically accepted ostracism begins the deep-seated homophobic thinking that is an integral part of the collective black psyche.

In elementary school, I recall when my class was assigned to write an essay on that proverbial subject: "What do you want to be when you grow up?" It is rare, of course, that children who are nine or 10 years old have any notion of what they want to do with the rest of their life, so needless to say, the responses were of the garden variety: law enforcement officer, firefighter, nurse, doctor, and teacher. However, there was one standout essay written by a classmate that got everyone's attention. The boy stood before the class and proudly read his essay declaring that he wanted to become a florist.

The boy's announcement became the impetus for ridicule and isolation that followed him relentlessly through grade school and beyond. My schoolmate's aspiration to become a florist was preposterously viewed as a unmanly pursuit and set in motion verbal assaults that would continue throughout his schooldays.[20]

Rappers like Ice Cube have underscored for another generation the clutch of slavery and its ability to produce a perverse self-inflicted hatred. When Ice Cube rapped on his *Horny Little Devil* CD that "true niggers aren't gay," his celebrity and abhorrent lyric were powerful instruments that added to the proliferation of discrimination against black LGBTs.[21]

Filmmaker Byron Hurt observed, "I would always defend hip-hop. But the more I grew and the more I learned about the sexism and violence and homophobia, the more those lyrics became unacceptable to me, and I began to become more conflicted about the music that I loved."[22]

It is this sort of hip-hop music that produces a distorted mix of intraracial discrimination and promotes the homophobic neurosis that is extremely damaging to impressionable minds. Perhaps the most damning thing about it is that it perpetuates a false definition of black masculinity and breeds an intraracial bias that continues to do the bidding of long-dead slave masters. Besides that, there is an irrefutable link to hip-hop's misogynistic treatment of black women, rampant homophobia, and heterosexism within the black community. However, identifying slavery as contributing to the problem is intended to make the historical connection. It should not be taken as an attempt to excuse modern-day moral denigration or to excuse Black pastors who participate in the hatemongering and exploitation of black LGBTs.

In his controversial book *Race Matters*, Cornel West says, "White supremacist ideology is based first and foremost on the degradation of black bodies in order to control them."[23] This comes off as a radical point of view, but West's assertion is supported by a considerable amount of evidence found throughout our history. That said, it would require an equal amount of evidence to overcome his theory. The point of view West offers is so straightforward that it gives the impression of summarily setting aside the endless exchange of beliefs about white domination throughout history and its effect on black culture then and now.

During President Lyndon B. Johnson's administration in 1965, scholar and former assistant secretary of labor Daniel P. Moynihan's provocative report on the "Negro family" was issued. In it, Moynihan ties the descent of the Negro family to its exploitation, in which there is no doubt that sexual manipulation, degradation, and control played an integral part. Here

Moynihan hypothesizes about the weakening of the black family structure, saying:

> At the heart of the deterioration of the fabric of Negro society is the
> deterioration of the Negro family. It is the fundamental source of
> the weakness of the Negro community at the present time. There is
> probably no single fact of Negro American life so little understood
> by whites. The Negro situation is commonly perceived by whites in
> terms of the visible manifestation of discrimination and poverty,
> in part because Negro protest is directed against such obstacles, and
> in part, no doubt, because these are facts which involve the actions
> and attitudes of the white community as well. It is more difficult,
> however, for whites to perceive the effect that three centuries of
> exploitation have had on the fabric of Negro society itself. Here the
> consequences of the historic injustices done to Negro Americans are
> silent and hidden from view. But here is where the true injury has
> occurred: unless this damage is repaired, all the effort to end discrimi-
> nation and poverty and injustice will come to little.[24]

This is not a frivolous postulation, but something that helps to explain
the averse and social marginalization of black homosexuals that is driven
by a racial hierarchy still at work today. The best evidence of its existence
is seen when blacks engage in the condemnation of black homosexuals
and make a conscious choice to dismiss the history and plight of the black
race. According to scholars and sociologists who have examined the issue,
when this is done, it fortifies the white hegemony that is at the crux of the
homophobic point of view now prevalent in the black community.
      Author Kelly Brown Douglas, explaining the need for a sexual dis-
course in the black community, elaborates on stereotypes and the white
assault on black sexuality:

> Carnal, passionate, lustful, lewd, rapacious, bestial, sensual—these
> are just some of the many terms that come to mind when thinking
> of the ways in which White culture has depicted Black people's sex-
> uality. This practice of dehumanizing Black people by maligning
> their sexuality has been a decisive factor in the exercise of White
> power in America. So crucial is the exploitation of Black sexuality
> to White dominance that White culture has left almost no stone
> unturned in its violation of Black bodies and intimacy. This violation
> is grounded in numerous sexually charged stereotypes. These stereo-
> types have been critical to the achievement of unprincipled racist

power . . . At the same time, these sexual stereotypes have impacted Black lives in such a way as to render sexuality a virtually taboo topic for the Black church and community.[25]

Douglas alludes to the bizarre power that sex has over the black community, while writer Ofari Hutchinson suggest that fear and a false sense of masculinity are at play. Hutchinson notes that in the past,

Black men mirrored America's traditional fear and hatred of homosexuality. They swallowed whole the phony and perverse John Wayne definition of manhood that real men talked and acted tough, shed no tears, and never showed their emotions. . . . Blacks listened to countless numbers of Black ministers shout and condemn fire and brimstone any man who dared think about, yearn for or God forbid, actually engage in the "godless" and "unnatural act" of having a sexual relationship with another.[26]

The theories offered by West, Moynihan, Brown, Hutchinson, and others who suggest reasons for the black community's vociferous homophobia are enormously persuasive. While this homophobia is not entirely explained by their hypotheses, these writers begin to shed light on the motivation of homophobes like Bishop Eddie Long and Reverend James Meeks, whose fanatical behavior and outrageous preaching about homosexuality and same-sex marriage undermine the faith-based funding concept, and demonstrate the degree to which a homophobic psychosis has infiltrated the Black Church.

Reverend Timothy McDonald, pastor of First Iconium Baptist Church in Atlanta and chair of African American Ministers in Action, goes as far as to suggest a link between receiving faith-based grants and homophobic rhetoric of some black clergy. "If you look at the black pastors who have come out with the faith-based money, they're the same ones who have come out with campaigns on the gay marriage issue."[27] On the matter of connecting the hatemongering, hyperhomophobia, and hypocrisy within the Black Church to faith-based funding, McDonald said what others may have been thinking but were reluctant to say. It was an insightful observation and an outright warning that faith-based funding had created an environment where infringement of the First Amendment, as well as religious and sexual-based discrimination, was becoming an acceptable tradeoff if it resulted in an infusion of faith-based cash.

Seeming to realize the extent to which faith-based funding had helped the Christian Coalition get into the black church, a fired-up Reverend

McDonald referred to the faith-based initiative program during a news conference of the Interfaith Alliance, saying that "It is hard to bark when there's a bone in your mouth . . . " McDonald was joined by Reverend Welton Gaddy, who stressed the initiative was a bad idea when it was conceived in 1999. Their caution about the effect that faith-based funding might have on the Black Church was summed up in a warning about the initiative's real effect when—putting it bluntly—Gaddy said, "It's an ill-conceived, unconstitutional experiment that creates government sponsored religion and threatens the integrity of democracy and the sanctity of religion."[28]

Opposition to the president's domestic agenda came from many sources including, the American Atheists, which took its turn threatening to petition the White House OFBCI, saying that it regarded faith-based funding as an encroachment of the First Amendment:

> Millions of American citizens who are Atheists, rationalists, agnostics or otherwise have concerns for the importance of the First Amendment separation of church and state, oppose your Executive Orders creating a special White House Office of Faith-based and Community Initiatives . . .
>
> It turns the "armies of compassion" into publicly funded "armies of conversion," and imposes a Religion Tax on the American people . . .
>
> No person should be compelled to worship, to believe in a specific religious creed, or financially support through any program or scheme, any church, mosque, temple or faith-based outreach.[29]

When the Episcopal Church passed two resolutions in 1976 entitling homosexuals to equal protection, love, acceptance, and concern it was light years ahead of virtually every other religion in U.S. society. If juxtaposing the Episcopal Church's action over three decades earlier, to what was happening as a result of faith-based funding during the Bush administration, including the deliberate campaign orchestrated by the Religious Right against LGBTs, the Bush initiative seems to have created religious acrimony.

The mounting hostility toward the black LGBT community seemed to support the contention of those who believed the warnings about pervasive and severe discrimination as a result of competition for faith-based funding. The increasing need for funding for a variety of projects and ministries would eventually lead to a scramble for cash during the Bush years. It was an era in which megachurch prosperity preachers like Reverend Creflo Dollar thrived. Dollar's "prosperity gospel" teaches that "You can be rich, healthy and trouble free. Jesus was rich and God wants you to be rich."[30] Dollar for dollar, Reverend Dollar—a televangelist and the senior pastor of the World Changers Church International, a megachurch in College Park, Georgia, with a membership that exceeds 30,000—leads the example of the megachurch prosperity preacher who thrived during the Bush administration while using the pulpit to rebuke homosexuals. While Dollar was not among the 10 black clerics named by the Southern Poverty Law Center (SPLC) in 2007 as one of the leading black religious voices in the antigay movement, he did manage to make Iowa Republican senator Chuck Grassley's list of six pastors known as the Grassley Six, who were targeted for investigation of the tax-exempt status of the ministries under their leadership.[31] Also coming under Grassley's scrutiny were Benny Hinn, Paula White, Eddie L. Long, Joyce Meyer, and Kenneth Copeland. Details of Grassley's investigation will be discussed later.

But it was Dollar who contradicted a couple of thousand years of teaching by theologians when he said, "Did Jesus have money? Well, the Bible was clear. Kings brought him gold." Dollar's statement prompted a response from Grassley that seemed to set the tone for the investigation. Grassley responded saying, "Jesus came into the city on a simple donkey ... What are disciples of his doing flying in jets?"[32]

Dollar is in the purest sense a prosperity preacher and as an early supporter of Bush's domestic agenda, it is not surprising that he was one of the most vocal advocates of faith-based funding. Dollar represented the very worst of black religious extremism by using vile and highly sexual references when talking about gay marriage and insinuating things about gays and their sexual acts. For example Dollar said, "I eat dinner on the dining room table, but if I take my dinner into the rest room and I try to eat it off the toilet stool, then I've extended that freedom far past the place where it was intended to be."[33]

Like most celebrity homophobic preachers, Dollar is unyielding, fixated, and impressed by his influence. His despicable declarations about homosexuals are no different than those of other religious fanatics like Bishop Long, who is quoted as saying that "The problem today and the reason society is like it is, is because men are being feminized and women are being masculine. You can-not say, 'I was born this way.' I don't care what scientists say!"[34]

Dollar's stance against gay marriage and his relentless lobbying of the Congressional Black Caucus to amend the Constitution to ban gay marriage should have warranted at least a mention on the SPLC's list of ill-famed ministers. The only logical explanation of why the popular televangelist eluded the dubious distinction most likely boils down to a matter of space. Nearly the entire spring 2007 edition of the SPLC's periodical was devoted to black ministers who preach hateful and divisive things about members of the black LGBT community.

Those, making the list in "Face Right," Brentin Mock's article exposing the shocking mistreatment of African American LGBTs and hatemongering that permeated Black Churches during the Bush presidency, is quite telling. Mock says, "In a community that has struggled to achieve its own civil rights, angry religious opposition to homosexuals is on the march."[35]

Mock's cutting-edge piece appeared in the *Intelligence Report* Spring 2007 edition. It presents the extremist views espoused by some black clergy regarding homosexuality and the LGBT community. Mock's story uncovers the aura of hate and animosity emanating from the pulpits of some the nation's largest and most prominent Black Churches, where on any given Sunday, a message of contempt toward members of the black LGBT community is spread.

Black clergy who were supportive of the Bush-era domestic agenda and joined the white-dominated Christian Right to viciously attack the LGBT community represent a fraction of black pastors who played a role in the damning proselytizing against black LGBTs. Following are five of those who routinely advocated derision toward LGBTs and whose inflammatory statements were reported in the SPLC story.

REVEREND GREGORY DANIELS, CHICAGO

The Reverend Gregory Daniels says if he "chose" not to be gay, so can others. And they should, he adds, because homosexuality is destroying black America. Reverend Daniels is a key player in the religiously based black antigay movement.

BISHOP WELLINGTON BOONE, NORCROSS, GEORGIA

A spokesman for the patriarchal and largely white Promise Keepers evangelical men's movement, sidekick to Focus on the Family leader James Dobson, and a popular guest on the *700 Club* hosted by Pat Robertson and his Christian Broadcasting Network. Bishop Boone preaches that unchecked homosexuality "will result in the ultimate destruction of society."[36]

REVEREND T. J. GRAHAM, NASHVILLE, TENNESSEE

The Reverend T. J. Graham has a hard time staying off the subject of homosexuality. When he was interviewed by the *Intelligence Report* last September about an anti-immigration rally that he'd helped organize, Graham had trouble keeping his focus on the Mexicans who he was supposed to be discussing. Again and again, his contempt for homosexuals kept spilling into the conversation.

"A homosexual called in and said he was born that way," Graham said at one point, referring to a caller to his WVOL-AM radio show. "You are not born that way. It's a choice."[37] A little later, he added that if any Klansmen showed up at his rallies, he'd be "supportive" of their presence there. Graham's outrageous statement reflects that his opposition to homosexuality is so virulent that he would consort with one of the most hateful white supremacist groups if they opposed LGBTs.

REVEREND JAMES MEEKS, CHICAGO

The Reverend James Meeks is a key member of Chicago's Gatekeepers network, an interracial group of evangelical ministers who strive to erase the division between church and state. A stalwart antigay activist, Meeks has used his House of Hope megachurch to launch petition drives for the Illinois Family Institute (IFI), a major state-level family-values pressure group that lauded him last year for leading African Americans in "clearly understanding the threat of gay marriage."

Meeks and the IFI are partnered with Focus on the Family, the Family Research Council and the Alliance Defense Fund, major antigay organizations of the Christian Right. They also are tightly allied with Americans for Truth, an Illinois group that said in a press release last year that "fighting AIDS without talking against homosexuality is like fighting lung cancer without talking against smoking."[38]

REVEREND WILLIE WILSON, WASHINGTON, D.C.

When a Washington, D.C., newspaper published the contents of an anti-gay sermon delivered by the Reverend Willie Wilson in 2005, it put a major dent into the Reverend Louis Farrakhan's Millions More Movement March scheduled for later that year. Even though Farrakhan and his march ally, New Black Panther Party leader Malik Zulu Shabazz, had repeatedly attacked homosexuals, Wilson's sermon, delivered at his Union Temple Baptist Church, was more inflammatory still. Despite Wilson's position as national executive director for the Millions More Movement, a commemoration of the Million Man March, his words stirred a hornet's nest within that movement.

"Lesbianism is about to take over our community," Wilson said in his sermon. And to gay men: "No wonder your behind is bleeding. It's destroying us."[39]

It is certainly credible to suggest that the deriding and hostile preaching against black LGBTs grew more raucous during the Bush years, a time when faith-based initiatives were touted by the administration. However, we may never know to what extent the competition for faith-based accelerated hostility against LGBTs. Still, there is no doubt that megachurch celebrity black ministers like Creflo Dollar, T. D. Jakes, Floyd Flake, and Eddie Long paved the way for other African American clerics to join forces with the traditional white-dominated Christian Right in a show of contempt for the LGBT community.

For example, Bishop Long supported Bush's candidacy for the presidency, and his ministry later receive a $1 million faith-based grant from the U.S. Administration for Children and Families. In an ironic and shocking twist, four former male parishioners of Long's New Birth Missionary Baptist Church in Lithonia, Georgia, a congregation of about 25,000 members, accused the flamboyant and outspoken pastor of using his spiritual leadership and authority over them to engage in sexual relationships when they were in their teens. Long, whose poisonous and humiliating slurs against LGBTs include him saying that homosexuality is worthy of death, originally denied the charges against him, but later settled out of court with his accusers.

When the scandal broke in 2010, longtime civil rights activist Julian Bond addressed the issue, saying that if proven, the situation would provide a rare public and flagrant example of sexual hypocrisy not uncommon in some Black Churches. Bond is former chair of the National Association for the Advancement of Colored People (NAACP) as well as an outspoken advocate for equality for gay, lesbian, bisexual, and transgender people. In 2006, he refused to attend the funeral of his longtime friend Coretta Scott King because it was held at Long's New Birth Missionary Baptist Church, one of the largest black churches in the nation.

Bond said this about Coretta Scott King: "I knew she was a big defender of gay rights. I knew that Bishop Long was a raving homophobe and I knew she was twisting in her grave if she were buried there and I'd be twisting in my grave eventually if I went to the funeral there, so I stayed

Atlanta Bishop Eddie Long. (AP Photo/John Amis, Pool, File)

away." Speaking of the allegations against Bishop Long, Bond said, "If they are true, it's typical of people who are raving homophobes who are secretly homosexual. They have this self-loathing, self-hate, and they have to let it come out some way."[40]

Continuing, Bond said, "It's sad to say, but if the charges against Bishop Long are true, it's going to be a victory for gay rights in black America. A sad victory."[41] Bond, by alluding to the deception of some gay black clergy who castigate others while hiding their homosexuality had addressed the continuing duplicity within the Black Church.

Make no mistake, there are moderate black religious leaders who are progressive in their thinking. They do not ascribe to hurtful ostracism and ill treatment of LGBTs even though many of them have the same desperate need for financial assistance as their religious brethren. They differ greatly in their treatment of members of the LGBT community, treating them with the love and acceptance shown to all parishioners.

There is no denying that in some Black Churches the hostility toward LGBTs continued to grow more hostile during the Bush administration. In 2005, a counter to the clamorous incendiary preaching against homosexuals was launched. Ironically, the response came in an open letter from Atlanta, considered the cradle of the civil rights movement during the 1950s and 1960s, and decades later referred to as the mecca for black gays.[42]

The challenge came in the 2005 open letter wherein an assembly of African American clerics spoke out after a condensed version of the open letter addressed to Martin Luther King, Jr., appeared in the *Atlanta Journal-Constitution*. The original letter was signed by Alton Pollard III, director of the black church studies program at the Candler School of Theology at Emory University. More than 50 black clergy and theologians from metro Atlanta joined Pollard in publishing the letter in the *Atlanta Daily World*, calling on African American churches to be more sympathetic to the political and spiritual struggles faced by gay men and lesbians. The action was taken to counter the area's growing reputation as "the epicenter of black religious backlash when it comes to issues of human sexuality."[43] Today, the spirit of the open letter continues to be critical to resolving issues related to the treatment of LGBTs by the Black Church.

The letter addressed to Martin Luther King, Jr., read in part:

> Sadly, many black people now have difficulty seeing their connections to other black people. We have embraced societal distinctions that separate us by age, education, gender, sexuality and class. We have forgotten the example set by so many courageous souls a generation ago ... The painful truth is that we now often violate and oppress our own in the name of religion.
>
> Always, at the center of the heart of the historic black-led struggle for freedom was the black religious experience. Black self-love was upheld as a divine imperative. Local black churches became ecumenical networks of nurture and resistance. At those beleaguered places of our most urgent human need common ground often could be sought and found in the church ... [44]

In 2006, Reverend Al Sharpton and other religious and civic leaders joined in chiding the inflammatory preaching of some black clergy against black LGBTs. Reverend Jeremiah Wright, Pastor Emeritus of the Trinity United Church of Christ in Chicago whose congregation at the time included U.S. senator Barack Obama, was a forceful opponent against antigay bias. Prior to his public break with Reverend Wright, Obama had looked to him for guidance related to faith-based initiatives issues.

A parishioner of Reverend Wright's congregation since 1987, Ronald Wadley, talked about the treatment of black LGBTs at Wright's church, saying, "It has always been a very welcoming place for LGBT individuals to come."[45] Wadley has participated in the church's same-gender-loving ministry program.

Prior to coming to Trinity, Wadley said, he was raised in a Baptist church that taught antigay messages. He applauded the leadership at Trinity for refusing to "gay-bash from the pulpit." Wadley continued, saying, "I'm a very vocal, very political, African-American gay man, and being able to also go to church and worship God and not have to feel like I'm going to hell because of who I am and who God created me to be is very important ... "[46]

Over the years, Reverend Wright has included LGBT-inclusive sermons and welcomed individuals with HIV/AIDS to his church. In fact, Trinity had one of Chicago's first church-run HIV/AIDS ministries. Toward the end of 2007, according to congregation members, Wright voiced his opposition to and disgust with antigay violence in a sermon following news of the murder of Trinity's openly gay choir director Donald Young.[47]

NOTES

1. Leviticus 18:29.

2. http://newsletters.cephasministry.com/04_01_pros_and_cons_faith_based.html. Accessed January 15, 2012.

3. Community Solutions Act of 2001.

4. http://cfed.org/assets/documents/SWFA/Timeline_on_Asset_Building_Policy_2009_July.pdf. Accessed January 15, 2012

5. http://www.globalethics.org/newsline/2002/12/16/bush-bypasses-congress-to-push-faith-based-initiative/. Accessed February 1, 2011.

6. Hamil Harris, "Bush proposal is worrisome," *Washington Post*, February 2001, B3; R. Drew Smith and Fredrick C. Harris, *Black Churches and Local Politics: Clergy Influence, Organizational Partnerships, and Civic Empowerment* (Lanham, MD: Rowman & Littlefield Publishers, 2005).

7. http://www.littleindia.com/october2003/Till%20Ethnicity%20Do%20us%20Part.htm. Accessed February 3, 2011.

8. http://www.globalethics.org/newsline/2002/12/16/bush-bypasses-congress-to-push-faith-based-initiative/. Accessed February 1, 2011.

9. http://www.rickross.com/reference/general/general411.html. Accessed February 4, 2011.

10. http://thebostonphoenix.com/boston/news_features/top/documents/00422453.htm. Accessed February 12, 2011.

11. http://www.au.org/resources/brochures/the-religious-rights-war-on-lgbt-americans/. Accessed February 2011.

12. http://www.interfaithalliance.org/news?start=180. Accessed February 21, 2011.

13. *New York Times*, February 2004.

14. Louis Farrakhan, "Savior's Day speech," Chicago, February 23, 2003, http://www.adl.org/special_reports/farrakhan_own_words2/on_homosexuals.asp. Accessed February 14, 2011.

15. Anthony Stanford, "On a day of rebirth, grieving a loss of faith," *Chicago Tribune*, March 23, 2008, http://articles.chicagotribune.com/2008-03-23/news/0803220263_1_religious-group-high-mass-doubt. Accessed February 22, 2011.

16. http://www.huffingtonpost.com/2010/11/14/jim-swilley-gay-pastor_n_783279.html.

17. Kelly-Brown Douglas, *Sexuality and the Black Church: A Womanist Perspective* (Maryknoll, NY: Orbis Books, 1991), 91.

18. Horace L. Griffin, *Their Own Receive Them Not: African American Lesbians and Gays in Black Churches* (Cleveland, OH: Pilgrim Press, 2006).

19. http://www.huffingtonpost.com/terrance-heath/are-blacks-more-homophobi_b_142543.html. Accessed February 6, 2011.

20. Anthony Stanford, *Aurora Beacon News*, October 6, 2010, http://beaconnews.suntimes.com/news/stanford/1872434-418/black-youth-church-african-american.html.

21. http://www.azlyrics.com/lyrics/icecube/hornylittledevil.html. Accessed February 9, 2011.

22. http://www.pbs.org/independentlens/hiphop/gender.htm. Accessed February 9, 2011.

23. Cornel West, *Race Matters*, 85.

24. Patrick Moynihan, "The negro family," http://www.dol.gov/oasam/programs/history/moynchapter2.htm.

25. Kelly Brown Douglas, *Sexuality and the Black Church*, 31.

26. Delroy Constantine-Simms, ed., *The Greatest Taboo: Homosexuality in the Black Community*, 2000.

27. http://www.democraticunderground.com/discuss/duboard.php ?az=view_all&address=221x27385.

28. http://www.interfaithalliance.org/news/208-unconstitutional-experiment-threatens-religion-and-democracy April 28 2006. Accessed February 3, 2011.

29. American Atheist Society, http://www.religioustolerance.org/ char_choi3.htm. Accessed February 14, 2011.

30. Creflo Dollar, "You can be rich, healthy and trouble free: Jesus was rich and God wants you to be rich."

31. "Grassley Six": Six prosperity preachers investigated by Iowa Senator Chuck Grassley.

32. http://www.religionnewsblog.com/16438/was-jesus-rich. Accessed January 15, 2012.

33. http://jasmynecannick.typepad.com/jasmynecannickcom/2006/ 11/putting_the_sep.html. Accessed January 15, 2012.

34. Bishop Eddie Long, http://www.splcenter.org/get-informed/ intelligence-report/browse-all-issues/2007/spring/face-right/the-preachers -mini-profile#.

35. Southern Poverty Law Center, "Brentin Mock face right," *Intelligence Report*, Spring 2007.

36. Ibid.

37. http://www.splcenter.org/get-informed/intelligence-report/ browse-all-issues/2007/spring/face-right/the-preachers-mini-profile.

38. http://www.splcenter.org/get-informed/intelligence-report/ browse-all-issues/2007/spring/face-right/the-preachers-mini-profile.

39. http://www.splcenter.org/get-informed/intelligence-report/ browse-all-issues/2007/spring/face-right/the-preachers-mini-profile#. Accessed February 18, 2011.

40. http://www.thegavoice.com/index.php/news/national-news-menu/ 1187-civil-rights-leader-julian-bond-speaks-out-on-eddie-long-same-sex -scandal?awesm=fbshare.me_ATmoB. Accessed December 4, 2012.

41. http://www.thegavoice.com/index.php/news/national-news-menu/ 1187-civil-rights-leader-julian-bond-speaks-out-on-eddie-long-same-sex -scandal. Accessed February 12, 2011.

42. http://www.inthelifeatl.com/community/. Accessed February 11, 2011.

43. Ryan Lee, "Black clergy unite to publicly support gay rights: Pastors offer 'a more hope-filled perspective,' February 4, 2005. Accessed February 17, 2011.

44. http://www.google.com/search?sourceid=navclient&ie=UTF-8 &rlz=1T4GGHP_en___US414&q=Jan.+17+in+the+Atlanta-Journal +Constitution+Pollard. Accessed February 17, 2011.

45. http://www.windycitymediagroup.com/gay/lesbian/news/ARTICLE .php?AID=17869. Accessed February 15, 2011.

46. http://www.windycitymediagroup.com/gay/lesbian/news/ARTICLE .php?AID=17869. Accessed February 15, 2011.

47. Ibid.

THREE

Faith in Money

Nor thieves, nor covetous, nor drunkards, nor revilers, nor extortioners, shall inherit the kingdom of God.[1]

The lure of faith-based funding gave the GOP and Christian Coalition their long sought after foothold in the Black Church. Among those joining the chorus praising President Bush's domestic program as a godsend were faith-based recipients and wannabes who hoped to benefit from an infusion of faith-based funding. Some, who were eyed as potential recruits, saw federal funding as a means of augmenting church coffers and bolstering their association with the Bush administration. A number of these cash-strapped ministers identified with the president's domestic agenda and were sympathetic to the antigay message emanating from the Christian Right and as a result were encouraged to join the battle to protect "family values."

In particular, black inner-city megachurch ministers whose moderate or extreme views on same-sex marriage and antigay issues were consistent with those of the Religious Right were at the very top of the list and were aggressively pursued. In some instances, recruitment was not always needed because relationships with the Republican Party already existed. For the most part, the preexisting alliances were centered on a shared opposition to homosexuality and same-sex marriage, for example, the one between powerful megachurch pastor Floyd Flake, a former Democratic U.S. representative from New York, that turned out to be important for the Republican Party, particularly in attracting other black ministers to the cause.

Encouraged by influential black ministers like Reverend Flake, a number of black ministers who routinely preached against LGBTs and same-sex unions, and who identified with the deeply rooted cultural aversion toward homosexuality within the black community were eager to participate and to spread the antigay message to black churchgoers. Courted by the Religious Right, these black ministers would be instrumental in furthering the antigay agenda and defeating same-sex marriage legislation.

Reverend Flake—who left Congress in 1997 to devote himself to his role as senior pastor of the 20,000-member Greater Allen A.M.E. Cathedral of New York Jamaica, Queens—openly condemned homosexuality and enthusiastically supported President Bush's faith-based agenda. As a member of the African American clergy, Reverend Flake was not alone in his stance toward the black Christian LGBT community; he was joined by other influential black megachurch ministers who ardently opposed same-sex civil unions and LGBT equality issues, and were willing to publicly denounce homosexuality to their massive congregations and the wider community. However, it was Reverend Flake's fondness for the politic arena that made his support for the president's domestic agenda an extremely valuable commodity to the Republican Party and Christian Right. Reverend Flake's desire for the limelight was noted in a November 30, 2002, article wherein Russ Baker describes an October 6, 2002, event at which Reverend Flake introduced President Bush in a way that can only be described as bizarre. Critics may have interpreted it not only as an indication of Flake's lingering proclivity for politics, but also his unbridled willingness to go to any lengths to maintain alliances with Republican heavyweights who controlled the federal purse string and as a result his ability to expand his church and related projects. Baker described the event in this way: "... The crowd at the Manhattan Institute—a mostly white, clubby, conservative think tank—enjoyed one of those delicious pinch-me moments: hearing a speaker improbably introduce George W. Bush as 'my homeboy.' ... Floyd Flake has been blurring party lines for some time now, not just warming up Republican crowds, but actually endorsing the candidacies of Republican New Yorkers Rudy Giuliani, George Pataki, and Alfonse D'Amato."[2]

In another notable instance, Reverend Flake appeared on the PBS's *NewsHour* on January 29, 2001. After attending the signing ceremony for the president's faith-based initiatives program, during the *NewsHour* appearance Reverend Flake talked about Bush's domestic program, vigorously defending the Republican domestic agenda.

During the broadcast, another *NewsHour* guest, Wendy Kaminer, a public policy fellow at Radcliffe College and a contributing correspondent of the *American Prospect* magazine. referred to faith-based initiatives, making her point by saying that "Charitable Choice bills allow for federal support of sectarian religious proselytizing. It's hard to imagine a more basic violation of First Amendment freedoms. And it's also impossible to imagine how you might enforce prohibitions on using federal dollars directly to proselytize without having federal bureaucrats policing the activities of sectarian groups, which they're not going to want."[3] Kaminer's position against the president's domestic plan continues to be a popular one used to imply a violation of the constitutional safeguards related to the separation of church and state. Kaminer's example, when used correctly, can be effective in putting evangelicals and conservatives on the defensive to explain how federal monies can be utilized by churches and faith-based organizations without violating a basic principle of the First Amendment.

When *NewsHour* host Gwen Ifill asked Flake to respond to Kaminer's assertion regarding the separation between church and state, Flake became defensive, referring to the church as a "basic institution," and its parishioners, saying, ". . . They deserve to have some of those benefits come back. And if they come back through that particular institution, that is all for the good because, again, those institutions are in the communities where those people are. They're in the communities where they serve the people. And the level of trust is far superior to the level of trust that they have for the government."[4]

As a former elected official and longtime religious leader, Reverend Flake's blunt and sometimes coarse criticism of same-sex marriage and homosexuality are a matter of record. In fact, "Flake is among a group of black clergy whose predilection for denouncing the immorality of homosexuality by comparing it to the irrationality of 'eating out of the toilet bowl,' is well known."[5] Reverend Flake's crude denunciation of homosexuality is strikingly similar to other black megachurch ministers who repeatedly use depraved descriptions to denounce the LGBT community. For instance, Atlanta megachurch preacher Reverend Creflo Dollar's inflammatory use of moral denigration and alienation of the LGBT community could be viewed as tantamount to psychological aggression. Throughout the Bush administration, the public rage and loathing by black ministers toward the LGBT community played to Conservative Right and white evangelicals whose primary mission was to generate, spread, and sustain this sort of reaction throughout Black Churches. This was incredibly important in the case of prominent black megachurch ministers with large voting-age congregations because it furthers the dehumanization of the LGBT community and strengthens support in the campaign against gay rights and same-sex unions.

Having developed more than $102 million worth of land, building new homes and hundreds of senior housing units by utilizing a variety of financing sources, including funding from the Department of Housing and Urban Development (HUD), Reverend Flake was no newcomer to controversy or the many ways that political relationships can translate into access to taxpayer dollars. For example, in 1990, the *New York Times* reported: "The complaints by an executive assistant, who said Mr. Flake had seduced her into an adulterous affair, stirred a former church trustee to come forward with allegations of fiscal improprieties. That in turn resulted in a 17-count Federal indictment last week, charging Mr. Flake and his wife with diverting thousands of dollars in church money to their own use."[6] However, on April 3, 1991, a judge ruled that the Flakes' use of the funds was not improper, and the charges against both were dropped.

In a more recent incident related to a 2006 real estate transaction in which Reverend Flake and his former chief financial officer, the Reverend Edwin C. Reed were involved, Reverend Flake's church came under intense media scrutiny. This case, according to the *New York Times*, involved properties that were built and subsidized with taxpayer money. The controversy involved a property that was sold by Reverend Flake's church to a for-profit organization for $14 million. Tenants who occupied the property were notified by mail, and the transaction was touted by New York mayor Michael R Bloomberg as an effort to preserve and build housing for moderate and low-income residents. However, the announcement about the sale did not disclose that the new controlling owners were Reverend Flake; the Reverend Edwin C. Reed, who was then the church's former chief financial officer; and two real estate developers, Peter G. Florey and Leonard T. D'Amico. According to the *New York Times*, "After taking ownership, Mr. Flake, one of the city's most politically influential pastors, and his partners decided how to split a $1.1 million fee for overseeing renovation work at the project. They also decided alone how much to pay themselves for their services from the $4.3 million in cash after expenses that the city expects the property to produce through 2018."[7]

As a former congressman and apart from his considerable political connections, Reverend Flake's knowledge of federal programs no doubt was useful during the Bush years when he and other black ministers effectively used mixed financing, a combination of both public and private funds, including faith-based and other federal sources of funding, to increase the size of their congregations and to expand their political influence. In fact, faith-based funding would become an important source of revenue depended upon by a number of Black Churches and other religious-based organizations.

More recently, Reverend Flake has expressed his displeasure with the Obama administration and changes in the faith-based program, saying in 2010, " . . . I am concerned about the controversy surrounding the program," while indicating that he had not received help from the Obama administration. Flake also said that he tries not to depend on the federal government for financial assistance, saying, "Once you accept, it drops you in the social bucket," indicating that people develop too much dependence on the government.[8]

In Chicago, a place of storied civil rights struggles where the iconic Reverend Martin Luther King, Jr., frequently visited to carry on the black freedom struggle and to fight for the underprivileged and numerous national black leaders honed their skills, an association with the Christian Right may have seemed not only unimaginable, but bordering on treasonous. However, there were no charges of betrayal when forces supported by the Conservative Right used biblical scriptures and faith-based funding to produce an odd but powerful alliance that coalesced over efforts to spurn members of the LGBT community and defeat same-sex marriage advocates. The association proved an overwhelming success for the Christian Right and an effective way of co-opting black ministers who were in dire financial straits and desperate for funding to maintain vital social services and ministries for their congregations. Emboldened by biblical scripture and financial need, some black minister could easily rail on against homosexuality and same-sex unions from the pulpit, and many members of their congregations expected and could enthusiastically support such condemnation.

During both Bush presidential terms, federal money and biblical scripture were used to connect the Black Church, Republican Party, and Religious Right. For nearly an entire decade, the bizarre relationship kept the antigay, same-sex marriage fight before black congregations and more blatantly than any time in recent memory Black Christian LGBTs were singled out and humiliated before their faith community. However, the use of biblical scripture by black religious and civic leaders to sway opinion is nothing new. An example of the brazen use of biblical scripture to influence black voters was seen during the 2010 Chicago mayoral race when U.S. representative Danny Davis (D-IL), a black man supporting a black mayoral candidate, shamelessly suggested in a radio ad that the Bible would consider a black person who didn't vote for his candidate to be "worse than any infidel."[9]

The uncommon relationship between black clergy and white evangelicals appeared to form quickly and without much difficulty regarding moral invectives related to same-sex marriage, resistance to LGBT equality, and faith-based funding. The mutually shared animosity toward the LGBT community was the glue that held these two unlikely allies together, allowing them to overlook differences that would have otherwise been a deal breaker. This was discussed in an April 6, 2001, article by *Chicago Tribune* religion reporter Julia Lieblich and gives a sense of the power that faith-based funding had in affecting opinion and influencing black clergy and civic leaders to do things that they might otherwise not consider. It also speaks to the desperation of some black ministers and gives a sense of their perspective at the time on faith-based funding. "... Rev. Walter B. Johnson, pastor of the Wayman African Methodist Episcopal Church, didn't vote for President Bush and rarely sings his praises, so when the administration announced its controversial faith-based initiative Johnson had to think long and hard about whether to sign on. In the end, Johnson joined other African-American ministers in Chicago and nationwide who are emerging as the most unexpected and vocal supporters of Bush's faith-based plan ..."[10] While this article is certainly not overwhelming confirmation that most black ministers supported Bush's faith-based program, as restrictions on the stream of funding were lifted and funds were made available, the number of black ministers who favored the use of faith-based money increased. And the funding that had started in the infancy of the Bush presidency as a trickle, blocked time after time by politics and untimely events, began flowing with the signing of Executive Order 13279 on December 12, 2002.

As black megachurch ministers gave their support to President Bush's domestic agenda, more and more of them who openly or secretly opposed same-sex marriage and the LGBT community's demands for equality united with the band of antigay intolerants whose mission was to defeat legislation favoring LGBT causes. However, the reality is that while they may have found common ground in their attempt to stall the fight for fairness being waged by the LGBT community, in some cases, their alliances were beginning to show signs of the strain that had put them at odds for generations. For example, it was obvious that one particular relationship was tenuous and beset with racial discord reminiscent of the pre–civil rights era:

> White leaders of the Christian Right who had long sought to recruit blacks to a unified anti-gay crusade had at last found the common ground needed to build a lasting partnership with an anti-gay agenda as its objective. One effort launched by conservative Christian organizations funneled money to black anti-gay churches through programs such as the Christian Coalition's ill-fated Samaritan Project.

The project raised money for black churches that promoted family values. However, the Samaritan Project fell apart when a lawsuit was filed by black employees against the Christian Coalition in 2001. The lawsuit claimed that black workers were required to enter the meeting facility through a back door and that the white and black groups were segregated during breaks. The issue was ultimately settled in an out of court agreement.[11]

During a Congressional Black Caucus forum attended by Representative Emmanuel Cleaver II (D-MO), who is also a minister, Bishop T. D. Jakes, Reverend Floyd Flake, and Chicago pastor and Illinois state senator James Meeks, an audience member asked if the pastors who had accepted faith-based grants had "sold out." Bishop Jakes responded to the question defensively, saying, "Government grants are minuscule compared to the dollars that mega churches generate. . . . If the government says we give you 30 cents on every dollar, you have to put in 70 cents to match the dollars and then the media comes along and says you have been bought. The real story is most faith-based money is flying over the black community."[12]

Bishop Jakes may have handily dodged the question by not addressing whether the funds should be accepted and what, if anything, is expected in return. However, Bishop Jakes's response almost certainly heightened speculation that black clergy who accepted faith-based funding, or who were considering doing so, were to some extent touchy about it and reluctant to explain the appearance of a burgeoning alliance with the Republican Party and white evangelicals. This was something that if delved into could potentially boomerang and trigger problems with liberal and moderate black churchgoers.

Still, T. J. Jakes's hypersensitivity doesn't negate what is seen as an enormous triumph by white evangelicals, one that brought on board black pastors who hailed from some of the country's largest megachurches to participate in a hugely effective multiethnic national effort against the acceptance of homosexuality and same-sex marriage, which had at its core a mutual contempt for members of the LGBT community. In fact, opposition to the LGBT community resonated with so many that the oneness and a shared fanaticism with black moralists over the issue of homosexuality and same-sex marriage brought homophobic white and black ministers together in lock step. Their unity and rigid stance against homosexuality and forbidding any aberration of male-female gender roles was used, quite effectively, to advance a crusade of intolerance and to solidify support for Bush's faith-based agenda.

Brentin Mock's outstanding 2007 SPLC piece discusses how black cultural homophobia and the allure of federal faith-based dollars was used by the Christian Right to cozy up to black clergy and to successfully develop what would otherwise seem an inconceivable association. In this article, Mock talks about how black ministers predisposed to oppose homosexuality and same-sex marriage were targeted by the Conservative Right with financial inducements in order to transmit its morality message to black churchgoers. However, it must be said that the black ministers who were receptive to the financial stimulus were already likely engaged in hate-mongering against black Christian LGBTs and as a result were primed and eager to treat them as if they were members of a counterculture. Mock said, "In addition, the faith-based funding initiatives of the current Bush Administration provide financial incentives for black preachers to promote a marriage agenda that's hostile to gays and lesbians, through federal programs such as the $1.5 billion Healthy Marriage Initiative. That initiative provides funding to religious groups, mostly in inner-city areas, to promote 'healthy marriages,' defined as 'married families with two biological parents.' "[13]

Championed by the Conservative Right and Moral Majority, campaigns like the Healthy Marriage Initiative used financial reward, moral supremacy, and fear to propagate the prospect of a spreading malignant sexual deviancy and destruction of the American family structure and garner support for their antigay agenda. For example, after Bishop Long received a $1 million faith-based grant, in what might be perceived as quid pro quo, the megachurch minister intensified his already scurrilous attack on the black LGBT community by encouraging his mammoth congregation and other black ministers to voice their objections to homosexuality and same-sex marriage.

In 2004, after Bishop Eddie Long received the faith-based grant from the Administration for Children and Families, Esther Kaplan, a critic of the Bush administration and well-known commentator and author of the 2005 book *With God on Their Side: George W. Bush and the Christian Right* told the Atlanta gay newspaper the *Southern Voice* that "It cannot be bad for your career as a black minister at this point to speak out against gay marriage."[14]

Efforts by the Bush administration to forge relationships with religious organizations were exceedingly ambitious and highly successful. The extent to which the administration was willing to go in order to expand its domestic agenda and association with the religious community is seen in the president's directive to the federal agencies who were associated with the (OFBCI). It is here that the president sought to coordinate the services of federal agencies by eliminating regulatory, contracting, and other programmatic obstacles to the participation of faith-based and other community organizations in the provision of social services. Prior to this unilateral action, there was not nearly enough funding to implement the Bush plan, so for faith-based proponents and religious organizations that were likely to benefit from the action, it was a godsend when funds were finally made available. During fiscal year 2005, more than $2.2 billion in competitive social service grants were awarded to faith-based organizations. Between fiscal years 2003 and 2005, the total dollar amount of all grants awarded to faith-based organizations (FBOs) increased by a whopping 21 percent, with the majority of these grants being distributed through state agencies to local organizations in the form of federal formula grants distributed to recipients based on how much funding they qualified for.

As reflected in Table 3.1, by 2007, the federal government was providing more than 19,000 direct, competitive awards to U.S. nonprofit organizations to aid the homeless, at-risk youth, recovering addicts, returning offenders, people infected or affected by HIV/AIDS, and others. The grants totaled more than $15.3 billion, with FBOs winning more than 3,200 grants in 2007 that totaled over $2.2 billion.[15]

The Bush administration's efforts to build partnerships in the black community were mainly focused on religious groups who in turn sought to get others to join their faith through evangelizing. Faith-based service providers could then be counted on to steer potential clients to beliefs that were in keeping with their viewpoint on homosexuality and same-sex marriage. However, to successfully prosecute this ambitious strategy and execute the president's faith-based funding program as it was intended, it would be necessary to retool and implement major changes in the way federal programs operated. For instance, religious and community faith-based organizations wanted an assurance that their operations would not be hampered by excessive federal restrictions, auditing, and oversight, something that had long prevented their participation in federal funding programs. Fully appreciating the impact that the program's effectiveness would have on President Bush's domestic agenda, the consensus within the administration was to move away from the massive federal efforts of the past toward programs that were streamlined and grounded in personalized relationships with communities and faith-based neighborhood groups. Changes related to reducing government oversight went a long way toward building trust and was viewed as the optimal approach to creating partnerships and using faith-based programs to demonstrate success with government and religious organizations working together.

Table 3.1 Federal Competitive Funding Won By Faith-Based and Secular Non-Profits FY06

Agency	Total Awarded	Secular	%	Faith-Based	%
Department of Health and Human Services	$9,774,274,710	$6,786,010,680	69.4	$723,171,246	7.4
US Agency for International Development	$3,884,458,053	$2,962,398,068	76.3	$552,363,250	14.2
Department of Housing and Urban Development	$2,054,962,792	$1,232,496,540	60.0	$512,014,071	24.9
U.S. Department of Agriculture	$1,811,016,754	$602,890,595	33.3	$193,038,168	10.7
Department of Justice	$645,485,827	$297,284,488	46.1	$73,091,780	11.3
Department of Labor	$157,088,195	$117,430,278	74.8	$15,536,283	9.9
Department of Education	$191,663,976	$68,502,686	35.7	$15,221,243	7.9
Corporation for National and Community Service	$573,020,592	$382,114,158	66.7	$69,892,379	12.2
Department of Commerce	$285,534,489	$58,301,191	20.4	$8,552,860	3.0
Veterans Administration	$69,158,052	$43,204,424	62.5	$20,790,952	30.1
Small Business Administration	$12,246,842	$10,250,756	83.7	$989,192	8.1
TOTAL	$19,458,910,282	$12,560,883,864	64.6	$2,184,661,424	11.2

Notes:
1. FY06 data are from a review of 134 competitive programs at HHS (65), HUD (11), DOJ (14), DOL (11), ED (5), USDA (20), DOC (6), VA (1), SBA (1), and 35 competitive program areas at USAID (26) and CNS (9). Percentages based on amounts awarded.
2. CNS used its own internal data collection method that differs in some ways from the standard process, notably that it included some programs from which grants to FBCOs came via state subgrants rather than directly from the federal government.
3. In a review of awarded totals from the seven agencies for which data are available in FY05, the amount to faith-based rose from 11.2 to 11.3 percent, while the amount to secular nonprofits fell from 66.2 to 65.1 percent.

A bold and unprecedented federally driven approach was used to gauge the viability of public-private partnerships and to address societal problems, something especially important and ultimately quite effective in the black community. With key players in place and funding available, the president's armies of compassion began attacking the need and leveling the playing field throughout communities in the manner that candidate Bush had so often talked about. The strategy referred to as the "determined attack on need" focused on a wide range of social issues like hunger, crime, homelessness, and HIV/AIDS, and it left little doubt that faith-based funding would be used to target the social problems that plagued the inner city and threatened minority communities. A robust White House commitment of no less than a dozen federal agencies and a cadre of governmental departments began working on the all-important mission of expanding and enhancing partnerships with nonprofit groups, frequently interacting with social service organizations that had no previous experience working with the federal government.

Acting as faith-based centers, federal agencies were pivotal to the success of the faith-based agenda. Guided by the OFBCI, they would lead the charge by implementing what amounted to an historic and transformational method for the government to interact with churches and faith-based groups. One crucial change paramount to the federal government's effort was to foster new and lasting relationships with churches and faith-based organizations absent the restrictive requirements of the past. Another important change that had previously been a sticking point was that eligibility for federal funding would no longer require that churches and faith-based service organizations eliminate symbols of religious affiliation or discontinue their efforts to evangelize as a condition of receiving federal funds. By far, this was the most significant change and one that played extremely well to black ministers whose ability to sell the Republican agenda to churchgoers almost certainly hinged on this crucial stipulation.

Because these were issues that had plagued faith-based funding efforts over the years, no one was surprised when the program came under fire by faith-based funding opponents for being laden with controversy and charges of First Amendment violations. However, the administration prepared to take immediate action to head off other potential problems and hoped to avoid a recurrence of the debacle that occurred during the mid-1990s. The last thing it wanted was a repeat of anything resembling the embarrassing and controversial affair that occurred when the Nation of Islam received federal funding from HUD, only later to become the target of a sweeping investigation that would severely strain partnerships and trigger a humiliating episode for the Clinton administration.

Under the Clinton administration, HUD had given contracts totaling more than $15 million to Chicago-based companies linked to the Nation of Islam to provide security at public housing projects in Chicago and a number of major cities throughout the country. Then, as a mid-level manager working for HUD, I vividly recall the political and racially charged climate that ensued when U.S. senator Robert Dole (R-KS) and U.S. representative Peter King demanded to know why a federal agency had contracted with the Nation of Islam to provide security at public housing projects in Baltimore, Chicago, Philadelphia, Cleveland, and Pittsburgh. Nation of Islam minister Louis Farrakhan, viewed by some as a fanatic and anti-Semitic—and who had on a number of occasions used his pulpit to attack Jews, Catholics, and others—was the source of the political firestorm that played out over several months. Representative King, a fervent critic of Farrakhan, who some viewed as stoking the fires of racial discord, said this when opposing the federal contracts: "You can't separate the message from the messenger when the messenger is as evil as Louis Farrakhan."[16]

Given Minister Farrakhan's well-known hate-filled rhetoric, King's motive is difficult to refute. King and others who opposed the federal government's contractual agreement with the Nation of Islam repeatedly cited Farrakhan's anti-Semitic message as reason to terminate funding. However, a significant and rather ironic hitch in the mounting political opposition was that Farrakhan's Nation of Islam was, according to experts, achieving measurable—some say remarkable—results. The Nation of Islam had contracted with the federal government to oversee tenant protective services at some of the nation's worst public housing projects, where gang activity and open-air drugs sales were rampant. In fact, a number of leaders had heaped praise on the results achieved by the Nation of Islam. Irrespective of the politics or motives, public housing professionals, residents, and politicians alike who had commended the achievements of Farrakhan and the Nation of Islam and its ability to establish rapport with residents of public housing communities and to achieve quantifiable results were put in an awkward position that almost entirely broke along party lines.

The Nation of Islam's success in meeting its contractual obligations and effecting change gave credence to the belief that politics was the real motive for King's attempt to end the contractual agreement with the federal government. According to the Anti-Defamation League, "Henry G. Cisneros, Secretary of Housing and Urban Development, says doing business with the Nation Islam is like doing business with B'nai B'rith, Catholic Charities, Lutheran Social Services United Church Homes,

Habitat for Humanity, and the Salvation Army."[17] Secretary Cisneros, a Clinton cabinet member, defended the Nation of Islam contract and set the tone for the debate over federal funding and the rights of religious organizations to participate in federal programs when he fought to maintain the relationship with the Nation of Islam. Nonetheless, amid a heated partisan environment, increasing controversy, and political pressure, it became an insurmountable issue that ended in the termination of all of HUD's contracts with the Nation of Islam. In the end, it turns out that the justification used to terminate the Nation of Islam contracts would just several years later be immaterial since the faith-based funding policies supported by the Bush administration contradict King's objection and the action taken against the Nation of Islam. This is because under Bush administration guidelines, which require examining the effectiveness of the program being offered by a religious organization, action to defund the Nation of Islam would not have been taken. Even if the Nation of Islam were proselytizing and distributing copies of its *Final Call* newspaper that some say encourages anti-Semitism and racial separation, this would not justify denying participation in the faith-based funding program. During the Bush administration, Farrakhan would condemn Bush's faith-based funding proposal, calling it an effort by the Republicans to woo black clergy. "Bush is not foolish," Farrakhan told a crowd of about 4,000. "He wants to win you, preacher."[18]

The federal government's reputation (which some say is well deserved) for being difficult to deal with was the primary reason given by religious groups who vowed to steer clear of the Bush administration's faith-based funding no matter how desperate their financial situation. The persistent belief held by religiously based organizations that the acceptance of federal funding would encumber their organizations with red tape was quickly identified by the Bush administration as the single biggest impediment to the success of faith-based funding. From the beginning, just as he had when he was governor of Texas, President Bush sought to revise the widespread perception. For example, an immediate hurdle to overcome involved rumors that were fueling speculation that acceptance of faith-based funding would bring legions of bureaucrats who would require rigorous reporting, federal oversight, and the elimination of all religious symbolism associated with the faith-based organization. The ultimate deterrent was fear that the organization's financial records would be subjected to federal oversight, audit requirements, and Internal Revenue Service (IRS) regulators. These assumed disincentives, along with the general suspicion that the acceptance of faith-based funding would interfere with efforts to evangelize, were enough to dissuade many faith-based organizations representing every denomination. These and other worries were enumerated in a report titled "Unlevel Playing Field: Barriers to Participation by Faith-Based and Community Organizations in Federal Social Service Programs," in which major hindrances were identified and addressed by the Bush administration. The August 2001 report identified 15 obstacles viewed as barriers by faith-based and grass-roots community organizations that perceived government programs as a problem. It was believed that eliminating these obstacles was key to the success of the president's domestic agenda and primarily hinged on the ability to quash negative rumors about the acceptance of faith-based funding and to remove the components that were perceived by potential participants as burdensome. The government's comprehensive report concluded that the end goal was to make all groups feel welcome and open to building lasting partnerships with the government. Toward this end, President Bush took drastic measures, mandating that federal agencies eliminate barriers that impeded or gave the appearance of obstructing the formation of partnerships with capable faith-based and community nonprofits possessing the ability to assist their communities.

A major change assigned the responsibility of conquering the 15 problems identified in the report to the heads of the federal agencies that administered the programs. Suddenly saddled with the herculean task of collaborating with faith-based community organizations, developing viable strategies tailored to their agency's specific mission, and being held solely responsible for success of the program, there was reason for optimism that the relationships between faith-based groups and the government would improve. However, first the effort would require both the creation and expansion of programs that targeted urban centers and the societal problems that plagued them. It was also agreed that a renewed and fortified diligence to garner trust, mostly through the active pursuit and encouragement of alliances with black faith-based groups, was essential. If successful, the concentrated effort focusing on issues that directly affected African American and minority communities would go a long way in helping to strengthen existing relationships and to form new partnerships with faith-based groups that had previously been reluctant to participate.

Expounding on a host of problems, the federal report identified specific obstacles that had prevented faith-based groups and the federal government from enjoying a productive working relationship. At the top of the list was the need to change the mindset of government officials whose longstanding suspicion of faith-based organizations had been viewed as a serious problem that hampered any real chance for a partnership. This, along with identifying and eliminating unnecessary restrictions on religious activities undertaken by faith-based groups as well as reducing the burden of reporting requirements, was viewed as a significant hurdle that if eliminated would go a long way toward bolstering the rapport between the federal government and faith-based organizations.

Getting there would require the involvement of over a dozen key federal agencies and departments overseeing Centers for Faith-Based Community Initiatives (CFBCI) and collaborating with local nonprofit groups that had partnered to fulfill the president's domestic objectives. By taking on delicate issues that were known to hamper already fragile alliances, these participating federal agencies worked to build relationships grounded in trust and driven by the underlying and acute need for funding. Once the bond with the Faith-Based Community Organizations (FBCOs) was achieved, federal agencies like the Department of Health and Human Services (HHS) and HUD were able to focus on problems like at-risk youth, urban poverty, and teenage pregnancy by utilizing an army of more than 4,000 FBCOs advocates.

In a study conducted by Dr. David Bositis from the Joint Center for Political and Economic Studies, a staggering 750 Black Churches throughout the nation were examined to gain information related to the faith-based funding initiative. The study as seen in Table 3.2, sheds light on the perception of faith-based funding in the Black Church.

Titled "Black Churches and the Faith-Based Initiative," the study yielded a broad range of results having to do with the how faith-based initiatives were viewed by black ministers. For starters, the study corrects the long and widely held misconception that Pentecostals and evangelicals are solely members of the white Religious Right. Refutation of this widely held misinterpretation is illustrated when the study talks about blacks who self-identify as Pentecostals and evangelicals.

The study also reveals that nearly three-quarters of the black ministers who were surveyed had heard about faith-based initiatives, and that about 70 percent of evangelicals and Pentecostals held a favorable few of the program. The study also makes known that for black ministers who expressed an opposition to faith-based funding, the opposition was mostly centered on their unwillingness to compete for federal funding. This reluctance was in part driven by a belief that faith-based funding was being taken from other government services and would result in the government withholding services in some other area where assistance to poor and minority communities was desperately needed. Then, there were those who were simply leery of the government and were fearful that by entering into a contractual relationship with the government, they might lose their church- and religious-based programs to Uncle Sam.

Table 3.2   National Survey of Black Churches on Faith-Based and Community

Do you have a generally favorable or unfavorable view of the Faith-Based Initiative?		
	Favorable %	Unfavorable %
Baptist	55	21
Methodist	54	28
Evangelical/Pentecostal	68	11
Nondenominational	60	13
Progressive Theology	55	22
Moderate Theology	46	27
Conservative Theology	70	13

Why do you view the Faith-Based Initiative unfavorably?		
	Opposed to Involvement with Government (%)	Separation of Church and State (%)
Baptist	23	8
Methodist	25	13
Evangelical/Pentecostal	19	14
Nondenominational	10	30
Progressive Theology	26	19
Moderate Theology	14	9
Conservative Theology	29	8

	Won't Compete for Funding (%)	Government Controls (%)
Baptist	20	15
Methodist	13	17
Evangelical/Pentecostal	14	24
Nondenominational	–	30
Progressive Theology	22	17
Moderate Theology	13	23
Conservative Theology	11	13

Source: Joint Center for Political and Economic Studies National Survey of Black Churches on Faith-Based and Community.

According to Dr. Bositis, evangelical and Pentecostal ministers as well as churches with a conservative theology had a favorable view of faith-based initiatives. Results from the study support the widely held belief that the government was trying to shift responsibility for the social safety net to religious-based organizations. Another interesting conclusion captured in a survey was that 47 percent of the Black Churches receiving funding were located in the Northeast region of the country, while only 26 percent were located in the South. According to the study, African American churches in states that voted largely Democratic in the previous two presidential elections were more likely to get faith-based grants than churches in states that voted Republican.[19]

It is possible to use the study's findings and demographics to demonstrate that both the Republican Party and Religious Right's strategy, amplified to reach out to black religious leaders and churchgoers in the northern United States was achieved, and that significant inroads were made in connecting with the black faith community. However, they could also be used to show that southern black ministers, who were believed to be more in tune with the Bush domestic agenda, were in actuality not as interested as was previously believed.

As previously mentioned, in 2007, Senate Finance Committee ranking member Iowa senator Charles Grassley (R-IA) sought to determine the use of federal monies by some prosperity and celebrity televangelists, Eddie Long, Joyce Meyer, Kenneth Copeland, Creflo Dollar, Benny Hinn, and Randy White. The six—who became known as the Grassley Six— would be the target of Grassley's investigation into how the millions of dollars in federal grants and monies from church members had been used. Deliberately or otherwise, some of the ministers targeted by Grassley's investigation had been major supporters of President Bush and longtime Republican supporters, putting Grassley at odds with the Republican Party and powerful Christian Coalition, and from the outset prompting speculation related to the motivation for the inquiry. Minority ministers caught up in Grassley's investigation—Eddie Long and Creflo Dollar—had to some extent also supported the president's domestic agenda, especially Bishop Long.

Nonetheless, Grassley's highly publicized probe got off to roaring start by targeting the financial dealings of these powerful megachurch pastors, investigating, for example, salacious claims that one had spent up to $5,000 for presidential suites when traveling. Another allegation was that several of the ministers owned private jets and were paid outrageous salaries. In an interview with National Public Radio (NPR) Grassley said, "There's enough questions being raised that we felt it should be further investigated."[20] Several of these megachurch pastors whose palatial houses of worship can take up an entire city block and who enjoy rock star status also use their pulpits to denounce members of the LGBT community. Grassley claimed that he was duty-bound to act on complaints from constituents who cited extravagant and lavish lifestyles, inferring poor federal oversight.

The homophobic Long took exception to the investigation, labeling the federal inquiry unjust and an attack on religious freedom and property rights. Others, for example, like Ken Behr, president of the Evangelical Council for Financial Accountability, complained that the majority of churches in the country don't file financial statements nor are they subjected to the degree of transparency sought by Grassley. While the six ministers targeted by the investigation were not in Behr's group, he said the Senate inquiry did not infringe on the separation of church and state because the inquiry did not relate to church doctrine. According to Behr, the inquiry was focused on issues related to taxes and asked questions such as "Were perks actually taxable benefits? Were gifts that were given to the ministry actually what's called a pass-through transaction, where the individual gives directly to another individual rather than using the church in between?"[21]

Explaining that he had to be sure that the millions of dollars donated were being used appropriately and not for personal gain, Grassley said, "My business is the enforcement of the tax laws and the integrity of the tax code and making sure that trustees of charitable giving are true trustees."[22] Grassley added that complaints about the pastors' extravagant lifestyles and questions about whether the churches' tax-exempt status was being abused was one factor that justified the investigation. As the debate continued, the Grassley Six were faced with the looming threat of IRS scrutiny and congressional hearings, yet for the most part they refused to cooperate.

The scope of the investigation was significant and much of Grassley's probe unprecedented, as it sought audited financial statements, names of associated churches, board members' names and addresses, the names of those serving on financial compensation committees, and records related to executive compensation and expenditures. One church being investigated, Joyce Meyer Ministries, placed its financial records on its website, and Meyer indicated that even though she was not required to do so, she would reply to Grassley's requests. In all, six letters were sent to the megachurch ministers in an effort to investigate claims of over-the-top lifestyles. Grassley sought specific answers related to the six ministries and also wanted to determine if any had violated their tax-exempt status.

For example, the letter sent to the College Park, Georgia, megachurch prosperity preaching couple Creflo and Taffi Dollar asked—among other things—for specific information related to the purchase of two Rolls-Royce vehicles. It also inquired into compensation, including cash and noncash gifts, loans, and personal use of assets paid to the Dollars by the ministry and other tax-exempt entities. The letter included a detailed list of expenses for the Dollars' residences in Georgia and New York.

Then, there was Grassley's letter to Bishop Eddie Long, pastor of a 30,000-member church in Lithonia, Georgia, which inquired about Long's compensation and whether he had personally benefited from church donations. Of particular interest was Grassley's 2005 claim that Long no longer received a salary but instead something referred to by a church spokesperson as a "love offering." The letter received by Long also sought information regarding the purchase of a home in Atlanta on behalf of a nonprofit operated by Bishop Eddie Long Ministries (BELM). The charity ended its operations in October 2002, and in December 2003, Long executed documents giving up interest in the home while the charity reportedly compensated him with a $1.4 million six-bedroom, nine-bath home on 20 acres of land. Grassley wanted to know who donated more than $3.5 million to BELM and if the megachurch preacher personally benefited from the donations.

Grassley's three year, highly touted probe ended inconspicuously in 2011 when the six televangelists—who hail from some of the country's largest churches—were not charged with any crime, assessed any penalties, or even called before Grassley's committee. In fact, only two of the Grassley Six—Joyce Meyers and Benny Hinn—fully cooperated with the Senate probe, and in the end, none were found to have violated the law. In what turned out to be an impotent conclusion to the Senate investigation, a recommendation was made that the Internal Revenue Service implement measures to ensure that religious organizations do not abuse their tax-exempt status. That said, with more than 1 million religious nonprofit organizations in the country, meaningful self-regulation seems little more than a lofty dream.

Disenchanted with the outcome, religious watchdog groups criticized Grassley for naming the Evangelical Council for Financial Accountability (ECFA) to lead the commission, commenting that doing so allowed the ECFA to protect large religious organizations at the expense of grassroots donors. Rod Pitzer of MinistryWatch.com said that Grassley's conclusions were "far less than we could have hoped for."[23] Suspicion related to the ineffective outcome of Grassley's investigation prompted speculation that the probe may have been a smoke screen used by the Religious Right to take attention away from religious extremists and self-appointed moralists who were receiving millions, and the operatives who funneled federal faith-based funding while campaigning against equality for LGBTs and the passage of same-sex marriage legislation. Evangelical ruse or not, some thought that the time and money spent investigating the Grassley Six would have been put to better use by ensuring that federal monies were not awarded to religious organizations that employed discriminatory tactics or waged political war against the LGBT community.

Iowa Senator Chuck Grassley. (AP Photo/Susan Walsh)

The question of whether taxpayer-supported religion is leading the country toward a theocracy has been hotly debated for some time. Some say that one of the gains made by the Christian Right over the past decades has been to help transition America from a secular to a religious government. The organization TheocracyWatch raises awareness about the invasive role of organizations like Focus on the Family and the National Association of Evangelicals, and their relationship with the federal government. Using a variety of methods, the organization informs people about things such as what former U.S. representative Christopher Shays (R-CT) had to say about the Republican Party: "This Republican Party of Lincoln has become a party of theocracy . . ."[24] Shays's statement may have shocked and even frightened some people because it portends the theocratic quest of organizations like the Christian Right establishing control over all facets of U.S. society in the name of God. On the other hand, to those whose mission it is to usher in religious rule over every segment of U.S. culture in God's name, it represents the hope that ultimately religion will reign over our government. For example, people like the late D. James Kennedy, the former pastor of Coral Ridge Ministries, asked his devotees to exert godly control over every part of human society. At a 2005 conference, Kennedy urged parishioners to do so by saying, "Our job is to reclaim America for Christ, whatever the cost. As the vice regents of God, we are to exercise godly dominion and influence over our neighborhoods, our schools, our government, our literature and arts, our sports arenas, our entertainment media, our news media, our scientific endeavors—in short, over every aspect and institution of human society."[25] Here Kennedy seems to cover every conceivable aspect of U.S. society. He is joined by Tea Party activists and others, such as 2012 presidential candidates Rick Santorum, U.S. congressional representative Michelle Bachmann (R-MN), and Texas governor Rick Perry, whose views to an increasing degree seem to bend toward Dominionism and theocratic thinking, causing great concern to those who are opposed to the direction of the United States' religiously influenced politics.

Neither Perry nor Bachmann are pledged Dominionists, but both are affiliated with extreme subgroups of evangelical Christianity, and Santorum is associated with the most conservative wing of the Catholic Church. In particular, Perry and Bachmann's religious affiliations and sway with the Christian Right prompted concern during the 2012 presidential election regarding the question of the separation between church and state. It is for this reason that the U.S. electorate is urged to listen more carefully to what political candidates say about their religious views in order to find out if subtle changes in their position are temporary and are being made to garner voter trust.

Despite the public's recognition of the increasing connection between religion and politics, the link has not affected evangelicals and religious extremists, who aim to not only increase their presence and might on the political stage, but to set the tone for castigation of the LGBT community. The quest for acceptance and equality by same-sex union advocates is increasingly being addressed openly by politicians who quote biblical verses to make their point. In fact, some evangelical politicians believe that they are appointed by God as the planet's caretakers. Sara Diamond defined this belief as Dominionism, which is a growing political tendency that has taken root within the evangelical and Christian Right movement advocating the belief that they have been singled out and biblically directed to occupy all secular institutions until Christ returns.[26]

According to Chip Berlet, a senior analyst at Political Research Associates who monitors and analyzes the organizations, leaders, ideas, and activities of the U.S. political right, "In its generic sense, dominionism is a very broad political tendency within the Christian Right. It ranges from soft to hard versions in terms of its theocratic impulse."[27] Soft Dominionists believe that biblically defined immorality propagates mayhem. Their belief also includes elements of a theocracy because they think that the nation's prominence has been weakened by liberal secular humanists, feminists, and homosexuals. Hard Dominionists want an outwardly Christian theocracy in the United States and do whatever is necessary to make their intentions known. Hard Dominionists also believe that our Constitution and Bill of Rights are addendums to the Old Testament and that anyone who does not accept these views should be considered a second-class citizen.

An integral part of the campaign to convince black ministers to support the principles of Dominionism and to incorporate what is considered by mainstream America as a harsh, divisive, and unyielding theocratic view aims at what they have in common—an opposition to homosexuality and same-sex marriage. Homophobic black ministers who preach that homosexuality and same-sex marriage are morally wrong and who rail against fair treatment for the LGBT community continue to be aggressively courted by Right Wing Republicans and Dominionist factions that advocate a theocracy.

Years after the Bush presidency, the granddaughter of a Ku Klux Klan (KKK) member, Alice Patterson—who is head of the Texas, Louisiana, Arkansas and Oklahoma Church Mobilization for Governor Perry's The Response prayer rally—explained that she is focused on reaching entire cities for Christ and that the effort includes bringing blacks back to the Republican Party. Black ministers inclined to respond to Patterson's bodacious call represent a subgroup of radical black ministers who not only share in the intemperate ideology, but have gone beyond the pale by backing a viewpoint that essentially says, "If you don't follow the Christian faith, you could be punished by death."

Though it is true that some black ministers have extremist positions related to homosexuality and same-sex marriage, most wouldn't dare to associate with this sort of uncontrolled fundamentalism that has the real potential to splinter an already fragile Black Church. However, because of issues like abortion and gains made by the LGBT community related to same-sex marriage and rights for LGBTs, Patterson's campaign to lure blacks to the GOP shouldn't be nonchalantly dismissed. It is very likely that these efforts are being duplicated by Dominionist groups seeking to fulfill their mission and take apart government by radically limiting its power.

Frankly, even given the agreed upon motives like standing against gay marriage advocates and homosexuality, as a matter of practicality, a theocratic government would be difficult to sell to an overwhelming majority of black ministers. This is in part because of the hard struggle against white supremacy to gain a seat at the table where blacks now not only compete, but are courted by established political powers. So in spite of the extraordinary spread of evangelical Christianity, if moving toward a theocracy means dismantling what was fought for by blacks since the dawning of the nation and has at its roots the concept of remaking society, to do so would not be a smart move for blacks. This is especially true given the 2012 reelection of the United States' first African American president.

NOTES

1. Corinthians 6:10.Holy Bible.
2. www.prospect.org/cs/articles?article=the_ecumenist November 30, 2002. Accessed March 3, 2011.
3. http://www.pbs.org/newshour/bb/politics/jan-june01/churchstate _1-29.html. Accessed February 19, 2011.
4. http://www.pbs.org/newshour/bb/politics/jan-june01/churchstate _1-29.html. Accessed February 19, 2011.
5. http://thedailyvoice.com/voice/2008/12/michael henry adams piece oo1441.php. Accessed February 29, 2011.
6. http://www.nytimes.com/1990/08/06/nyregion/congressman-flake -s-indictment-good-works-or-greed.html. Accessed March 2 2011.
7. http://www.nytimes.com/2010/06/18/nyregion/18flake.html ?_r=2&src=me. Accessed March 3 /2011.
8. http://thespiritualherald.org/article.php?id=98. Accessed May 28, 2011.
9. Eric Zorn, *ChicagoTribune.com*, February 27, 2011, http://blogs. chicagotribune.com/news_columnists_ezorn/. Accessed March 5, 2011.
10. "Black clerics open arms to bush's funding plan," *Chicago-Tribune.com*, April 6, 2001, http://articles.chicagotribune.com/2001-04 -06/news/0104060123_1_urban-churches-faith-based-initiative-african -american-ministers. Accessed March 5, 2011.
11. http://www.splcenter.org/get-informed/intelligence-report/ browse-all-issues/2007/spring/face-right. Accessed September 3, 2011.
12. http://test.blackenterprise.com/2007/01/01/black-churches-missing -out-on-federal-aid/2/. Accessed September 3, 2011.
13. http://www.splcenter.org/get-informed/intelligence-report/ browse-all-issues/2007/spring/face-right. Accessed September 3, 2011.
14. http://www.splcenter.org/get-informed/intelligence-report/ browse-all-issues/2007/spring/face-right. Accessed September 3, 2011.
15. http://www.allgov.com/agency/Council__for_Faith_Based_and _Neighborhood__Partnerships. Accessed 03/12/2011.

16. http://www.jweekly.com/article/full/4089/jewish-democrats-chastise-kemp-for-cozying-up-to-farrakhan/. Accessed September 3, 2011.

17. http://www.adl.org/presrele/natisl_81/2377_81.asp. Accessed September 3, 2011.

18. http://www.thefreelibrary.com/Faith-Based+BACKLASH.-a0752 49714. Accessed March 4 2011.

19. http://religionclause.blogspot.com/2006/09/study-of-black-churches-and-faith.html. Accessed March 24, 2011.

20. http://www.npr.org/templates/story/story.php?storyId=16860611. Accessed September 3, 2011.

21. http://www.npr.org/templates/story/story.php?storyId=16860611. Accessed September 3, 2011.

22. http://global.christianpost.com/news/more-questions-raised-in-probe-of-preachers-30344/. Accessed September 3, 2011.

23. http://www.worldmag.com/webextra/17543. Accessed September 3, 2011.

24. http://www.nytimes.com/2005/03/23/politics/23repubs.html?pagewanted=print&position. Accessed September 3, 2011.

25. http://www.theocracywatch.org/relig_inst.htm. Accessed June 23, 2011.

26. http://www.theocracywatch.org/relig_inst.htm. Accessed September 3, 2011.

27. http://www.theocracywatch.org/relig_inst.htm. Accessed June 23, 2011.

FOUR

The Black LGBT Struggle

If a man lies with a man as one lies with a woman, both of them have done what is detestable. They must be put to death; their blood will be on their own heads.[1]

Going back to the roaring 1920s on Chicago's south side in historic Bronzeville, black homosexuals, gays, and transgenders congregated in some of the city's famed nightclubs. Black gays were visible and to an extent genuinely accepted in spite of their flamboyance, effeminate mannerisms, and homosexuality. Back then, black LGBTs or "queers" as they were mostly referred to, were restricted to certain areas within the city. They were tolerated for the most part as long as they stayed in their place and did not attempt to blend in with the wider black community. Decades before the formation of family values organizations like Focus on the Family and the protests of radical evangelicals who organized to systematically oppose homosexuality, same-sex marriage, and to demonize the LGBT community, life as a black homosexual was difficult but distinctly different from today.

In his 2009 doctoral dissertation at Northwestern University, Tristan Cabello's *Bronzeville in the Life: Urban Boundaries, Race and Homosexuality in Black Chicago, 1935–1985*, the history of African American gays and lesbians on the south side of Chicago is explored. In his work, Cabello referred to the visibility of queers on Chicago's south side, and their acceptance from the turn of the century to the early 1980s when the AIDS crisis, and anti-gay attitudes swept across America, saying, "On the streets, working-class African American queers were also tolerated.

For example, Lorenzo Banyard, a Cabin Inn drag entertainer, remembers riding streetcars to the West Side, dressed in drag, without incident. Professional drag entertainers were indeed respected because of their relatively well-paying jobs, which often enabled them to provide for their families' needs."[2]

At first blush, it sounds as if Cabello is suggesting an idealistic existence for black homosexuals who lived during this period, in part, because he is focusing on one segment of Chicago's black LGBT community and not the everyday existence and experiences of the typical black homosexual. However, to my way of thinking, the treatment of black LGBTs decades ago depicts a life of isolation, bias, and disparagement still suffered by black LGBTs. In fact, the black cultural prejudice against LGBTs practiced then continues today as many black LGBTs are forced to conceal their sexual identity in modern society in order to avoid being shamed by the black community and church.

As Chicago's black gay population increased and a class structure in black communities developed, biases inside the homosexual community became an issue. These prejudices, often supported by black ministers warning against the immorality of homosexuality, caused homophobic attitudes to deepen within the black community. With little support from black civic and religious leaders, the ill treatment of black LGBTs was amplified and as a result, the division within the black community increased. With little to tamp down the negative perception of black homosexuals, African American gays from downtrodden communities were an easy target for black religious leaders who cast aspersions on their sexuality. Some black ministers used LGBTs to illustrate how the march toward impending moral decay, if not halted, would result in the doom of the black family structure and eventually all of black culture.

Taken literally, which is precisely what some black ministers do and advise members of their congregations to do, biblical scripture is used to promote the idea that homosexuals are not only immoral, but are subject to punishment by extreme measures. This sort of thinking is buttressed by Right Wing white fundamentalists and radical evangelical factions that use the Bible to justify their strident repudiation and vitriol against homosexuality, and has proven to be a powerful deterrent to the rights of the LGBT community.

As far as the Black Church's aggressive stance is concerned, the inequitable treatment and subjugation of black LGBTs executed by some black ministers is extraordinarily complex, problematic, and contradictory. For instance, according to some black gay activists, black ministers contribute considerably to the phenomenon of black gay and bisexual men concealing their sexuality identity and perpetrating a heterosexual life-style known in the black community as the down low, or the DL. According to some black religious leaders, the DL is the cause of a host of societal problems afflicting contemporary black culture. Without a doubt, the DL is the focal point for the continuing raging debate about unnatural social dysfunction that exists in modern-day black culture.

Some LGBT advocates claim that black ministers are participating in the public degrading of homosexuals and are deliberately instigating unfair treatment and hostility toward the black LGBT community, all in an effort to protect the Defense of Marriage Act (DOMA) and to halt same-sex unions. This is a troubling accusation on a number of levels, the first of which is that it contradicts the longstanding reputation of the Black Church as a bastion for fair treatment and humaneness, principles the Black Church has claimed to uphold since blacks were brought to this country in irons. Given the prolific history of the Black Church, the allegations made by gay rights advocates are for many blacks disconcerting and difficult to accept. However, the mean-spirited proselytizing against black homosexuals is a matter of record and springs from the pulpit of some of the country's most renowned Black Churches, where eminent black ministers encourage abhorrent treatment of members of the black Christian LGBT community. The effect has been a rise in homophobic attitudes that are flourishing within the spiritual and secular black experience.

In the new millennium, in a world of Oprah and tell-all revelations, the fact that some black men are living on the DL isn't shrouded in the secrecy it was only a few decades ago. Still, many black gay and bisexual men continued to be prisoners of fear because of the consequence related to divulging their sexuality or being outed. As a result, many choose to conceal their homosexuality. However, this promotes the speculation by members of the black community and religious leaders that black LGBTs are the source of the social ills that are eroding an already fragile black family structure. Add to that mounting evidence that the charade perpetrated by black gay and bisexual men living on the DL is increasing the spread of HIV/AIDS and destroying traditional norms within the black community, and the allegations are potentially volatile. Armed with scientific data from the Centers for Disease Control and Prevention (CDC), the claims of antigay activist are not dismissed as convoluted and are extremely powerful when leveled by powerful black ministers.

The speculation about black men living on the DL and the consequence of covering up their true sexuality identity continues to feed the rancor and extremism that play out in Black Churches and throughout black urban America. That being the case, there is little doubt that the robust opposition to homosexuality within black culture and the conscious choice of black LGBTs to live clandestinely is largely related to the vigorous religious and secular rejection of their departure from acceptable ethnic sexual norms.

Something else that is arguably an issue that creates confusion in black culture is that some black men living on the DL do not consider themselves gay or bisexual. This may stem from the fact that sexual designations that are not in keeping with ethnic standards are not considered acceptable. Because homosexuality is considered distasteful to most blacks, any sexual designation that is contrary to the all-important inherent masculinity prized in black culture is considered taboo. To compensate for what is seen as a ludicrous social and religious quandary, black culture responds by driving gay and bisexual black men to live their lives on the DL. Many black LGBTs believe that if they are to avoid the rebuke of a black community whose stance against homosexuality is unwavering, they must conceal their sexual identity.

In *Exploring Black Sexuality*, Robert Staples talks about the DL with remarkable frankness, offering realistic explanations that provide insight into the black cultural perspective as it relates to homosexuality. While it is likely that some will vehemently oppose Staples's assertions about the reasons that some black men live on the DL, what is clear from the outset is that he makes no attempt to excuse the behavior of black gays and bisexuals who work to deceive society. Here Staples candidly explains the reasons for and repercussions of black males living on the Down Low, offering credible explanations that are rational and worth considering:

> As for the Down Low Black males, they often see being gay in very stereotyped ways; the effeminate, weak, *unmasculine* model often portrayed in the media. That may be why they deny being gay while engaging in same-sex behavior. That image is not part of the collective Black identity. For centuries, Black men were treated as boys, denied even the title of mister. During slavery, all their masculine prerogatives were stripped away by plantation owners....
>
> Even today, Black males are denied real power. Within families, they are told that women were in control, they were marginal and ineffective figures within their own family.
>
> Of course, there are other explanations for Down Low behavior. Gay advocates have long claimed there is no such thing as a bisexual—only a man who can perform sexually with both men and women. The obvious implication is that such men are true homosexuals and in denial

because of the stigma attached to it . . . Another explanation is that the homophobia among Afro-Americans keeps many true homosexual Black men from coming out as exclusively gay, because Euro-American males are economically secure, they have nothing to lose by coming out of the closet.

The hype over the threat of Down Low men to heterosexual Black Women creates a cloud of suspicion over all heterosexual Afro-American men. Since Down Low men are just as masculine as all Afro-American men, there is no way to distinguish them except to catch them in "in flagrante delicto."[3]

Staples's attention to the paradoxical conflict within black culture as it relates to the black community's shared perspective is instrumental. It conveys a number of logical reasons that help to explain the conflict and enduring pervasiveness of homophobia that has managed to permeate every layer of black culture. These are in fact the motives that shape the way that black secular and religious institutions contend with issues related to homosexuality and same-sex marriage. It is also what will continue to prevent blacks from responding like other ethnic groups, many of whom have changed their mindset and broadened their acceptance of the LGBT community.

Author, pastor, and HIV/AIDS activist Pastor Terry Angel Mason is well acquainted with the angst of black LGBT Christians who in black churches across the country are made to feel inferior and to silently suffer utter hopelessness. Mason seems to identify with the difficulty associated with changing the opinion of black LGBTs held by their communities, families, and black religious leaders. Mason's heightened awareness and history of emotional stress is indicative of what black men living on the DL experience in a culture where heterosexism and homophobia are predominant. Mason's observations go to the core of what is widely viewed as being among the main reasons given by black gay and bisexual men who decide that there is no alternative to living on the DL. Mason straightforwardly describes what it is like for black men on the DL who are chastised in black houses of worship: "Imagine sitting in church for years, surrounded by hundreds of people (lonely and feeling rejected) hearing sermon after sermon, hating who I was and what I was, on the brink of suicide and a nervous breakdown. I was convinced that God detested the most important part of who I was and I felt trapped in a condition not of my own doing and hell-bound."[4]

Even the slightest chance of being subjected to this sort of revile and mistreatment motivates black gay and bisexual men to choose a life of secrecy on the DL. Having witnessed how others have been degraded and treated like immoral deviants is more than enough for many black LGBTs to consider the risk and to opt for the protection that concealment offers. This is especially true when they know that by living as openly gay or bisexual, they would in the view of the black community be considered the reason for the breakdown of the black ethos. As far as moral beliefs are concerned, living openly as a gay or bisexual is equal to other social ills plaguing the black community like drugs and crime. There are those who consider a deviation from acceptable sexual norms to be the top factor in the obliteration of black culture. This is a crushing indictment of men living on the DL and one that is passionately preached by black clergy Sabbath after Sabbath. Incredibly, the contentious message is readily accepted as the gospel truth by some black churchgoers. Black ministers who rebuke those living on the DL to proselytize the immorality of homosexuality and the looming consequences to black culture realize the potency of the message and its proven track record to generate malice toward the black LGBT community. They are savvy and quick to point out an extensive theological basis for their agitation and prepared to provide a litany of reasons why God-fearing Christians should be similarly outraged by homosexuality and efforts to legalize same-sex marriage.

Individuals like hardline antigay activist Rod Parsley, author of *Silent No More*, is infinitely skilled at using despicable language and imagery to create animosity toward the LGBT community. In a chapter of his book titled "The Unhappy Gay Agenda," Parsley argues that gay people are susceptible to depression and deviance, including their "substantially higher participation in sadomasochism, fisting, bestiality, ingestion of feces, orgies."[5] By describing homosexual acts in this manner, Parsley manages to evoke unbridled ridicule and hatred toward homosexuals, and to provoke like-minded thinkers whose over-the-top viewpoint has gained entry into the black secular and religious experience.

On the other hand, in his book *Their Own Receive Them Not*, author Horace L. Griffin talks about the struggle of black men living on the DL. Griffin describes how difficult it is to comprehend the intense and continuous effort that is required to conceal one's true sexuality. From a heterosexual perspective, this can be truly mindboggling and even bizarre. To further illustrate an absurdity that seems to go on without end, Griffin touches on a point that is central to the DL experience, explaining that men living on the DL are apt to vigorously defend and even justify their deceptive behavior.

Griffin believes that the DL is used mainly by black men who are unable to deal with the reality of their sexuality or the repercussions that might result from revealing their sexuality to their families and community. Instead of coming out, these men conceal their sexual identity in spite of the risks to themselves and others. Because of an overwhelming reluctance of blacks to consider something other than traditional sexual norms, the predicament for black men on the DL remains, and more often than not, covering up their sexuality is seen as the best way to circumvent the stinging and malicious ostracism exclusive to black culture.[6]

Some people—like J. L. King, the author of *On the Down Low*—long pretend to be straight. King admits that intrinsically unprincipled behavior that begins with sexual deception causes enormous pain for women who are duped by black men living on the DL. Living duplicitously in both the heterosexual and homosexual world is a conscious choice that is made with full knowledge of the ramifications to others. The decision to do so is often planned and is carried out using unsuspecting women to shield their homosexuality from the watchful eye of a strident homophobic black culture while hurting the innocent.[7]

The cerebral and occasionally controversial hypotheses from notable scholars like Frances Cress Welsing, Michael Eric Dyson, bell hooks, Cornel West, and others offer thought-provoking and abundant rationales for the DL phenomenon, and their opinions about the acceptance of homosexuality by blacks vary widely. To date, however, all of the analysis by leading black intellectuals has not provided a definitive explanation for the surge in public derision toward black LGBTs, or if it has intensified as a result of faith-based funding competition during the Bush years.

Welsing is a psychiatrist, activist, and writer who did not mince words in her jaw-dropping *The Isis Papers: The Keys to the Colors* (1990), which presents views on homosexuality and homophobia in the black community that appear as audacious now as they were over two decades ago. Welsing's study related to urban black males, which was completed 10 years before Bush took office, doesn't back down from the reality of homosexuality or the black community's downright failure to retool and confront it as other ethnicities have.

Emphatic when discussing homosexuality and the black community's handling of it, Welsing says that "Homophobia in communities of color is rampant . . . to the tenth power of the white mainstream. Why?, Because the struggle for human rights against white supremacy has been disproportionately explained as the need to achieve 'manhood' rights, from the period of the slave trade to the present."[8]

Welsing's assertion not only rings true, but calls to mind an initiation familiar to black males who are inducted early in life and made to understand the importance of demonstrating manliness and the consequence of failing to do so. The manhood rights that Welsing refers to are seen as an essential tool to the survival of black males growing up urban America, where living and surviving in economically depressed communities is connected to the black urban experience. In an environment where masculinity is reinforced and virility routinely put to the test, proving one's manhood is fundamental to surviving. Equally important in black culture is conformity to the definition of intrinsic masculinity traits defined by black culture. These characteristics are akin to a sort of Darwinism wherein failure to comport could bring an immediate reverberation and after-effects lasting throughout one's lifetime.

Still relevant is Welsing's work relating of the pursuit of manhood as defined by black culture and the struggle against white domination. Welsing's candidness concerning black submissiveness toward matters of sexuality in the black community is similarly powerful and equally provocative when she describes the insidious destruction:

Black male passivity, effeminization, bisexuality and homosexuality are being encountered increasingly by Black psychiatrists working with Black patient populations. These issues are being presented by family members, personnel working in schools, and other social institutions, or by Black men themselves. Many in the Black population are reaching the conclusion that such issues have become a problem of epidemic proportion amongst Black people in the U.S., although it was an almost nonexistent behavioral phenomenon amongst indigenous Blacks in Africa.[9]

However, during the time when Welsing's work was critically acclaimed, it was also severely critiqued. Welsing's peer Matthew Chance critiqued Welsing's work titled "Afrocentricity vs. Homosexuality: The Isis Papers," Chance offers an example of the contrast in thinking by black intellectuals on the issue of homosexuality in the black community. Here Chance questions the validity of Welsing's observations:

The author, angry with the American Psychological Association's relatively recent repeal of their former opinion that homosexuality constitutes poor mental health, prescribes a distinct position for Black people. Black psychiatrists must understand that whites may condone homosexuality for themselves, but we as Blacks must see it as a strategy for destroying Black people. Welsing argues that homosexuals or bisexuals should neither be condemned nor degraded, as they did not decide that they would be so programmed in childhood. The racist system should be held responsible. Welsing believes the task of professionals who concur with her should be proactive treatment and prevention of homosexuality among Black people.[10]

Chance continues countering Dr. Welsing, calling her premise "retrogressive ideas." Chance suggests that Dr. Welsing's Afrocentrist idea of a revolt against the white power structure is destined to fail. Whether one agrees with Welsing or Chance does not matter because there is no denying that a particular familiarization and preparation of adolescent black males, which begins early in life, is exclusive to the black experience and is not Welsing's invention. What occurs in the neighborhoods, churches, and homes of young black males both directly and subtly culminates in a collaborative drumming in of an awareness that any hint of femininity in black males will be perceived and treated as repugnant and forbidden in black culture.

It is very possible that to an outsider, this might appear a questionable and even cruel practice. However, for generations of black males, it has been viewed as an essential readying and toughening to prepare young black boys who are destined to encounter harsh realities that will necessitate an unwavering show of manliness. Therefore, it is not unusual to witness an African American parent publicly and nonchalantly reprimanding a black male child, using harsh verbal or sometimes physical chastisement, for acts perceived as effeminate, or behaving like a "sissy." In black culture, such behavior by a boy is considered disgraceful and abhorrent. Needless to say, the punitive actions do not actually purge the perceived effeminate trait, change, the conduct, or resolve the underlying issue. However, it is generally felt that as long as the behavior is not openly exhibited, the individual can elude the scorn and ostracism of the black community. Therefore, learning early on to suppress feminine tendencies is crucial. While controlling effeminate mannerisms and sexual impulses may facilitate assimilation into black culture, down the road it is a safe bet that sexual maturation will ultimately end in an internal struggle that could prove detrimental to the individual, the family, and as a growing body of evidence seems to suggest, all of black culture.

Veteran Chicago human rights activist Kit Duffy, who served as liaison between the city and the gay and lesbian community, enjoyed the utmost confidence of Chicago's first black mayor, Harold Washington. In the mid-1980s, Mayor Washington expressed his belief that Duffy's role would likely expand as issues related to the protection of gay rights in areas such as city employment which were proving to be a growing concern.

Washington, who was already building his legacy years before he became Chicago's first black mayor, had built a rainbow coalition long before the Reverend Jesse Jackson laid claim to the term. The gay community celebrated Washington for his brave and unyielding work as a state senator and congressman who sponsored a variety of gay rights legislation and also established a committee on gay and lesbian issues, and a human rights ordinance prohibiting discrimination based on sexual orientation. In the minds of Chicagoans, white and black, Mayor Harold Washington was a forerunner in the equitable treatment of members of Chicago's LGBT community.

Discussing the treatment of members of Chicago's LGBT community, Duffy shared a recollection of something that occurred several decades ago. At an event, a prominent black Chicago alderman loudly announced that in his ward sissies are liked. Duffy was quick to add that the alderman doing the shouting did not perceive his words as wrong, nor were they intended to malign members of the LGBT community. In fact, the alderman likely viewed his statement as entirely supportive, and his proclamation was more his way of expressing the differences in perceptions of sexual orientation that exist in diverse communities and in the black community, which is to a great extent viewed as a gender role issue rather than the political identity it is perceived as in white and affluent areas.

Duffy elaborated, saying, "Those differences in perceptions are really important and key to understanding that what is often interpreted as hate and bias actually is an entirely different understanding of sexual orientation. That difference even exists among gays . . . you will find a whole different perception in the South, for example, and between older and younger gays."[11]

During his tenure as mayor and following his sudden death in 1987, Mayor Harold Washington's reputation was besmeared. In the aftermath of Washington's untimely death when School of Art Institute of Chicago student David K. Nelson, Jr., depicted the beloved Washington wearing only a bra, G-string, garter belt, and stockings Washington's supporters—black and white—were outraged. After a brief showing in a private student exhibition, angry African American aldermen accompanied by Chicago Police Department officers removed the picture.

It is true that rumors related to the much-loved Mayor Washington's sexuality were persistent, and the issue was discussed by members of the black community during Washington's tenure as mayor. For example, the innuendo about Washington, who had been a life-long bachelor and his somewhat sudden engagement to be married, was thought by some to be a ruse to conceal his homosexuality. Surreptitious discussions related to Washington's sexuality became relatively common. However, the issue of Nelson's painting rapidly became racially charged and threatened to taint Mayor Washington's legacy and strain race relations. Nelson's characterization of Washington was peculiarly perceived as an affront to the communal strength of the black community. Because Nelson is white, his actions were seen as exceedingly egregious. Nelson's rendering of Washington was viewed as an attack on a man who was revered for his prodigious accomplishments and virile stand in the face of political and racial adversity. For the black community, the painting was enormously controversial.

A quarter of a century later, not much has changed, and opinions about homosexuality within the black community continue to contribute to the homophobia and rigid mentality that is almost entirely based on irrational beliefs about the LGBT community and antigay propaganda intended to defend DOMA. While there has been some progress, regrettably, the perception of homosexuality in the black community represents the prevailing attitude that has helped to sustain the aura of profound misunderstanding that engulfs black LGBTs and affects the way they are treated by their friends, families, and faith community. So it is not surprising that when black religious leaders demonstrate dogged opposition to homosexuality, same-sex unions, or anything seen as an aberration to traditional sexual mores, it nourishes the intimidation that helps to drive gay and bisexual black men underground. Escaping the stigma and wrath of family members, and the real possibility of being ostracized by members of their race and religion, demonstrates what they are up against. Some homosexual and bisexual black men opt to escape the vilification by marrying women, procreating, and doing whatever is necessary to put on the appearance of fitting in and living by ethnically defined sexual standards and church dogma. However, when their masquerade is under threat of being revealed a hoax, it adds to the problem. There is also the real potential that their lives and those of their loved ones will be wrecked by the havoc that results from a number of social ills associated with living on the DL, including sexually transmitted infections (STIs) and HIV/AIDS. The insidious ravages of these diseases can indiscriminately affect every aspect of black culture.

A number of years ago, I found myself involved in an irrational homophobic episode when I convinced myself that my son was exhibiting feminine tendencies. Attempting to camouflage it as innocuous parental concern, I slyly mentioned his behaviors to my wife, pathetically couching them as probably nothing to worry about. However, I was actually consumed by it and had somehow convinced myself that his behaviors were a reflection of my own masculinity. Looking back, it was all so ridiculous because at the time, my son was only five years old. However, this illustrates the power that the specter of homosexuality has in black culture and on the stability of the black family structure.

In her 1989 essay "Homophobia in the Black Communities," author, feminist, and social activist bell hooks discusses the perception that blacks are more homophobic than other groups. She illustrates black men's nearly automatic homophobic responses when confronted by homosexuality by discussing the puzzling contradiction of how they are conditioned to respond to issues related to it. Hooks asserts that black men have accustomed themselves to respond to LGBT issues in a way that is considered acceptable and expected even though their true belief may be entirely different. Above all, they are conditioned to respond in a manner consistent with masculinity. Hooks writes:

> Black communities may be perceived as more homophobic than other communities because there is a tendency for individuals in black communities to verbally express in an outspoken way antigay sentiments. I talked with a straight black male in a California community who acknowledged that though he has often made jokes poking fun at gays or expressing contempt as a means of bonding in group settings, in his private life he was a central support person for a gay sister. Such contradictory behavior seems pervasive in black communities. It speaks to ambivalence about sexuality in general, about sex as a subject of conversation, and to ambivalent feelings and attitudes toward homosexuality.[12]

The complexity of the habituated homophobic response that hooks so aptly describes depicts ways that blacks cope with issues related to homosexuality. Yet she also manages to effectively express the absurd and illogical bias that thrives throughout black culture, which is almost entirely associated with a perceived need to disassociate from all matters related to homosexuality or male weakness, real or imagined. This is mostly achieved through a sort of behavioral sham learned early by black males.

In *Race Matters* (1993), his first book, Cornel West talks about the issue of sex in the black community by connecting it to race. A master at making a legitimate association with almost any societal issue to race relations, West employs his trademark device to explain how race and sex are inextricable, persuasively suggesting that "it is virtually impossible to talk candidly about race without talking about sex . . . "[13] Here West exposes another facet of the multidimensional problem of race and sex in the black community.

Peeling away all pretension, West explains black sexuality by juxtaposing black male and female heterosexuals and homosexuals to illustrate the intricacy and bizarre nature of sexuality in black culture. The manner in which West illuminates the differences is a pragmatic and potent dose of sexual realism that is an everyday occurrence in black culture. West deals with the issue by asking,

> Is there a way out of this Catch-22 situation in which black sexuality either liberates black people from white control in order to imprison them in racist myths or confines blacks to white "respectability" while they make their own sexuality a taboo subject? Or put another way, the ways out for black men differ vastly from those of black women.

Black male sexuality differs from black female sexuality because black men have different self-images and strategies of acquiring power in patriarchal structures of white America and black communities. Similarly, black male heterosexuality differs from black male homosexuality owing to the self-perceptions and means of gaining power in the homophobic institutions of white America and black communities. The dominant myth of black male sexual prowess makes black men desirable sexual partners in a culture obsessed with sex.[14]

Another controversial thesis comes out of the Kennedy and Johnson administrations in the 1960s. Written by then-sociologist and later U.S. senator Daniel Patrick Moynihan, "The Negro Family: The Case for National Action" reported on the high level of pregnancies by unwed black mothers, the number of female-headed households in black communities, and black men's high unemployment rates. The controversial report, known as the Moynihan Report, concluded that the black family was dysfunctional due to a "tangle of pathologies" largely because of matriarchy and feminized or absent Black males.[15] Moynihan's report contributed to the notion that feminization of black men was weakening the black family. This premise would undoubtedly strengthen the stand against homosexuality in the black community as black civic and religious leaders honed their message to combat the ominous threat.

Extremely provocative at the time, Moynihan's assertion that dwindling virility in the black community is relevant a half century later. Societal issues like high unemployment, incarceration, and recidivism are infinitely more complicated when black men choose to live on the DL. Given the proliferation of maltreatment and the way that homosexuals are marginalized in modern black culture, Moynihan's report is still relevant. However, Moynihan's report, a tangle of pathologies, is I believe revolutionary in another way, as it contributed to the emergence of what is acknowledged by blacks and whites as the most radical and virile black movement in modern times, the Black Panther Party.

The progressive theory that emanated from a declaration by the Black Panther Party addressing the issue of gay rights was brazen. It spoke volumes about the open-mindedness and practicality of the Black Panther Party as well as the ironic treatment of homosexuality in black culture. It was 1970 when Black Panther Party founder Huey P. Newton wrote this about homosexuality:

> We have not said much about homosexuals at all, but we must relate to the homosexual movement because it is a real thing. And I know through reading, and through my life experience and observations that homosexuals are not given freedom and liberty by anyone in society. They might be the most oppressed in society.
>
> We should be careful about using these terms that might turn our friends off. The terms "faggot" and "punk" should be deleted from our vocabulary . . . Homosexuals are not enemies of the people.[16]

Decades later, it is apparent that Newton's appeal for a change in blacks' attitude as it relates to the treatment of black LGBTs has yet to materialize. Not very long ago, National Basketball Association (NBA) great Kobe Bryant's antigay rant against an NBA referee drew national attention and is indicative of the treatment that members of the LGBT community endure. The attitudes of Bryant and like thinkers prevail because they are parroting the sanctioned stance of black culture, its political leaders, and the powerful Black Church. This being true, there is little reason to believe that Newton's courageous and politically astute appeal will soon be realized.

Believers the world over strive for a religious experience that makes them feel like they are part of their community and congregation. The need to belong is no different for devout black LGBTs whose faith alone is not enough to ensure an equitable religious experience or an unfettered opportunity to find fellowship with other parishioners. The Human Rights Campaign (HRC) reports that approximately 25 percent of the world's Christians are Pentecostal or charismatic, which is a form of the Christianity that emphasizes the work of the Holy Spirit, spiritual gifts, and modern-day miracles.

According to a U.S. think tank, the Pew Forum, approximately 3.4 percent of charismatic Christians are Americans.[17]

There is a history of condemning homosexuals by Pentecostal congregations and a strict requirement to denounce homosexuality. For example, the International Pentecostal Holiness Church doctrinal statement explicitly states: "We have maintained a strong position against premarital, extramarital, and deviant sex, including homosexual and lesbian relationships, refusing to accept the loose moral standards of our society. We commit ourselves to maintaining this disciplined lifestyle with regard to our bodies."[18] This overtly strident doctrine sets forth clear parameters that require total conformity. The Pentecostal precept is similar to those of traditional Black Churches, where deviation from conventional sexual norms is denounced. The growing conflict within the Pentecostal church and traditional Black Church is the source of fierce criticism by black LGBTs who consider church dogma unfair and oppressive to them.

Describing what sounds like a verbal crucifixion, one black Pentecostal blogger talked about the mistreatment of black gay Pentecostal Christians, saying that his intention was to expose the mistreatment and hypocrisy that exists within the black Pentecostal church. The blogger states that black Pentecostal clergy do not openly welcome homosexuals to their churches and in fact work to keep them away, saying, ". . . Pentecostal clergy may allow a gay person to remain (at some low capacity) in the church under Don't ask–don't tell policy. This is usually reserved for guys who have masculine mannerisms."[19] The account is consistent with the practice of conditioning black males and rebuking those who fail to adhere to the sexual behaviors deemed acceptable in black culture.

Antigay strategies run the gambit. However, the use of HIV/AIDS and religious extremism is an effective tactic against black LGBTs. Right Wing political groups like GOProud use religious extremism and the dreaded illness to contest same-sex marriage and LGBT advocates who seek equal treatment under the law. Aside from the polarizing effect that it has on the LGBT community, the volatile mix of fanaticism and science produces a brand of intensely venomous contempt aimed at anyone who does not comport to Christian Right values and the corresponding definition of acceptable sexual standards. Made stronger by homophobic black ministers armed and emboldened with data from the CDC that reveals a sharp increase in HIV/AIDS infections among young black men, the tactic is extremely effective.

The antigay stance is fortified by recent statistics that demonstrate that black communities are seeing a disproportionate rise in new HIV infections. For example, in 2009, blacks accounted for 44 percent of new

HIV cases, a rate that was about eight times that of whites. This is crucial to black ministers and secular sympathizers, who continue to link the epidemic of HIV/AIDS to black LGBTs and in the process, reinforce their campaign to stop the legalization of same-sex unions. Skilled at utilizing CDC data to demonstrate a correlation to the spread of HIV/AIDS, they scare the bejesus out of black churchgoers and are able to fend off claims of divisive tactics by claiming to be protecting their flock against the ravages of the secular world. Homophobic black ministers who embark on this clever crusade of blending scripture and scientific data, under the pretext of fighting the devastating disease, are subtly promoting condemnation for the black LGBT community under the guise of religious duty. Such devices can lead to what amounts to the sanctioning of a psychological and spiritual flogging chiefly aimed at gay and bisexual black men, who are more likely to keep secret their homosexuality. More often, the possibility of suffering inhumane treatment and discrimination leads to a decision to conceal one's sexual identity. Consequently, when powerful black religious leaders make incendiary statements about homosexuals, using their megachurches to spread the word that the menacing HIV/AIDS epidemic is the fault of gays and bisexuals, they are ramping up hostility toward black LGBT Christians. When these antigay antagonists say incendiary things about the LGBT community and talk about homosexuality as an unhealthy lifestyle that is sinful in the eyes of God, they are participating in a very effective campaign against LGBTs and same-sex marriage. They know that one sure way to strengthen the effort against same-sex marriage and homosexuality is to talk about issues like HIV/AIDS that affect communities and family stability. They also know that an attack that uses scientific data is nearly impossible to refute and will be viewed by most as a legitimate reason for dressing-down the LGBT community.

Another undeniable truth is that the lives of black families throughout America are being devastated by the feared disease. One alarming indicator comes from the CDC: "in 2006, black men accounted for two-thirds of new infections (65%) among all blacks. The rate of new HIV infection for black men was 6 times as high as that of white men, nearly 3 times that of Hispanic/Latino men, and twice that of black women."[20] According to the CDC, by the end of 2008, an estimated 240,627 blacks with AIDS had died.[21] Terrifying statistics like these promote fear, and ultimately, blame is aimed at the LGBT community. The feared disease, now 30 years old, continues unabated, terrorizing black communities as it did the white gay community during the mid-1980s when the deadly disease emerged. Now, homophobic black ministers seem eager to directly link homosexuality to the rise of HIV/AIDS, increasing divisiveness in the black community.

Countering the claims of antigay extremists is difficult when AIDS has killed nearly 30 million people worldwide, causing a paradigm shift to address behavioral, social, and economic aspects that contribute to the disease. However, in black and Hispanic communities, the effort is made more difficult by the persistence of issues related to disparities like abject poverty, an explosion of drug use, and homelessness, all things that plague minority communities and economically disadvantaged people.

According to the CDC, the precipitous growth will ultimately result in more women contracting of HIV/AIDS than men.[22] This data and other CDC statistics demonstrate why efforts by religious zealots and antigay protagonists to legitimize the stigma of HIV/AIDS have been incredibly effective.

Consider this:

- By race/ethnicity, African Americans face the most severe burden of HIV in the United States. At the end of 2007, blacks accounted for almost half (46 percent) of people living with a diagnosis of HIV infection in the 37 states with long-term, confidential, name-based HIV reporting. In 2006, blacks accounted for nearly half (45 percent) of new infections in the 50 U.S. states and Washington, D.C. Compared with members of other races and ethnicities, they continue to account for a higher proportion of cases at all stages of HIV—from new infections to deaths.

- In 2006, black men who have sex with men (MSM) represented 63 percent of new infections among all black men, and 35 percent among all MSM. HIV infection rates are higher among black MSM compared to other MSM. More new HIV infections occurred among young black MSM (aged 13 to 29) than among any other age and racial group of MSM.

- In 2006, the rate of new HIV infection for black women was nearly 15 times as high as that of white women and nearly 4 times that of Hispanic/Latina women.

- At some point in their lifetimes, 1 in 16 black men will be diagnosed with the HIV infection, as will 1 in 32 black women.

- From 2005 to 2008, the rate of HIV diagnoses among blacks increased from 68 out of every 100,000 persons to 74 out of every 100,000. This increase reflects the largest increase in rate of HIV diagnoses by race or ethnicity.

- In 2008, an estimated 18,328 blacks were given an AIDS diagnosis; the number had remained relatively stable since 2005.

- By the end of 2007, an estimated 233,624 blacks with a diagnosis of AIDS had died in the United States and five dependent areas. In 2006, HIV was the ninth leading cause of death for all blacks and the third leading cause of death for both black men and black women aged 35 to 44.[23]

According to a November 2011 CDC report, "African Americans face the most severe burden of HIV of all racial/ethnic groups in the United States (US). Despite representing only 14% of the US population in 2009, African Americans accounted for 44% of all new HIV infections in that year. Compared with members of other races and ethnicities, African Americans account for a higher proportion of HIV infections at all stages of disease—from new infections to deaths."[24]

Reverend Willie T. Barrow, an African American and former national executive director of Operation PUSH, a social justice organization, who lost her son Keith to AIDS in 1983, has an entirely different perspective than many black clergy on the issue of homosexuality and HIV/AIDS. In an interview with *JET* magazine, a reflective Barrow said, " . . . When I found out that he was gay I never ostracized him." Barrow publicly revealed her son's cause of death at a health conference in Chicago, saying, " . . . I feel such an urge to speak because I think we are killing too many people with short-sightedness. If we are really going to be religious, then Jesus said, pick up people, not crush them down . . ."[25]

It must be said that not all black gay and bisexual men choose deception to avoid the humiliation that revealing their sexuality could bring. In recent times, a growing number have acted with audacity and for a variety of reasons have come out to claim their sexuality. In doing so, they risk the wrath of significant others, family members, and ministers. J. L. King's 2005 best-selling *On the Down Low: A Journey into the Lives of "Straight" Black Men Who Sleep with Men* set the stage for a string of confessional books and guest appearances on the *Oprah* show where gay and bisexual men told of their lives on the DL.[26]

In acutely apparent opposition to the rash of tell-all confessionals, writer Irene Monroe tells the other side of the DL phenomenon in a 2005 article that deftly captures the anger of a black woman who talks about the effects of black men on the DL and how their deception and twofaced lives affect others:

DL may stand for "down low," but for Chicagoan Gladys Overton, "the DL stands for black men just 'damn lying.'" For Overton, the long-term effect of secrets and lies contributes to the alarming health crisis among African-American heterosexual women. According to the Kaiser Family Foundation, a nonprofit health organization, African-American women account for 72 percent of all new HIV cases in women, and they are 23 times more likely to be infected with the virus than white women. What is also unnerving is that 67 percent of African-American women with HIV contracted it from heterosexual sex. And two ways that the virus is contracted heterosexually is through intravenous drug use and African-American men on the down low . . .

Many African-American men on the DL say there are two salient features that contribute to their subculture—white gay culture and the Black Church. DL men deliberately segregate themselves from both black and white gay cultures as an alternative black masculinity that only wants to have sex and socialize with other black men. But class is a factor here, too. While many gay African-American men have the economic mobility to reside outside of the black community and are likely to intermingle with the dominant gay culture, most DL men don't.[27]

Given the visceral response of women like Overton, the negativity toward black men who live on the DL is not soon to change. And while an increasing number of black men live as openly gay and bisexual, as a rule, homosexuality continues to be perceived as a perversion that directly threatens the black family, fatherhood, and all of black culture. So as blacks confront the rise of HIV/AIDS in their communities at a time when other ethnicities are experiencing a retreat of the disease, it makes it harder for even the most liberal black minister to counter the claims of antigay forces or to openly support the black LGBT fight for equality and the legalization of same-sex marriage.

Whether mockingly murmured in the pews of black churches or bombastically shouted in a public setting, the ridicule aimed at black LGBTs existed long before Bush-era faith-based initiatives came along. While it is true that rampant homophobia and ill treatment of black LGBTs existed prior to the implementation of Bush's domestic agenda, the likelihood that the Republican Right and Christian Coalition exploited the black community's already homophobic predisposition to stimulate its family-focused, anti–same-sex marriage campaign in the black community is convincing. It is also entirely conceivable that some black ministers did not entirely understand the inherent probability for discrimination in President Bush's domestic agenda, and that others may have been confused. However, the fact remains that a number were on board and in hot pursuit of the federal faith-based funding that represented financial relief and an opportunity to expand their ministries. One black minister who appears to have understood the ramification is Reverend Jesse Jackson, who aptly characterized the state of flux that the Black Church was in over faith-based funding and social service programs funded by the government. Jackson appears to recognize the impending conflict, warning others that "the church must not . . . compromise its independence."[28]

Chicago reverend James Meeks, who preaches to his congregation of more than 20,000 at the House of Hope, is a member of the Illinois Senate and is an example of a black leader whose power in both the secular and spiritual world greatly affects the black LGBT Christian community and its efforts to attain equality. As an outspoken critic of homosexuality and equality for LGBTs, Meeks's influence in legislative matters and in his role as a minister is occasionally difficult to differentiate, and as a result, he is a disquieting figure for the LGBT community. Meeks is generally viewed as a dependable obstructionist to gay rights measures, and his remarks about homosexuality are often insensitive and inflammatory. The megapreacher has given ample reason for the concern of the black LGBT community, preaching against homosexuality and even sponsoring a controversial and tactless Halloween-themed event in 2006 called the Night of Terror—a tour of hell featuring gays and abortionists burning for their sins.[29]

In another example, "Throughout his career, Meeks has made several homophobic and offensive comments. In 2006, he called homosexuality 'an evil sickness' and also campaigned against an Illinois LGBT non-discrimination bill while serving in the Illinois state legislature."[30]

During his 2010 failed mayoral campaign, Meeks tried to dial down the heat after being named by the SPLC in 2007 as "one of the leading black religious voices in the anti-gay movement." As a Chicago mayoral candidate, he continued to stoke the fire, asking, "If homosexuals can endorse a candidate, why can't a church?"[31] Meeks has also told members of his congregation that they have a duty to support candidates who are guided by Christian values. And in what sounded like a carefully crafted politically safe statement, Rick Garcia, the former public policy director of Equality Illinois', credited the usually homophobic Meeks with making an effort, telling the *Chicago Tribune*, "There is still a good deal of skepticism there, but we also have respect for someone who might become mayor; and he has respect for us as a politically active community."[32]

The SPLC article observed that "Meeks and the Illinois Family Institute (IFI) had partnered with Focus on the Family, the Family Research Council and the Alliance Defense Fund, major antigay organizations of the

Christian Right. They also are tightly allied with Americans for Truth, an Illinois group that said in a press release last year that 'fighting AIDS without talking against homosexuality is like fighting lung cancer without talking against smoking."[33] The SPLC also noted that the number of far-right hate groups continues to climb for the second year in a row. "The SPLC documented 1002 hate groups operating in the U.S., a 7.5 percent increase from the year before. It was the first time that more than 1,000 hate groups were recorded since the organization started tracking them in the 1980s."[34]

The viewpoint of people like Reverend Meeks is not monolithic among black ministers. Therefore, it is important to say again that laying the explosion of HIV/AIDS in urban America at the door of LGBTs is not something that all black religious leaders do. That said, some black ministers who may want to modify their position on the issue of homosexuality and same-sex civil unions find it exceedingly difficult to do so at a time when black communities are experiencing a rise in HIV/AIDS. This is especially true given scientific data from the CDC, the federal agency charged with protecting people and saving lives, which correlates risky homosexual behavior to the spread of HIV/AIDS among blacks.

In addition to HIV/AIDS, other issues like class distinction, and secular and religious factors continue to shape views about black sexuality, causing them to vary greatly, from liberal to ultra-conservative. These dynamics bear heavily on the opinion of the black LGBT community and have a tremendous effect on the acceptance of homosexuality and same-sex civil marriage by black culture.

NOTES

1. Leviticus 20:13.

2. http://www.outhistory.org/wiki/Queer_Bronzeville_%3A_An _Overview. Accessed April 18 2011.

3. Robert Staples. *Exploring Black Sexuality* (Lanham, MD: Rowman & Littlefield Publishers, 2006).

4. http://loldarian.blogspot.com/2011/02/author-activist-terry-angel -mason-on.html. Accessed March 24, 2011.

5. Brentin Mock Southern Poverty Law Center.

6. Horace L. Griffin, *Their Own Receive Them Not: African American Lesbians and Gays in Black Churches* (Pilgrim Press, 2006).

7. J. L. King, *On the Down Low: A Journey into the Lives of "Straight Black" Men Who Sleep With Men* (New York: Broadway Books, 2004).

8. Matthew Quest, http://www.spunk.org/texts/pubs/lr/sp001715/ isispap.html. Accessed March 21, 2011.

9. Frances Cress Welsing, *The Isis Papers* (Third World Press, 1991).

10. Quest; Ibid.

11. Kit Duffy, Chicago activist and former liaison to Chicago LGBT community, interview with author.

12. bell hooks, "Homophobia in black communities," in Delroy Constantine-Simms, ed., *The Greatest Taboo: Homosexuality in Black Communities* (Los Angeles: Alyson Books, 2001).

13. Cornel West, *Race Matters* (Boston: Beacon Press, 1993). http://books.google.com/books?id=p89c2eTJgJgC&lpg.

14. Ibid., 87, 89.

15. Daniel Patrick Moynihan, "The negro family: The case for national action" (Office of Policy Planning and Research, 1965). http://www.dol.gov/oasam/programs/history/webid-meynihan.htm.

16. Charles Earl Jones, *The Black Panther Party (Reconsidered)* (Baltimore: Black Classic Press, 1998). http://books.google.com/books?id=hxpCxS661Q8C&dq=black+panthers+on+homosexuality&source=gbs_navlinks_s.

17. http://religions.pewforum.org/affiliations. Accessed April 14, 2011.

18. http://www.hrc.org/issues/13444.html. Accessed April 14 2011.

19. http://humandiginity.wordpress.com/about/. Accessed April 13, 2011.

20. http://www.cdc.gov/hiv/topics/aa/. Accessed April 14, 2011.

21. http://www.cdc.gov/hiv/topics/aa/ Accessed December 19, 2012.

22. http://www.cdc.gov/hiv/topics/women/index.htm Accessed December 19, 2012.

23. http://www.cdc.gov/hiv/topics/aa/. Accessed April 14, 2011.

24. www.cdc.gov/hiv/topics/aa/PDF/aa.pdf. Accessed April 14, 2011.

25. Willie T. Barrow, http://books.google.com/books. Accessed 14, 2011.

26. *On the Down Low: A Journey into the Lives of "Straight" Black Men Who Sleep with Men* April 5, 2005.

27. Irene Monroe, "The Lie of Living 'On the Down Low,' " *Witness*, March 25, 2005, http://www.thewitness.org/article.php?id=866.

28. http://newsletters.cephasministry.com/04_01_pros_and_cons_faith_based.html. Accessed April 14, 2011.

29. http://www.nbcchicago.com/blogs/ward-room/Meeks-on-gay-rights-hes-no-Harold-Washington-102861034.html#ixzz1Ir7LWQp8. Accessed April 13, 2011.

30. http://www.huffingtonpost.com/2010/12/09/james-meeks-courts-gay-vo_n_794499.html. Accessed March 25, 2011.

31. http://articles.chicagotribune.com/2010-12-11/news/ct-met-chicago-mayor-meeks-sermon-20101211_1_meeks-mayoral-candidate-churches. Accessed December 4, 2012.

32. Kristen Mack and John Chase, *Chicago Tribune*, Thursday, October 7, 2010.

33. Brentin Mock 2007 SPLC Report.

34. http://www.indypressny.org/nycma/voices/464/news/news_August 1, 2012.

FIVE

Same-Sex Marriage

Who knowing the judgment of God, that they which commit such things are worthy of death, not only do the same, but have pleasure in them that do them.[1]

According to polling, a majority of Americans agree that sexual orientation should not affect a person's civil rights. The LGBT community and its advocates have long maintained this stance, saying that their civil rights are endangered because of their sexual identity. LGBT activists have appealed to the government to intercede, asking to be provided protection against discriminatory acts as was done for black Americans during the 1960s civil rights movement. On the other hand, those who oppose homosexuals and same-sex marriage take the position that those involved in homosexual relationships should not be recipients of additional public or legal advantages beyond those afforded any other U.S. citizen.

Encouraged by social conservatives and evangelicals, opponents of homosexuality and same-sex marriage—some of them extreme—challenge the entire LGBT equality movement. They counter the demand of LGBTs for fairness and equality with their self-imposed and narrow view of sexual intercourse to be as God intended it—a human connection or bond between a man and woman. Anything beyond the confines of this parameter is perceived as immoral. In spite of court decisions favoring the LGBT community, antigay extremists continue their vigorous pushback against same-sex marriage and LGBT equal rights protections. They are particularly unsympathetic to gay activists who demand the same rights afforded heterosexual couples, and who call for the rescission of Defense of Marriage Act (DOMA). These antigay forces vow to protect what they consider society's most important institution and defend their position by suggesting dire consequences if any form of same-sex marriage is allowed by the courts. They justify their inflexible position by cleverly asserting that it would be discriminatory to single out one variety of relationship for special treatment while denying that same benefit to others.

Antigay groups are tough on the issue of same-sex marriage. They are quick to point out that the freedom of the LGBT community (like any other) to form organizations does not necessarily mean that federal and local laws should require their participation in churches and professional organizations where they do not share the common goal. This shrewd approach is quite effective when arguing that free association allows organizations to have ethical and religious criteria. The defined standards could by their very nature, for example, exclude members of the LGBT community whose practices are contrarian to the conviction in the sanctity of traditional marriage between one man and one woman. These extremists firmly oppose LGBT rights and believe that homosexuality is abnormal, immoral, and an unhealthy variant of human relationships. At the core of their belief is that same-sex marriage defies the traditional marriage bonds between a man and woman, which are essential for a strong and secure society. They further their position by vehemently opposing legal recognition of domestic partnerships of any kind and dismiss even the possibility of providing health care and death benefits to same-sex couples. They are intensely focused on safeguarding the DOMA, a bill signed into law by President William Jefferson Clinton on September 21, 1996, giving states the "right" to refuse to acknowledge the validity of same-sex marriage performed in other states. Antigay groups are also pushing a constitutional amendment against same-sex marriage intended to forever protect the traditional institution of marriage between a man and woman

In 2010 when Vice President Joe Biden commented on the growing acceptance of same-sex marriage by saying, "I think the country is evolving, and I think there is an inevitability for a national consensus on gay marriage," surely his intent was not to speak for all Americans.[2] However, Biden's comment suggesting a trend has been seen in several states, including Maryland, where same-sex marriage legislation was approved in February 2012. A few days earlier in New Jersey, conservative Republican governor Chris Christie vetoed a bill legalizing same-sex marriage, saying, "I continue to encourage the Legislature to trust the people of New Jersey and seek their input by allowing our citizens to vote on a question that represents a profoundly significant societal change. This is the only path to amend our State Constitution and the best way to resolve the issue of same-sex marriage in our state."[3]

Gay marriage legislation in other states will likely face strong opposition as social conservatives and evangelicals, along with major segments of U.S. society, strongly disagree with the vice president's optimistic prediction. Leading the opposition are African Americans and Hispanics, whose resistance to same-sex marriage is formidable. In fact, blacks and Hispanics were instrumental in overturning same-sex civil union laws in several states, including California. Higher courts have reversed rulings banning same-sex marriage, and many in the black community and many black ministers remain resolute in their opposition to same-sex marriage and appear prepared to counter any political efforts that encroach on ethnic and black religious tradition.

However, it is not just blacks and Hispanics contradicting the vice president's confidence in Americans' acceptance of same-sex marriage. Biden's comments present a stark contrast to the opinions of televangelists like Pat Robertson of television's *700 Club*, who has said that the legalization of same-sex marriage would destroy the United States. Discussing the issue of same-sex marriage in 2011, Robertson explained his position, saying, "In history there's never been a civilization, ever in history, that has embraced homosexuality and turned away from traditional fidelity, traditional marriage, traditional child-rearing and has survived."[4] The reality is that Robertson's viewpoint is shared by a considerable percentage of the electorate. The resistance is comprised of 26 percent evangelicals and born-again Christians who are motivated by their religious conviction to oppose any form of same-sex marriage. The religiously inspired opposition supports a constitutional ban against any effort that threatens the sanctity of marriage between a man and a woman.

The outlook related to same-sex marriage is increasingly hopeful as was evidenced by a March 2011 *Washington Post* and ABC News poll which reported that "more than half of Americans say it should be legal for gays and lesbians to marry."[5] In a number of states, battles rage on as passionate adversaries fortify their positions in political and religious arenas. Antigay activists challenge efforts by employing a variety of strategies that include garnering support from social conservatives who share their view. Nonetheless, the 2011 survey and landmark legal victories have strengthened the hope of LGBTs. For example, LGBTs are heartened by reports indicating that among registered voters, growing support for same-sex marriage has increased from 32 percent in 2004 to 53 percent in 2011, and that the percentage opposed to gay marriage declined to 41 percent in 2011, a reduction of 18 points from the 2004 survey. This was the first time in the United States that a majority of people favored some form of legalized same-sex civil or domestic unions.[6] Clearly, the issue has the potential to prompt strong disagreement, has riled the conservative wing of the GOP, and has sparked ardent disapproval from evangelical Christians.

The noticeable shift in the public's mindset, as substantiated by polls like the one just mentioned, brings cautious optimism and seems to bode well for LGBT advocates who have waited for a long time for signs of acceptance by fellow Americans. But to antigay adversaries like the Christian Right, social conservatives, and family values organizations, the shift is seen as an infringement not only on traditional marriage, but also on the separation between church and state. The staunch opposition from well-organized evangelicals against highly motivated pro-LGBT forces, which include younger people, liberals, political moderates, and progressive Catholics, has helped to stem the tide of resistance to same-sex marriage. The effort has so far resulted in trending that leans more toward tolerance of gay rights and an acceptance of some form of same-sex marriage. The unexpected support from Catholics and others whose acquiescence was not long ago considered highly improbable bring hope to the LGBT community. In spite of these advances, black LGBTs continue to face dogged repudiation and resentment from an increasingly tough opposition comprised predominantly of blacks ministers, social conservatives, and evangelical Christians.

The intense adverse reaction of many blacks to the prospect of same-sex civil marriage is striking even without the preposterous proclamations of people like black minister Gregory Daniels, who received national attention when he made the absurd vow to ride with the KKK against gay marriage. However, refusal by an overwhelming majority of black religious leaders and churchgoers to embrace same-sex marriage, or to adjust their stance on LGBT equality issues, does to some degree validate Daniels's over-the-top objection to what is believed sinful, unnatural, and a destructive force in the black community. Given this, it is reasonable to conclude that the longtime political and religious differences that separate diehard opponents and proponents of same-sex civil marriage are not likely to change or to move toward meaningful compromise anytime soon.

Polling that repeatedly shows growing and broad public support for equal rights for gay people provokes strong emotions. The topic has the potential to become heated, especially when same-sex marriage is the issue. This is rather surprising, considering that almost 90 percent of Americans are in favor of equal rights at work, over 60 percent were in favor of overturning

"Don't ask, don't tell" when it was finally repealed in 2011, and the country remains almost equally split on the issue of same-sex marriage.[7]

In the black community, a plethora of mostly groundless phobias and a deep-rooted resentment toward homosexuality help create an odd blend of accusations rooted in ethnic taboos that are unique to the black experience. The powerful homophobic mindset of blacks compels many black homosexuals to live in the shadows, concealing their sexuality. In fact, until very recently, open discussions in the black community about homosexuality and same-sex marriage were not at all common. The rigidity of some black ministers makes it nearly impossible to work toward a meaningful change in blacks' thinking as it relates to homosexuality. As a result, it comes as no surprise that the Black Church and religious-based organizations are perceived as being at the heart of the muddled contradictions surrounding and powerful indignation toward the black LGBT community. Gay rights advocates believe that as long as powerful black ministers refuse to compromise on the issue of same-sex marriage, it will continue to be a nonstarter in the black community.

Black LGBTs may be justified in thinking that the Black Church is responsible for the continuing standoff and discriminatory treatment of black LGBTs. As far as same same-sex marriage goes, there has been little budging by the majority of black ministers, who are almost wholly supported in their unyielding stance by churchgoers and the broader black community. On this issue, not only are they united, but they become instantly vocal and intense when depicted as intolerant of LGBT equality–related issues. Antigay clergy are quick to argue that their firm stand against efforts to legalize same-sex marriage is intended to save the black family and defend the sanctity of traditional marriage between one man and one woman. In this, they are quite convincing and in absolute lockstep with former president George W. Bush, who made no bones about the sacredness of marriage, unequivocally expressing his position on the issue of same-sex marriage by pledging that "Marriage is a sacred institution between a man and a woman . . . I will work with congressional leaders and others to do what is legally necessary to defend the sanctity of marriage."[8] This stand is one of the few things on which blacks agreed with him. However, President Bush's compelling pledge to do what is legally necessary to defend the sanctity of marriage, never quite expounded on how the legal recognition of same-sex marriage would adversely impact traditional marriage or for that matter, any form of matrimony.

President Bush's statement and talk of a federal constitutional amendment banning same-sex marriage was responded to in a letter from Julian

Bond, chairman of the National Association for the Advancement of Colored People (NAACP) to the Massachusetts State Senate. In this letter, Bond wrote, "The NAACP vigorously opposes President George W. Bush's attempt to pass a federal constitutional amendment banning same-sex marriage. . . . We also oppose state-level attempts to do the same thing. . . . There is no such thing as a moderate or 'compromise' amendment that in any way enshrines treating one group of people differently than others."[9]

However, it is important to point out that even progressive white church leaders like Bill Hybels, senior pastor of the 7,000-plus congregation at Willow Creek Community Church in Illinois, have been accused of promoting an antigay position and opposing same-sex marriage. Hybels was forced to defend his church against an online petition launched by political organizer and strategist Asher Huey. Seeming to explain his church's position on homosexuality, Hybels said, "We challenge homosexuals and heterosexuals to live out the sexual ethics taught in scriptures, which encourage sexual expression between a man and a woman in the context of marriage."[10]

In 2004 when President Bush pressed for a constitutional amendment to protect the institution of marriage and restrict marriage to two people of the opposite sex, he did so by taking a shot at a handful of judges whose rulings on same-sex marriage had resulted in confusion. Bush made it clear that the significance of this issue should not be decided by an activist court, saying, "If we're to prevent the meaning of marriage from being changed forever, our nation must enact a constitutional amendment to protect marriage in America."[11] The president's admonishment of judges who were thought to be advancing efforts to legalize same-sex marriage spoke directly to the nation's citizenry: ". . . Decisive and democratic action is needed because attempts to redefine marriage in a single state or city could have serious consequences throughout the country."[12]

In that same year, a candidate for the U.S. Senate, Barack Obama, publicly supported civil unions while opposing same-sex marriage. In a *Chicago Tribune* interview, Obama stood on his religious conviction to avoid controversy, alienating the LGBT community by tiptoeing around the same-sex marriage issue. He said, "I'm a Christian. And so, although I try not to have my religious beliefs dominate or determine my political views on this issue, I do believe that tradition, and my religious beliefs say that marriage is something sanctified between a man and a woman."[13]

By 2007, as a presidential candidate, Obama's views had not dramatically changed on homosexuality and morality. In what was considered by some a political blunder and others a brilliant strategy, the presidential hopeful came dangerously close to the third rail of politics from the viewpoint of the LGBT community. Revealing how he felt about the issue of homo-sexuality, Obama said, "Homosexual acts between two individuals are immoral ..." His position on the issue played well in the black commu-nity and among moderates.[14]

As far as same-sex marriage is concerned, during this period, neither Bush nor Obama held an ambiguous position or one open to compromise. In fact, there was little difference between the two on the issue, and both enjoyed support from the black community for their stance on same-sex marriage. Because the United States' first black president did not originally support same-sex marriage, differences between Obama and Bush were negligible from both a religious and a societal viewpoint. If there was any distinction at all, it related to strategies used by Bush to suppress the LGBT community and same-sex civil union legislation, and his very frank public opposition to legalization of same-sex marriage. For example, during the 2004 presidential election, George W. Bush was able to dramatically increase support among black voters in Ohio by rallying them around the issue of defeating same-sex marriage equality efforts championed by LGBT advocates. The number of blacks voting Republican was up over 7 percent from the 2000 presiden-tial election, the highest percentage increase was seen among blacks who attended church services more than once a week. Black voters overwhelm-ingly supported Bush, increasing from 52 percent in 2000 to 69 percent in 2004. The impressive gain was in part due to the use of antigay campaigns that played to black churchgoers and an unbending homophobic African American culture.[15]

Surely there were and continue to be moderate voices within the black community on the issue of LGBT equality and same-sex marriage. How-ever, they are often stifled by the more vocal and extreme homophobic adversaries of gay rights and same-sex marriage. Yet even now, what trig-gers the ire of the black community and black liberal religious leaders is attempts by LGBT advocates to compare the fight for LGBT parity to the storied struggle for racial equality waged during the civil rights era. It is here that the vast majority of black ministers and civic leaders who might daringly publicly support the black LGBT cause either retreat or make it perfectly clear that there is no connection to the civil rights strug-gle. For many blacks, any attempt to link the hallowed civil rights move-ment to the black LGBT community's quest for fair treatment runs a real risk of being labeled irreverent to the black experience.

In a 2004 article, author and inspirational black gay activist Keith Boykin discussed the black church and its handling of the same-sex civil union issue. Boykin chose to focus on what the Reverend Jesse Jackson said when he spoke out against same-sex marriage and rejected comparisons between the civil rights movement and LGBT equality. Jackson could not go wrong voicing the opinion of many blacks when talking about the unmerited and inaccurate comparisons between today's battle for fair treatment of LGBTs and racial equality fought for during the civil rights movement. Driving home his point, Jackson left no room for comparison or comprise. "Gays were never called three-fifths human in the Constitution," he said, and "they did not require the Voting Rights Act to have the right to vote."[16]

Jackson's forthright observation is shared by prominent black ministers and community leaders whose views by and large mirror the sentiment of the broader black community. In fact, powerful indignation results when attempts are made to compare the two or to piggyback the civil rights movement to advance LGBT equality or same-sex marriage. While it may not be the opinion of the entire black community, unity on this issue is overwhelming and reflects the intense reverence conferred on those who fought against racial discrimination decades before issues related to LGBTs or same-sex marriage were on the table. Moreover, LGBT advocates who have tried to equate their fight to the civil rights movement seem more likely to impede their efforts and further damage an already tenuous relationship with powerful black religious leaders.

Boykin is obviously disappointed in Jackson's viewpoint and the fact that an overwhelming majority of blacks share in his thinking that LGBT equality and same-sex marriage are entirely detached from the fight for civil rights. Yet Boykin's disappointment and noticeable umbrage appear an overreaction that fails to consider the historical basis for the black community's position, and that the illogicalities toward homosexuality have existed for generations and are not likely to soon change. LGBT activists who attempt to tie LGBT equality to the civil rights movement, believing it a good idea, weren't just wrong; rather, they remarkably overlooked a history of several hundred years in which opposition to homosexuality was consistently linked to attaining racial equality through strength. Conscious or not, ignoring this important fact seems to have created friction and further disaffected black religious and civic leaders, resulting in further hindering progress and building alliances. Moreover, Boykin's reaction to the position taken by liberal black clergy like Jackson and former U.S. congressman Walter Fauntroy, whose record on reformist causes are well known in the black community, is similarly surprising since it implies that Boykin had not considered the possibility that black leaders might respond in a manner consistent with how they have for generations.

That said, Boykin does offer persuasive reasoning that is shared by black LGBTs and same-sex marriage advocates who believe that blacks' opposition to the LGBT community and its effort to legalize same-sex marriage is the height of hypocrisy. Plainly put, the very notion that blacks would unite to resist an effort that has as its purpose the achievement of equal rights for any group strikes black LGBTs and gay rights supporters as utterly preposterous. Boykin makes this argument by comparing the denial of matrimonial rights to blacks who wanted to marry whites only decades ago to that of gay people now who are denied the right to marry, with the support of a majority of the black community. In spite of this, since Boykin's opinion piece appeared in the *Village Voice* in 2004, the black community and its religious leaders have not wavered on the issue of same-sex marriage, continuing to dig in their heels when comparisons between LGBT equality and civil rights are suggested. A similar response is seen when blacks who support laws banning discrimination against the LGBT community immediately draw a line of demarcation when the issue of same-sex marriage is discussed.

In a shrewd move and an accentuation of his dissatisfaction, Boykin refers to questions posed by the late reverend Peter Gomes, a black Republican minister, related to the way that the Black Church responds to homosexuality. Gomes's probing seems to go directly to the heart of the issue when he questions whether the black church had succumbed to the devices of the white religious right. Gomes asserts that, "I'm sure they're being co-opted, but they don't need a great deal of co-optation . . ." "I think they come to the prejudice on their own."[17] Gomes, a conservative Republican, Harvard theologian, author, and Baptist preacher who gave the benediction at Ronald Reagan's second inauguration, turned out to be a great example demonstrating that even among the most conservative ranks, LGBTs are represented. Gomes had come out over two decades before following a particularly bitter and inflammatory magazine article by an antigay Right Wing student magazine that quoted Sigmund Freud and used the book of Leviticus to deprecate homosexuality as an "immoral" and "pitiable" path to misery and disease. A Christian who happened to be gay, Gomes was the perfect conservative to take up the cause and in a *Washington Post* interview asserted his reasons for doing so, saying, "I now have an unambiguous vocation, a mission, to address the religious causes of homophobia . . . I will devote the rest of my life to addressing the religious case against gays."[18]

Taking a decidedly moral road, Gomes said, when speaking to a crowd of Harvard students, "These wicked writings are hurtful, divisive and most profoundly wrong." Gay people, he contended, were victims not of religion but of, "people who use religion as a way to devalue and deform those whom they can neither ignore nor convert."[19]

Yet even with examples like Gomes, few believed that changing the mindset of blacks would be easy. In a telling illustration of the difficulty ahead, determined black antigay, same-sex marriage antagonists, even while voting overwhelming to elect the nation's first African American president, voted their religious and cultural conviction, leading the charge to overturn same-sex marriage laws in California and Florida. In what may have seemed contradictory to onlookers, the clear-cut, unapologetic, and unmovable stand against homosexuality and same-sex marriage boils down to what has aptly been expressed as "just the way things are." The attempts to define same-sex marriage as political, indifferent, or discriminatory are generally mischaracterized and inconsistent with the black ethos.

In fact, there are few things as far-reaching and entirely unyielding in the black community as the resistance to the efforts of the LGBT community to force the acceptance of homosexuality or the legalization of same-sex marriage. In a stunning show of strength, in 2008, the LGBT movement suffered an astounding defeat when California voters approved a ban on same-sex marriage, which was in large part propelled by black voters. In the end, the vote—which overrode a previous court decision legalizing same-sex marriage—was powered by 50 percent of Hispanics and the full-throated retaliatory reaction of 70 percent of African Americans. Calling the ban against same-sex marriage unconstitutional, the 2008 measure banning same-sex marriage and limiting marriage to a man and a woman was overturned by a federal appeals panel in a vote of 2 to 1 in 2012.[20]

In Illinois, where a law authorizing same sex civil unions went into effect in 2011 to give gay and lesbian couples some of the same rights as married couples, support for same-sex marriage increased from 12 percent in 1988 to 40 percent in 2010.[21] Data from Equal Illinois, an LGBT advocacy group, shows that in the first month following passage of the state's bill allowing civil unions, more than 1,600 licenses were issued to LGBT couples taking advantage of the new civil union law. The law made Illinois the sixth state to join the short list of states permitting same-sex marriage, which at the time included Washington, Oregon, Nevada, California, and the District of Columbia. These locales recognize domestic partnerships and empower the clergy to preside over civil unions for same-sex couples.

Northwestern University political science professor Andrew Koppelman expressed his opinions about the inevitability of same-sex marriage, referring to it as a "social movement." He said, "This has been a spectacularly successful social movement. In about 10 years, they've reached the point where a quarter of the population of the United States lives someplace that at least has civil unions. And that's from nothing."[22] Professor Koppelman's opinion should raise the spirits of LGBT advocates and lend hope to those who have toiled to achieve equality. However, even as optimism increases that sooner or later legalized gay marriage will be the law of the land, a majority of states have constitutional amendments banning same-sex marriage. In fact, in 2011, in 31 states and among ethnic groups like blacks and Hispanics, the sentiment to permit same-sex marriage has not trickled down. To illustrate, in the Black Church and among black voters, opposition to same-sex marriage is intense as ever. In liberal states like New York where the gay rights movement is said to have started, Archbishop Timothy Dolan—a fierce opponent of the same-sex civil union bill—spoke out repeatedly about the dangers of characterizing marriage as anything other than between a man and woman in a "loving, permanent life-giving union to procreate children."[23] Despite Dolan's warning as well as the vigor and big pockets of traditional marriage supporters who spent in excess of $2 million to defeat New York's same-sex civil union bill, a robust grassroots campaign to legalize gay marriage led to the bill's passage in 2011. Some theorize that the legislative success in New York may have provided the momentum for other states to legalize gay nuptials. New York joined Iowa, Massachusetts, New Hampshire, Vermont, and the District of Columbia. Civil unions were also approved in Delaware and Hawaii. According to a report by the Independent Democratic Conference, more than 21,000 gay and lesbian couples from New York were likely to marry within the first three years of the approving legislation.[24]

In Chicago, the resistance to gay marriage is led by influential members of Chicago's black clergy. One religious and political leader, Reverend James Meeks—who was running for mayor of Chicago in 2010—had this to say about a proposed bill allowing same-sex marriage: "I don't think that a person should vote on a bill of that magnitude based on the next office . . . I think they should base their vote on what they believe. And I believe that this is a bill about marriage, and I believe that the sanctity of marriage should be protected, and it should be between a man and a woman."[25] This declaration was bold yet not far removed from the opinions of a lot of black ministers who from the pulpits of churches large and small, urban and rural, often sermonized about the nonvirtuous aspects of and damning judgment awaiting people who engage in sexual behavior that is not sanctioned by biblical scripture.

Countering this prohibited morality view were people like John Knight, director of the Lesbian, Gay, Bisexual, Transgender Project of the American Civil Liberties Union of Illinois, who touted the same-sex union legislation as a significant achievement, speaking of it as though it were a watershed and symbolic moment for the advancement of LGBT issues and all of Illinois. "Illinois is taking an historic step forward in embracing fairness and extending basic dignity to all couples in our state," Knight proudly proclaimed.[26]

Not surprisingly, Meeks and other gay rights antagonists quickly responded by standing on former president George Bush's personal and political creed, which soundly asserts that any law permitting civil unions paves the way for the legalization of same-sex marriage. In the black community, just talk of legalizing same-sex marriage is enough to prompt a predictable and visceral reaction to homosexuality, one predominately driven by a predisposed and ethnically identifiable brand of homophobia unique to black culture. Add to this societal and political complexities that correlate to the rapidly changing acceptance of homosexuality in mainstream thought, and the result is a contrast that strongly suggests the beliefs about homosexuality that has prevailed in black culture for generations will likely endure.

Even the powerfully persuasive and shocking speculation presented by the late author Manning Marable in his 2011 book *Malcolm X*, which suggest that the audacious black Muslim leader who preached black supremacy and was arguably the most virile black figure of the twentieth century had a homosexual encounter, is likely to have little effect on the black community' viewpoint as it relates to homosexuality.[27] This impenetrable veneer supports the sea of contradiction that engulfs the issue of homosexuality within black culture, and so Marable's findings—while no doubt dramatic—are likely to be viewed as a scholarly study gone too far and therefore pose absolutely no threat to the legend and manliness of the great Malcolm X.

During a 2004 meeting at the Sweet Holy Spirit Gospel Baptist Church in Chicago, black religious leaders from various denominations committed to collecting 50,000 signatures in Black Churches throughout the city to support efforts to prevent same-sex marriage. This signature drive aimed to caution local and state politicians that if they were to support same-sex marriage, they should not expect the same support that the Black Church had provided black politicians for generations. Opponents of homosexuals and same-sex marriage know and are willing to use powerful ultimatums such as this because of the lingering effect they have on black and white politicians throughout the country, urging them to contribute to the defeat of same-sex union legislation.[28]

In 2011 as part of the effort to advance LGBT issues in Illinois, the American Civil Liberties Union filed a class-action lawsuit on behalf of transgenders who wanted their birth certificates changed to the sex they identify with. The suit alleged that prior to 2005 the state would change the gender on birth certificates despite the fact that the individual had not undergone any form of genital surgery. Cleverly timed, it was potentially groundbreaking litigation and is—along with gay foster parenting and adoption rights—the type of legal challenge that could impact same-sex marriage laws throughout the nation by incrementally challenging ambiguity in state laws. Moreover, this method of piecemeal litigation seems promising and is gaining popularity with LGBT moderates as a viable and less confrontational alternative to advance legislative change and parity for the LGBT community. Given the sheer scale of the legal and societal challenges confronting LGBTs, it is difficult to argue against employing a strategy that has already proven not only rational, but effective in achieving the desired objective.

Similarly, litigation was brought in 2011 by three Catholic Charities' heads in Illinois dioceses. Catholic Charities sought protection for religious organizations from legal action when turning away same-sex couples in civil unions who sought to adopt. Much like the strategy employed by same-sex marriage advocates, the Catholic Charities' lawsuit streamlined the focus of its litigation. In the case initiated by Catholic Charities and supported by opponents of homosexuals and same-sex marriage, the petitioners claimed that they were compelled by their faith and asks that the court resolve the question of whether new antidiscrimination policies that accommodate civil unions should prevent social agencies from considering sexual orientation and marital status when reviewing applications for foster care and adoption. The litigation asked the judge to resolve the issue in order "to avert an imminent risk of irreparable harm to many thousands of vulnerable and needy children, families and adults across the state of Illinois and to avoid the collapse of a critical network of social services."[29] Catholic Charities' requested the court's permission to refer couples in civil union to other agencies. Responding to the contentious issue of whether religious organizations that receive public funds to license foster care parents are breaking antidiscrimination laws if they reject LGBT couples, Sangamon County circuit judge John Schmidt ruled that the state did not have to renew its contract with Catholic Charities of Illinois to provide publicly funded foster care. In doing so, the ruling dissolved the long-lasting relationship between the state and Catholic Charities, allowing for the transfer of children to other social service agencies.

Catholic Charities is among a group of religious entities that received financial support from faith-based funding during the Bush administration. The organization continues to receive this funding from the Obama administration. While taking these monies, the organization vigorously affirms its opposition to same-sex marriage, taking its longstanding position that it and other religious organizations are not required to negate their beliefs when performing charitable works. Catholic Charities' assertion of rights is an example of the existing disapproval of same-sex marriage and also suggests that disagreement is not geographically exclusive or confined to a particular ethnic group. Catholic Charities' legal stand reinforces the fact that obstacles related to homosexuality and same-sex marriage exist throughout U.S. society and are prevalent among religious-based organizations.

It is almost certain that the vocal bias against same-sex marriage heard in Black Churches throughout the land significantly contributes to the prejudice that leads to the ostracism of black LGBTs. The denouncement of LGBTs plays out as verbal torment when some black pastors preach about the immorality of homosexuality and stigmatize black Christian churchgoers who are lesbian, bisexual, gay, or transgender. Black ministers who publicly expound on the immorality of homosexuality are seen as contributing to polling that consistently substantiates what is already known in the black community—many blacks are keenly opposed to same-sex marriage of any kind. In fact, according to the Pew Research Center, almost half of all African American churchgoers reported that black ministers routinely express negative opinions about homosexuality.[30]

Proof of the widespread ridicule that black LGBTs regularly face is upheld in a survey conducted by the National Gay and Lesbian Task Force. The survey looked at 2,645 black LGBTs throughout the United States. The study indicates that 53 percent of those evaluated reported an incident of racial discrimination, and a whopping 42 percent of respondents reported being discriminated against because of their sexual orientation. Some reported being victims of racism while attending white gay events and suffering disparagement from black heterosexual organizations, their families, and also in churches and by religious-based organizations. For members of the black LGBT community, the high incidence of victimization and discrimination based on sexual orientation, gender identity, and race comes as no surprise.[31]

Speaking at a Human Rights Ecumenical Service at Atlanta's Tabernacle Baptist Church—which is known as an LGBT-supportive and -inclusive black institution—reverend and human rights activist Al Sharpton talked about the Mormon Church, its support of California's Proposition 8, and the unified effort of black megachurch pastors to mobilize their congregations against homosexuality and same-sex marriage. Using his potent trademark language, Sharpton discussed the immorality of not using power to end social ills like poverty but to instead, as Sharpton put it, "break into people's bedrooms and claim that God sent you." The message was frank and directed at black ministers in California who, according to Sharpton, had done nothing to stand against police brutality or to prevent the overturning of affirmative action, yet quickly mobilized to, "prevent consenting adults from choosing life partners."[32]

Going further than any nationally known black minister had dared, Sharpton talked about the hypocrisy of homosexual clergy who are sexually involved with members of their own sex, saying, "I am tired of seeing ministers who will preach homophobia by day, and then after they're preaching, when the lights are off they go cruising for trade ... When Bush took us to war chasing weapons of mass destruction that weren't there you had nothing to say. But all of a sudden, when Proposition 8 came out, you had so much to say, but since you stepped in the rain, we're going to step in the rain with you."[33]

As brutally candid and controversial as Sharpton's insinuation of same-sex indiscretion by black clergy seems, it is nothing new. Sex scandals within the Black Church didn't start with the 2009 salacious allegations against Atlanta megachurch preacher Eddie Long, nor did they end in 2011 when Bishop Long settled out of court with his four male accusers for an undisclosed sum. What Sharpton was talking about predates all of this. But along the way, what the iconic civil rights leader managed to accomplish on the national stage with his candor was drawing attention to the broadening chasm that exists within the Black Church and community over the issue of homosexuality and same-sex marriage. As black religious leaders and LGBT advocacy groups toil to find common ground over which to coalesce, the dispute over efforts to attach the legalization of same-sex marriage to the civil rights struggle hampers the already narrow prospect for building an enduring and meaningful alliance. In the end, though, all of this seems to have aided in driving home the point that continued attempts to join the battle for same-sex marriage with the civil rights movement will only further distance the black religious community and make achieving a cultural shift in mindset in the black community toward homosexuality or any form of same-sex unions all the more difficult.

In fact, some say that even a tangential association of the two will lead to a toughened stance by antigay black clergy, whose power and passionate position against equality for LGBTs could include a political fortification of their resistance to same-sex marriage. As a matter of fact, it may already be in the offing as intensified haranguing of the black LGBT community by social conservatives and black clergy conveys their message that same-sex marriage equates to the annihilation of what remains of the black family structure. The burgeoning strategy could mean that the already tepid support from moderate black clerics and support of black liberals could be waning and in serious jeopardy. If true, and a unified effort opposing black LGBTs materializes it will not come as a shock to the black community, which for the most part stands united in its belief that the emergence of openly gay individuals demanding the right to marry would be counterproductive to the stabilization of an extremely fragile black family structure. In fact, if this is embraced by homophobic black religious leaders as a stratagem, it could prove a very effective way of reeling in moderate and liberal black ministers who have already strayed—in their estimation—too far by welcoming black LGBT Christians to their congregations and creating ministries to accommodate them.

To assess the power at the core of the challenge to same-sex marriage in the black community, one only has to look to the results of a survey that revealed that seven in 10 African Americans voted yes on Proposition 8, the 2008 California ballot measure overruling a state Supreme Court judgment that legalized same-sex marriage and bringing almost 20,000 gay and lesbian couples to California state courthouses to legitimize their relationships. Similar measures in Florida and Arizona were also passed, and exit polling revealed that no ethnic group more forcefully rejected the attempt to legalize same-sex marriage as blacks. For many blacks, there was no ambiguity whatsoever when they helped to elect the first black president in 2008 while simultaneously and prodigiously rejecting the legalization of same-sex marriage.[34]

Eventually, the California victory was overridden in 2010 when U.S. district judge Vaughn Walker ruled that the California's Proposition 8 ballot initiative denying marriage rights to same-sex couples was "unconstitutional under both the due process and equal protection clauses." Vaughn's ruling observed that "Proposition 8 fails to advance any rational basis in singling out gay men and lesbians for denial of a marriage license. Indeed the evidence shows Proposition 8 does nothing more than enshrine in the California constitution the notion that opposite sex couples are superior to same-sex couples."[35]

Vaughn's ruling created a firestorm and was viewed as a victory for the LGBT community as well as same-sex civil union advocates. However, in the end, the victory may have fortified resistance to same-sex marriage, especially within the Black Church and in urban communities where growing resentment to LGBT equality by zealous antigay black religious traditionalists, egged on by Christian Right factions, propelled Proposition 8 and similar efforts intended to fight same-sex marriage on every front.

Once again, offsetting the sometimes acrimonious standoff is the more subtle and incremental approach to move toward accepting LGBT equality issues and ultimately same-sex marriage. This tactic is generally viewed as an effective strategy to persuade those who are sitting on the fence. In the black community, the piecemeal weakening of the illogical refusal to accept homosexuality on any terms seems better than the confrontational strategies that have so far miserably failed. So while it is too soon to tell if this or any other will yield results, it is by and large agreed that going forward using the least provocative approach should be considered first. So for now, strategies like the one used several years ago when a Boston civil rights group challenged the legality of DOMA—which defines marriage as a legal union between a man and a woman but to the surprise of many does not argue that gays and lesbians are entitled to marry under the Constitution—are seen as more effective.

It's an astute and pragmatic alternative that focuses on the narrower argument that it is unconstitutional to discriminate against legally married gay couples. This method of using the court system to challenge laws in select states throughout the country is growing, and reasonable LGBT advocates respect the sensibility of it as an effective way to ultimately lead to the legalization of same-sex marriage throughout the land. It offers the promise—even with its limited use—of real change within the Black Church and community.[36]

In a cavalcade of high-profile disclosures, one celebrity after another continue to reveal their true sexual identity. When it was reported that the National Basketball Association (NBA) had been informed by Phoenix Suns president Rick Welts that he was gay, the news was both shocking and meaningful, especially to the black community. While Welts is white, the majority of professional basketball players are black. Therefore, it is an industry in which any discussion of homosexuality parallels the taboos of the black community. Intolerance toward homosexuals is notorious in professional basketball. Therefore, the coming out of a player, coach, or for that matter anyone associated with the NBA is likely to cause a stir and unknown consequences.

Saying that he is gay, Welts explained why he decided to reveal his sexual preference, saying that he wanted to "pierce the silence that envelopes the subject of homosexuality in men's sports . . . and most of all he wants to feel whole, authentic," he did so in one of the last industries to deal with homosexuality—professional sports. In declaring his homosexuality, Welts indicated that his aim was to encourage LGBTs who were interested in a sports career to pursue their ambitions.[37]

Then there was African American CNN anchorman Don Lemon, who revealed his homosexuality in his 2011 book titled *Transparent*, in which he talks about his life and sexuality, creating a seminal moment for network news organizations and members of the black LGBT community. Lemon's revelation came a quarter of a century after Max Robinson's death. Robinson was the first black network news anchor in the United States and the first television journalist to die of AIDS at the height of the HIV/AIDS epidemic.[38]

In the book, Lemon, who has been a CNN anchor since 2006, claims to have made no secret of his sexuality and talks candidly about his life as a homosexual. Lemon brings attention to the irony of being a black homosexual versus a white gay man by saying, "I guess this makes me a double minority now." But what Lemon—who was raised in a traditional black Baptist church—says when describing what prevents the acceptance of homosexuality by the black community and church is extraordinarily raw. "It's quite different for an African American male. It's about the worst thing you can be in black culture. You're taught you have to be a man; you have to be masculine. In the black community they think you can pray the gay away."[39]

When Lemon talks about his fear of being an outcast and of how the black community would respond to the disclosure that he is a homosexual, one can imagine that his apprehension was akin to what Max Robinson must have felt decades earlier when he struggled on two pioneering fronts, working as the news industry's first black anchor and working hard to conceal his sexuality. However, if Robinson had been exposed, it would almost certainly have brought his career to a screeching halt.[40]

Prior to Lemon's daring admission, network television seems to have been conspicuously silent on the issue of an openly homosexual black man anchoring a network news program. To the black LGBT community, Lemon's revelation and the high-profile nature of his profession are particularly important because of the potential they have to affect the black community's perception of a gay black man, and to create a different and transformational thinking among blacks. Consequentially, Lemon and Welts might be the most recent impetus to bring about a cultural breakthrough in the black community's acceptance of homosexuality.

On the political front, during a 2010 *Good Morning America* interview, Vice President Joe Biden seemed to predict that the country was moving toward a growing acceptance of same-sex marriage. Biden's bold statement and comparison of changes in the military allowing LGBTs to openly serve and same-sex marriage were somewhat overly hopeful and do not represent the way sections of American society, like social conservatives, the Christian Right, evangelicals, and a largely homophobic black community perceive the issue.

Whether at some point blacks will join other ethnic groups who are beginning to show support of some kind same-sex marriage mainly depends on how black religious leaders respond to the elimination of

"Don't ask, don't tell" (DADT). For example, if the repeal of DADT is mostly successful, and by that I mean implemented with minimal complications, it could represent a dramatic turning point on the issue of homosexuality, even within black culture. While transformational thinking doesn't entirely depend on the smooth transitioning of a U.S. military in which heterosexuals and homosexuals serve together harmoniously, the specter of major complications associated with the elimination of DADT would further impede acceptance of homosexuality in black culture and likely rule out any chance of concession related to the issue of same-sex marriage.

One variable that has the potential to affect the black community's perception of LGBT causes is our current economy. Because the legalization of same-sex marriage could over time conceivably offer LGBT couples some of the rights and protections that a marriage license affords traditional heterosexual couples, such as access to family courts, death benefits for surviving spouses, child custody, pension rights, and domestic violence protections, a united campaign that includes equal opportunity for LGBTs and centers on economics could conceivably be useful to the LGBT fight for fairness.

For instance, the federal government uses census data to allocate over $400 billion to states and communities every year. Census information is used for a variety of things, including determining where retail stores, schools, hospitals, new housing developments, and other facilities are located. Another use of census data is determining the boundaries of state and local legislative and congressional districts, something that is extremely crucial to every U.S. citizen as well as to special interest groups like LGBT advocates and their detractors.[41] To demonstrate the importance of census data, in 2010 for the first time, the U.S. Census counted same-sex couples who identify themselves as spouses. Because in previous census counts these individuals had been classified as unmarried partners, this change is significant as it relates to the LGBT community's relationship with the federal government. Going forward, this seemingly subtle nuance has the potential to affect the entire country in a myriad of ways not yet fully known. Yet what is already clear is that being recognized with a status equal to heterosexual couples by the U.S. Census progress in the LGBT community's fight for equality is in a step in the right direction toward the legalization of same-sex marriage. In addition, this recognition seems to suggest a substantial strategic paradigm shift in the way that the federal government deals with the LGBT population. This being the case, there is no doubt that religious institutions, including the Black Church, are cognizant of changes in federal policy, which are obviously driven by the increasing political might of the LGBT community.

Beginning in 2010, another important change reflected in the U.S. Census is seen in the way that issues associated with LGBT households are phrased. Consider, for example, the wording of this statement from the 2010 Census questionnaire: LGBT people living with a spouse or partner can identify their relationship by checking either the 'husband or wife' or 'unmarried partner' box. The 2010 Census fact sheet provides an explanation of the process this way: The person filling out the form (Person 1) is asked to identify how all other individuals in the household are related to him or her. This change is noteworthy because it means that the census data is based on how individuals self-identify and how couples think of themselves as opposed to being forced to respond in predefined ways. For instance, same-sex couples who are married, or consider themselves to be spouses, can identify one other adult as a "husband or wife." Other same-sex couples may instead decide to use the term "unmarried partner." In general, people who identify as unmarried partners are in a close personal relationship but are not married, or do not think of themselves as spouses. And in the case of transgender individuals they are able to select the sex with which they identify.[42]

A decade ago, a first of its kind study titled "Black Same-Sex Households in the United States" conducted by the National Gay and Lesbian Task Force Policy Institute and the National Black Justice Coalition (NBJC), offered an evaluation of data that included demographics and personal experiences of black same-sex households. The study used data captured by the 2000 U.S. Census. A second edition was published in 2005. The pioneering report yielded surprising results and implications for black same-sex couples and prompted this observation by H. Alexander Robinson, strategic director of the NBJC, who stressed the magnitude of the report's findings: "As this landmark report makes clear, gay African-Americans are an active, involved, vibrant, and integral part of our communities. African-Americans make up 13% of the U.S. population. Black same-sex couples are 14% of all same-sex couples in the U.S. We are you . . ."[43]

The report did more than legitimatize black same-sex couples as an important segment of U.S. society. It also provided evidence that black LGBTs represent a considerable percentage of same-sex households and as such, should along with white LGBTs be considered potential victims of antigay organizations that might undertake, for example, a mission to divide the black and white gay communities. In addition, the joint report spoke to the strategy employed by antigay groups that speak as if black LGBTs are not victims of discrimination. The eye-opening findings suggest that another conceivable outcome might be that thousands of black same-sex couples who are raising children could be disproportionately affected if state and federal antigay marriage ballots initiatives are enacted. This dire situation is already a possibility as antigay antagonists in several states seek to do just that.

When confronting numerous hindrances, LGBT advocates like John Lewis, U.S. congressman (D-GA) and legendary civil rights freedom fighter, are among a handful of public figures who publicly speak out against the government's treatment of LGBTs and their exclusion from the rights of a civil marriage. Lewis says that denying LGBTs a basic human right such as a civil marriage degrades them and their families. Religious leaders like Al Sharpton agree with Lewis, as do other champions of LGBT equality and same-sex civil marriages. They do so even while risking being at odds with a formidable and united Black Church that is highly critical of homosexuality and same-sex marriage, and that encourages churchgoers to believe that anyone who participates or supports either is going against black moral tenets. Still, in the face of strong disapproval, as Lewis sees it, the ability for LGBTs to marry the person of their choice is a matter of basic human rights. In 2003, Lewis said this when discussing the issue:

> From time to time, America comes to a crossroads. With confusion and controversy, it's hard to spot that moment. We need cool heads, warm hearts, and America's core principles to cleanse away the distractions ... We are now at such a crossroads over same-sex couples' freedom to marry. It is time to say forthrightly that the government's exclusion of our gay and lesbian brothers and sisters from civil marriage officially degrades them and their families ... I have fought too hard and too long against discrimination based on race and color not to stand up against discrimination based on sexual orientation.[44]

Yet, Lewis' heartfelt statement does not seem to matter because blacks on the whole are insulted by any efforts that give the impression of associating LGBT equality and civil rights.

The relevancy of Lewis's observation as it relates to the LGBT struggle for equality is seen in the breakdown of statistical data. Data from the National Gay and Lesbian Taskforce provides a closer look at black same-sex couples residing in large metropolitan areas such as Chicago, where the Black Church is a major power. Focusing on six categories—demographics, income, family, residence, employment, and military service—Chicago, a city with a population of approximately 2.7 million people that is not unlike other urban centers such as Los Angeles or Atlanta.

For one, the data revealed that the 2000 US Census counted 3,954 black same-sex couples in the Chicago area, which represents 4.7 percent of all black same-sex couples in the United States and 16 percent of all same-sex households in the Chicago area. The report also revealed that the average age of individuals from black same-sex couples in Chicago was 42 percent and that almost 100 percent of black same-sex partners and 96 percent of black female same-sex partners were U.S. citizens. About 4 percent partnered black men and 5 percent of partnered black woman were born outside the United States. An examination of income revealed that the median household income for black male same-sex couples was $44,000, and for black female same-sex couples was $45,700.

The study showed that 59 percent of black female same-sex couples and 41 percent of black male same-sex couples were raising children; 42 percent of black female same-sex couples and 34 percent of black male same-sex couples were raising their biological children. Seventeen percent of black female same-sex couples and 7 percent of black male same-sex couples were raising children they were not biologically related to (fostered or adopted). According to the study, 57 percent of black male same-sex couples and 56 percent of black female same-sex couples report having lived in the same residence five years previously. 52 percent of black male same-sex couples and 44 percent of Black female same-sex couples owned their own homes. 59 percent of black men in same-sex households and 68 percent of black women in same-sex households reported working full time. Four percent of black men in same-sex households and 7 percent of black women in same-sex households worked part time. Thirty-seven percent of men and 24 percent of women in black same-sex households reported not working. Sixteen percent of black men and 16 percent of black women in same-sex households worked in the public sector. Fifteen percent of men and 4 percent of women in black same-sex couple relationships reported being military veterans.[45]

Following the study and after several years of relatively stable estimates of the percentage of same-sex couples reporting themselves as spouses (about 45 percent to 50 percent between 2005 and 2007), oddly in 2008 there was a surprising decline to 27 percent. The dramatic decline led some researchers to suggest that previous estimates of same-sex spouses from the American Community Survey (ACS), an ongoing Census Bureau survey that samples a small percentage of the population every year, were too high, indicating that the decline represented an improvement in the data.[46]

However, another plausible explanation for the decline in same-sex couples reporting as spouses, especially during the Bush years, could be a result of growing animosity and frequent shunning of black LGBTs by black megachurches preachers who were motivated by the allure of faith-based funding. Add to that a genuinely pervasive negative attitude toward LGBTs and same-sex marriage, the awesome power of the Black Church to influence large congregations, and an amalgamation of deterrents that may have had a significant impact on the data, possibly distorting federal census data and independent studies and the decline in same-sex couple reporting is not as much a mystery.

A decade later, the 2010 U.S. Census data seems to show a reverse in the decline as the number of same-sex couples gay and lesbian in Chicago had increased 40 percent. The surge in the number of same-sex households is not confined to inner cities, but is also seen in suburbs of large urban centers. For example, in Aurora, the second largest city in Illinois, an astounding 80 percent increase in female same-sex households was reported. And in Oak Park, Illinois, the reported number of female same-sex households grew by almost 65 percent. Even as dramatic as the increase is, it doesn't include individuals who identify themselves as LGBT because the U.S. Census does not count these individuals.[47]

In spite of the gains made by LGBT activists, the black community, black LGBTs, and the Black Church continue to be targeted by antigay groups, extremists, and same-sex marriage opponents hoping to promote their agenda. In 2012, an ethics commission accused the National Organization for Marriage (NOM) of employing secret tactics aimed at defeating marriage equality. Documents discovered as a result of the commission's investigation revealed a campaign by NOM to use tactics to divide gays and blacks. The NBJC responded to the unsealed court documents by saying that they exposed NOM as a hate group seeking to use African American faith leaders to push its antigay same-sex marriage agenda.

The commission's investigation disclosed a document detailing strategies employed or planned by the NOM to achieve its goal. A variety of schemes were aimed at the black community and described in detail.

> The strategic goal of this project is to drive a wedge between gays and blacks—two key Democratic constituencies. Find, equip, energize and connect African American spokespeople for marriage; develop a media campaign around their objections to gay marriage as a civil right; provoke the gay marriage base into responding by denouncing these spokesmen and women as bigots. No politician wants to take up and push an issue that splits the base of the party. Fanning the hostility raised in the wake of Prop 8 is key to raising the cost of pushing gay marriage to its advocates and persuading the movement's allies

that advocates are unacceptably overreaching on this issue. Consider pushing a marriage amendment in Washington D.C.; find attractive young black Democrats to challenge white gay marriage advocates electorally.[48]

NOTES

1. Romans 1:32.Holy Bible

2. "Joe Biden: Gay marriage in U.S. 'inevitable'" *ABCNews.com*, December 24, 2010, http://abcnews.go.com/GMA/video/joe-biden-gay -marriage-us-inevitable-12471729. Accessed May 12, 2011.

3. Angela Delli Santi, "New Jersey Gov. Chris Christie vetoes gay marriage bill as vowed," *MiamiHerald.com*, http://miamiherald.typepad .com/gaysouthflorida/2012/02/new-jersey-gov-chris-christie-vetoes-gay -marriage-bill-as-vowed.html#storylink=cpy. Accessed May 12, 2011.

4. Frances Martel, "Pat Robertson cites 'angel rape' during discussion of NY gay marriage law," *Mediaite.com*, June 27, 2011, http://www .mediaite.com/tv/pat-robertson-cites-angel-rape-during-discussion-of-ny -gay-marriage-law/. Accessed May 12, 2011.

5. Gary Langer, "Support for gay marriage reaches a milestone," *ABCNews.com*, March 18, 2011, http://abcnews.go.com/Politics/support -gay-marriage-reaches-milestone-half-americans-support/story?id=13159 608. Accessed May 12, 2011.

6. http://abcnews.go.com/Politics/support-gay-marriage-reaches-mile stone-half-americans-support/story?id=13159608#.UL5fVYU4yoQ. Accessed May 12, 2011.

7. Charlie Savage and Sheryl Gay Stolberg, "In shift, U.S. says marriage act blocks gay rights," *NYTimes.com*, February 23, 2011, http://www .nytimes.com/2011/02/24/us/24marriage.html. Accessed May 12, 2011.

8. November 18, 2003, http://lesbianlife.about.com/od/lesbian activism/a/Bush.htm. Accessed May 3, 2011.

9. Julian Bond, chairman of the NAACP, March 8, 2004. nbjc.org/ resources/jumping-the-broom.pdf. Accessed December 6, 2012.

10. *Chicago Tribune*, August 12, 2011. August 11, 2011| Manya A. Brachear.

11. http://www.nytimes.com/2004/02/24/politics/24TEXT-BUSH.html. Accessed December 11, 2012.

12. "Pres. Bush calls for constitutional amendment against gay marriage," *WatchBlock.com*, February 24, 2004, http://www.watchblog.com/ democrats/archives/000858.html. Accessed May 3, 2011.

13. "Obama opposes gay marriage," *After-Words.org*, September 24, 2004, http://after-words.org/grim/mtarchives/2004/09/Sep242301.shtml. Accessed May 12, 2012.

14. Kevin Robinson, "Barack Obama and the gay gaffe," *Chicagoist.com*, March 26, 2007. http://chicagoist.com/2007/03/26/barack_obama_and_the_gay_gaffe.php. Accessed May 3, 2011.

15. "At the crossroads: African American same gender loving families and the freedom to marry," National Black Justice Coalition 2009 Report, http://seven-generations.org/resources/NBJCreport_final.pdf. Accessed May 12, 2011.

16. Keith Boykin, "Whose dream?: Why the black church opposes gay marriage," *VillageVoice.com*, May 18, 2004, http://www.villagevoice.com/2004-05-18/news/whose-dream/. Accessed May 2, 2011.

17. Ibid.

18. Emma Brown, "The Rev. Peter J. Gomes, Harvard minister, dies at 68," *WashingtonPost.com*, March 1, 2011, http://www.washington post.com/wp-dyn/content/article/2011/03/01/AR2011030106964.html. Accessed May 1, 2011.

19. The Rev. Vernon Hill, Sermon, Grace Episcopal Church, March 6, 2011, http://www.graceepiscopalbakersfield.com/march-2011.html. Accessed May 3, 2011.

20. Robert Barnes, "California Proposition 8 same-sex-marriage ban ruled unconstitutional," *WashingtonPost.com*, February 7, 2012, http://www.washingtonpost.com/politics/calif-same-sex-marriage-ban-ruled-unconstitutional/2012/02/07/gIQAMNwkwQ_story.html. Accessed May 3, 2011.

21. *Chicago Tribune*, June 2, 2011.

22. 1 Rex W. Huppke, *Chicago Tribune*, June 2, 2011.

23. http://www.towleroad.com/2011/06/new-york-archbishop-condemns-move-toward-marriage-equality-says-it-redefines-natural-law.html. Accessed December 6, 2012.

24. http://www.reuters.com/article/2011/06/25/us-gaymarriage-newyork-idUSTRE75N5ZA20110625. Accessed December 4, 2012.

25. Ray Long and Monique Garcia, *Chicago Tribune*, December 2, 2010.

26. Andrew Stern, "Illinois allows civil unions for same-sex couples," *Reuters.com*, January 31, 2011, http://www.reuters.com/article/2011/02/01/us-illinois-gays-idUSTRE71006620110201. Accessed May 3, 2011.

27. Manning Marable, *Malcolm X: A Life of Reinvention* (New York: Viking, 2011.

28. Geneive Abdo, "Black ministers join drive against same-sex marriage," *ChicagoTribune.com*, May 27, 2004, http://articles.chicago tribune.com/2004-05-27/news/0405270335_1_black-churches-same-sex -unions-same-sex-marriage. Accessed May 12, 2011.

29. Manya A. Brachear, *Chicago Tribune*, June 8, 2011, http:// articles.chicagotribune.com/2011-06-07/news/ct-met-catholic-charities -legal-actio20110607.

30. Pew Research Center for the People and the Press. *Pragmatic Americans Liberal and Conservative on Social Issues*. August 6, 2006.

31. "At the Crossroads."

32. http://rodonline.typepad.com/rodonline/2009/01/al-sharpton -again-denounces-antigay-black-megachurchpastors.html. Accessed May 12, 2011.

33. http://rodonline.typepad.com/rodonline/2009/01/al-sharpton -again-denounces-antigay-black-megachurchpastors.html. Accessed May 3, 2011.

34. Karl Vick and Ashley Surdin, "Most of California's black voters backed gay marriage ban," *WashingtonpPost.com*, November 7, 2008, http://www.washingtonpost.com/wp-dyn/content/article/2008/11/06/ AR2008110603880.html. Accessed May 3, 2011.

35. Chris Rovzar, "Judge hands victory to Proposition 8 opponents, gay-marriage ban overturned," *NYMag.com*, August 4, 2010, http:// nymag.com/daily/intel/2010/08/judge_vaughn_walker_hands_vict.html. Accessed April 29, 2011.

36. David G. Savage, "Rights group takes a step-by-step approach on gay marriage," *LATimes.com*, March 2, 2011, http://articles.latimes.com/ 2011/mar/02/nation/la-na-gays-legal-20110303. Accessed May 11, 2012.

37. Dan Barry, "A sports executive leaves the safety of his shadow life," *NYTimes.com*, May 15, 2011, www.nytimes.com/2011/05/16/ sports/basketball/nba-executive-says-he-is-gay.html?_r=1&ref=danbarry. Accessed May 12, 2011.

38. Don Lemon, *Transparent* (Las Vegas: Farrah Gray Publishing, 2011).

39. Nardine Saad, "Don Lemon comes out in book 'Transparent,'" *LATimes.com*, May 16, 2011, http://latimesblogs.latimes.com/gossip/ 2011/05/don-lemon-gay-cann-anchor-transparent-book.html. Accessed May 12, 2011.

40. "Don Lemon Comes Out: CNN Anchor Reveals He's Gay In New Book," *HuffingtonPost.com*, May 16, 2011, http://www.huffingtonpost .com/2011/05/16/don-lemon-comes-out-cnn-anchor-gay_n_862308.html. Accessed May 12, 2011.

41. Williams Institute, "U.S. Census 2010," http://2010.census.gov/partners/pdf/factSheet_General_LGBT.pdf.

42. Ibid.

43. http://nbjc.org/news/001227.html. Accessed May 3, 2011.

44. John Lewis, "At a crossroads on gay unions," *Boston.com*, October 25, 2003, http://www.boston.com/news/globe/editorial_opinion/oped/articles/2003/10/25/at_a_crossroads_on_gay_unions/. Accessed September 4, 2011.

45. National Gay and Lesbian Task Force, "Black same-sex households: Chicago metropolitan area," Fact Sheet, http://www.thetaskforce.org/reports_and_research/black_same_sex_chicago. Accessed May 12, 2011.

46. Martin O'Connell, Daphne Lofquist, Tavia Simmons, and Terry Lugaila, "New estimates of same-sex couple households from the American Community Survey," Annual meeting of the Population Association of America, Dallas, Texas, April 15–17, 2010, http://www.census.gov/population/www/socdemo/hh-fam/SS_new-estimates.pdf.

47. "In the News: Census," *ChicagoTribune.com*, http://articles.chicagotribune.com/keyword/census. Accessed May 11, 2011.

48. Scott Wooledge, "Confidential court papers reveal anti-gay NOM's dirty racial strategies, 'sideswiping Obama' plot," *Dailykos.com*, Mar 27, 2012, http://www.dailykos.com/story/2012/03/27/1078093/-Confidential-court-papers-reveal-anti-gay-NOM-s-dirty-racial-strategies-sideswiping-Obama-plot. Accessed May 11, 2011.

SIX

Don't Ask, Don't Tell

And they called to Lot and said to him, "Where are the men who came to you tonight? Bring them out to us that we may have relations with them." But Lot went out to them at the doorway, and shut the door behind him, and said, "Please, my brothers, do not act wickedly."[1]

Prior to the last several decades, U.S. military policy related to homosexuality has as a rule been inflexible and extremely difficult to prevail over. Going back to the Revolutionary War, efforts to protect the military brand and root out those believed to be homosexuals or participating in homosexual acts (defined as anal and oral sex between men) were rigorously undertaken. As part of the induction process during World War II, inductees were subjected to psychiatric analysis in order to assess their views on homosexuality. It was also during this time that procedures were first developed to reject homosexuals. Three decades later, as a result of the civil rights movement, the legality of U.S. military policies toward homosexuals was challenged. It occurred in 1975 when Leonard P. Matlovich—a Vietnam War veteran, race relations instructor, recipient of the Purple Heart and a Bronze Star—became the first gay service member to sue the U.S. military and challenge the ban on gays. Matlovich would eventually become a hero to the LGBT community.[2]

Yet for some blacks, still today the mere contemplation of gays openly serving in the U.S. military initiates intense anger; the very premise of LGBTs serving would be counterintuitive to the black experience. For starters, to many, it would contradict the enormous importance that blacks place on masculinity and represent a blatant affront to the Black Church's view of homosexuality and acceptable sexual behavior.

African American baby boomers are, for example, more likely to perceive the September 20, 2011, striking down of "Don't ask, don't tell" (DADT) markedly differently than generations X and Y. However, this doesn't necessarily mean that a majority of older blacks disagree entirely with the repeal of DADT. Yet it does suggest that boomers are not as willing as younger blacks to accept open homosexuality in the U.S. armed forces, same-sex marriage, and equality for LGBTs. These differences are logical given that older blacks tend to identify with and hold sacred integration of the U.S. military and the civil rights struggle as watershed moments for the black race as a whole. Consequently, their backing of homosexuals openly serving in the U.S. armed forces and the repeal of DOMA is not as strong. On the other hand, blacks in generations X and Y are more likely to be less concerned with LGBTs openly serving, mostly because they don't identify as strongly with the historic desegregation of the U.S. military and or the civil rights struggle. Nonetheless, there are still younger blacks who embrace the same homophobic notions shaped in part by the views of their baby boomer parents and the prevailing contemporary thinking in the black community and church related to the issue of homosexuality.

What seems to matter isn't the well-documented history of black LGBTs fighting and dying for the freedoms enjoyed by all Americans, but rather the stubborn and impervious iconic machismo widely embraced by many blacks, despite the fact that it borders on irrationality. Through it all, homosexuality is still perceived as somehow defiling the gains and triumph over racial inequality achieved by past generations. In a disquieting and rather bizarre way, this absurdity speaks to what has so far been an inescapable cultural attitude toward homosexuality. This illogicality poses a serious dilemma for black LGBT military personnel who may hold out hope that they will benefit from the reversal of DADT.

The changes prompted by the repeal of DADT significantly affect the U.S. military and soldiers serving around the world. Chief among them is that homosexuals serving in the U.S. armed forces can no longer be separated from the military because of their sexual identity, and sexual orientation can't be used to bar an otherwise eligible person from serving. In addition, the military cannot request, collect, or maintain information about a soldier's sexual orientation except when it is needed for an appropriate investigation or official action. For example, Uniform Code of Military Justice (UCMJ) Article 125 is unchanged under the repeal of DADT. It allows, for example, the military to investigate allegations related to forcible sodomy or sodomy involving minors, or to investigate charges of sexual harassment.[3]

Also in preparation for the repeal of DADT and as part of the sensitivity training provided to U.S. military personnel, it was made clear that there would be no creation of separate living quarters or bathroom facilities, and that harassment or abuse based on sexual orientation is unacceptable and will be dealt with through appropriate channels.

So when President Barack Obama signed the repeal of DADT, effectively ending legalized discrimination against gays and lesbians who choose to serve openly in the military, it was considered an historic event. In fact, some LGBT advocates consider it the most important decree since 1965's Voting Rights Act.[4] However, unlike minorities, homosexuals are not considered by the law as a "protected class" and are therefore not able to file formal complaints related to acts of discrimination. Yet in spite of lingering issues that will take years to sort out through the courts, LGBT equality supporters like Evelyn Thomas—a Marine veteran who strongly favored the reversal of DADT and who was present at the signing of the repeal—said this when talking about what the repeal of DADT meant to LGBTs serving in the U.S. military now and in the future: ". . . The impact of our brother's and sister's right to serve our country and the freedom to serve in their true essence will forever change the social fabric of the Armed Forces and this bill will initiate a stronger military. The next step is to provide educational programs to service members so they may develop the knowledge, foundation, and skills to deal with LGBT issues that will manifest in the work environment."[5]

Thomas is right—the effect of the repeal of DADT is historic and transformational, and will make significant changes for LGBT military personnel. However, the repeal of DADT also leaves unresolved a number of problems that are exclusive to black gay and lesbian military personnel. It must also be said that the ending of DADT does not necessarily equate to the be-all and end-all for gays of every ethnicity serving in the U.S. military. It is hardly a revelation to black active duty personnel that the opposition to homosexuality, LGBT equality, and gay marriage will almost certainly continue to thrive in black culture in spite of the momentous reversal of DADT. Black LGBTs are acutely aware that widespread and growing disapproval of homosexuality is evidenced in polling from 1994 that showed 57 percent of blacks supported allowing gays in the military, versus some 48 percent who did in 2010. The same is true among black Protestants, whose support for gays serving in the military was 55 percent in 1994 and 46 percent in 2010. The retreat by blacks supporting gays serving in the military is not entirely surprising. In fact, it may be explained to an extent by the audacious push by LGBT activists who support same-sex marriage, and the pushback from Right Wing conservatives and the Christian Coalition to affiliate with black ministers in their stand against equality for LGBTs. Blacks backing off and trending toward a more traditional position on the issue of homosexuality is consistent with traditional black norms and in keeping with the ethnic paradoxical stance against homosexuality.

Throughout U.S. history, hiding homosexuality in black culture was exacerbated by systematic discrimination that was supported by a racially biased U.S. military policy toward LGBTs. U.S military policy toward blacks has been more prejudicial and unjust than toward any other ethnic group. The systemic prejudice leveled against black U.S. military personnel helps explain to some extent the irrational and pervasive homophobia that exists in the black community. For example, as service in the military was increasingly viewed as the ultimate proving ground for black men to demonstrate bravery, loyalty, and masculinity, disapproval of homosexuality was increasingly rejected by blacks who were striving to achieve racial equality. As a consequence, already homophobic attitudes were fortified to protect the gains made by black U.S. military personnel. This might seem preposterous to outsiders. Yet to begin to comprehend the assortment of puzzling contradictions presented by black-on-black homophobia, or to understand how blacks might respond to President Obama's 2011 order repealing DADT, it is necessary to consider the evolution of U.S. military policy as it relates to blacks.

During an interview prior to the repeal of DADT, Illinois human rights activist Mavis Bates may have best summed up the possible effect of repealing of DADT. Comparing it to desegregating the U.S. military over 60 years earlier, Bates asserted her perspective on the hotly debated issue with this question" "Was the military ready for integration? They didn't want it, but when it happened it became a strength because diversity makes us stronger."[6] Bates's point was that just like six decades ago when not all Americans agreed with President Harry S. Truman's order to integrate the U.S. military, many Americans at the start of the twenty-first century—including many blacks—disagreed with President Obama's decision to push the repeal of DADT through Congress during his first term. Blacks who side with military experts, evangelicals, and others who believe that allowing LGBTs to openly serve will undermine military order, morale, and discipline contribute to a monumental paradox. It is especially absurd given that the nation's first black president, in keeping a campaign promise to repeal the ban against gays openly serving and ending decades of discrimination against LGBTs, has been forcefully challenged by a solid black constituency that is resolute in its opposition to homosexuality and same-sex marriage. To LGBT advocates and onlookers, that the lifting of DADT—a discriminatory policy solely for members of the LGBT community—has come under attack by blacks, who have themselves been the victims of discrimination more than any other ethnicity throughout America's history, must seem absolutely surreal. In the end, with any luck, Americans will respond as they did during the Truman administration by relaxing their position on the issue and accepting the service of LGBTs in the U.S military.

It was more than a half-century ago, on July 26, 1948, when President Harry S. Truman signed Executive Order 9981 to desegregate the U.S. military. The order stressed "Equality of treatment for all persons in the armed services, without regard to race, color, religion or national origin."[7] Truman's order also established the President's Committee on Equality of Treatment and Opportunity in the Armed Services. Truman's actions effectively put an end to formal segregation of the U.S. armed forces, bringing to a close a divisive chapter in the country's history. The order was significant in another way because it represented a turning point for blacks not only related to the U.S. armed forces, but also related to seeing them as Americans who were deserving of equal treatment in every respect. President Truman's order mandated integration when he affirmed that:

> WHEREAS it is essential that there be maintained in the armed services of the United States the highest standards of democracy, with equality of treatment and opportunity for all those who serve in our country's defense:
>
> NOW THEREFORE, by virtue of the authority vested in me as President of the United States, by the Constitution and the statutes of the United States, and as Commander in Chief of the armed services, it is hereby ordered as follows:

> 1. It is hereby declared to be the policy of the President that there shall be equality of treatment and opportunity for all persons in the armed services without regard to race, color, religion or national origin. This policy shall be put into effect as rapidly as possible, having due regard to the time required to effectuate any necessary changes without impairing efficiency or morale.

> 2. There shall be created in the National Military Establishment an advisory committee to be known as the President's Committee on Equality of Treatment and Opportunity in the Armed Services,

which shall be composed of seven members to be designated by the President.

3. The Committee is authorized on behalf of the President to examine into the rules, procedures and practices of the Armed Services in order to determine in what respect such rules, procedures and practices may be altered or improved with a view to carrying out the policy of this order. The Committee shall confer and advise the Secretary of Defense, the Secretary of the Army, the Secretary of the Navy, and the Secretary of the Air Force, and shall make such recommendations to the President and to said Secretaries as in the judgment of the Committee will effectuate the policy hereof.

4. All executive departments and agencies of the Federal Government are authorized and directed to cooperate with the Committee in its work, and to furnish the Committee such information or the services of such persons as the Committee may require in the performance of its duties.

5. When requested by the Committee to do so, persons in the armed services or in any of the executive departments and agencies of the Federal Government shall testify before the Committee and shall make available for use of the Committee such documents and other information as the Committee may require.

6. The Committee shall continue to exist until such time as the President shall terminate its existence by Executive order.

Harry Truman
The White House
July 26, 1948[8]

Yet there were blacks who viewed President Truman's order as a mere formality. Some blacks rationalized that regardless of whether they shared the same barracks with whites, they (the black soldiers) had nothing to prove, having already demonstrated allegiance to the United States, shown courage, and most notably proven beyond a doubt their masculinity since the nation's birth. Pointing to the fact that blacks had valiantly fought and died in every conflict since the time of runaway slave turned sailor Crispus Attucks, a black man who was the first person killed by British redcoats during the Boston Massacre, a number of blacks and civil rights advocates downplayed Truman's Executive Order as a political necessity.

Nonetheless, when Executive Order 9981 was issued and the U.S. armed forces were ordered integrated, blacks were finally permitted to serve alongside whites and as a result, things began to slowly change for what some considered the better. Given the long history of discrimination suffered by blacks at the hands of the U.S. military since the beginning of the Republic, it would seem that the very idea of barring homosexuals from openly serving, or for that matter any capable American, would be seen as blatantly wrong by blacks. Yet the very opposite appears to be true; the U.S. military's biased policies that systematically discriminated against and victimized homosexuals during and prior to DADT did not provoke a sense of outrage by the black community. Even as the more than 2 million U.S. military personnel received training to prepare for the new U.S. military following the era of DADT and amid a celebratory atmosphere in which the *Marine Corp Times* magazine cover page exclaimed "We're Gay. Get Over it,"[9] there is great concern that among blacks, very little has changed with respect to their position on homosexuality, same-sex unions, and equality for LGBTs.

As the military transitioned to new regulations that allow gays to openly serve, gay recruits began signing up, and troops were reminded to treat each other fairly. With the abolishment of DADT, all pending investigations related to pre-repeal DADT violations were halted, as were DADT-related discharges. However, still an obstacle to LGBT active military personnel is that there will be no immediate changes to eligibility standards for military benefits or to the Defense of Marriage Act (DOMA), which prohibits gay service members and their spouses from receiving the full range of benefits that heterosexual troops and their spouses receive.

That aside, as DADT officially ended on September 20, 2011, LGBT U.S. military personnel and their supporters were comparing the expiration of DADT to the racial desegregation that took place in the South over 60 years ago. Few would argue that there are not similarities, especially related to the obvious inequities in military policies toward blacks and LGBTs serving in the U.S. military. Still, the inequality of blacks serving in a segregated U.S. military versus that of homosexuals serving under the flagrant biases of DADT is where many believe the comparisons end. The explanation given for drawing the line at comparing the two prejudicial systems is that blacks serving in a segregated U.S. military had no choice—they could not conceal their racial identity or escape the military's systematic racism and discriminatory policies. So given the unjust policies of the U.S. military and the condoned treatment of black soldiers by white soldiers during World War II, for example, when white soldiers spread rumors that black GIs were subhuman with tails like monkeys, it seems implausible that blacks would so staunchly support discriminatory military policies toward LGBTs. In fact, one might assume that the bigotry leveled against blacks during the time of a segregated military would have been all that was needed to influence them to relax their position on homosexuality and support the right of LGBTs to serve openly in the U.S. military. It is also reasonable to conclude that blacks would only have look to how demoralizing a segregated military had been to generations of black soldiers, their families, and the black community little more than 60 years ago to have empathy for the plight of LGBT military personnel serving prior to DADT's repeal. However, even as rumors spread that openly gay LGBTs would wreak havoc on U.S armed forces serving around the world and the obvious similarities to a racially segregated military became more apparent, there was little outrage from black leadership. Not only was there no wave of indignation and a show of support from the black community for active duty military LGBTs, but there was no indication that blacks would lessen their resistance toward homosexuality. In fact, quite the contrary seems true and despite the stark similarities, there is no hint of a mutual identification. Unfortunately, the reality is that the discriminatory practices leveled against blacks that are a scar on the nation's history are now commonly carried out by some blacks who demonstrate extreme prejudice toward black LGBTs. Having said that, the repeal of DADT is not likely to result in an immediate or major change in the treatment of LGBTs by the black community and church. Therefore, black LGBTs should prepare for a continuation of an ethnic form of don't ask, don't tell from their community, families, and places of worship.

That blacks were not considered equal to whites by the U.S. military until President Truman's order to integrate the armed forces explains to some extent how, over time, Truman's order became a defining moment for blacks. Some black military personnel and veterans came to view the U.S. military as the definitive proving ground for showing white America that blacks were innately loyal and brave. By the time equality for black soldiers finally came, some 182 years after the founding of the nation, the saga of denying parity to black soldiers was symbolic of their suffering, perseverance, and all they endured before finally being viewed as equal to white soldiers. Desegregation of the military was seen as pivotal to the black experience and was passed down through generations as a watershed event that has helped to facilitate perpetuation of the belief that military service is the definitive demonstration of black patriotism and masculinity. The emphasis on masculinity reinforces the strident homophobia that exists in contemporary black culture wherein blacks, and there are many who buy into this type of military machismo, will not soon likely support homosexuals joining the armed forces, much less openly black LGBTs.

Fast-forward to breaking news that Colin Powell, the first black chairman of the Joint Chiefs of Staff and secretary of state who initially opposed gays openly serving in the U.S. military had changed his mind, and Bob Dylan's unforgettable lyric "The Times They Are A-Changin" comes to mind.[10] General Powell's turnabout and the shifting attitudes of political and military leadership leading up to the repeal of DADT in the midst of a thinly stretched U.S. military fighting on two fronts may help to explain Powell's somewhat shocking metamorphosis. Could it be that the U.S. military, desperate for new recruits, had no choice but to acquiesce in order to augment the nation's dwindling armed forces?

Appearing on CNN's *State of the Union* in 2009, Powell made his surprising conversion public by calling for a review of the 18-year-old policy. In doing so, he explained why he had changed his position on the issue: "The policy and law that came about in 1993 I think were correct for the time." Powell added, "Sixteen years have gone by and I think that a lot has changed with respect to attitudes within our country. And therefore I think this is a policy and law that should be reviewed."[11] Whatever Powell's reasons may have been—political or otherwise—his reversal was of course extremely important to U.S. military personnel and especially so to black LGBTs and the broader black community. Whether Powell's unexpected about-face ultimately has bearing on black culture and the way that homosexuality and equality for LGBTs is viewed by the black community is yet to be seen. However, one thing that Powell's declaration did was create an immediate dilemma for hardcore black and white antigay religious and political extremists who had often referred to Powell's former opposition to homosexuals openly serving as being consistent with their self-ascribed family values. Suddenly without this opposition from Powell, conservatives lost one of their main supporters, a military expert who had steadfastly opposed homosexuals openly serving in the U.S. armed forces.

Regardless of how well intentioned Powell's change of heart may have been, black gay and bisexual men who are active members of the U.S. military but continue to live in secret on the DL may impede the transition of the U.S. military following the repeal of DADT. On the other hand, it is also possible that Powell's reversed stance on the issue will eventually result in blacks modifying their thinking on homosexuality and altering their seemingly inflexible stance toward same-sex marriage. Few expect that results will be immediate, but there is at least hope that the black community will respond incrementally and in some cases favorably to the repeal of DADT and as a result encourage more black leaders and clergy to lend support to the fair treatment of black LGBTs.

There is even optimism that there is a chance in the future for an acknowledgement by the Black Church that the epic battle for civil rights during the 1960s will be linked to the ongoing struggle by members of the black LGBT community for fairness and equality. If the black community is ever able to put behind it the idea that military service and masculinity go hand in hand, it is also conceivable that a relaxed position toward homosexuality could evolve. However, as long as the Christian Right and Black Church are at the forefront, setting the tone on issues like same-sex marriage and equality for LGBTs, a more realistic possibility is that some blacks—at the urging of progressive black leaders—will minimally relax their position. So a transformation, like Powell's, related to the acceptance of homosexuality by the Black Church and community is not likely in the foreseeable future.

In the short term, what the repeal of DADT really means to black LGBTs currently serving or intending to serve in the U.S. military is an extraordinarily complex state of affairs that are difficult to predict. The situation is so complex that not only is it necessary to first consider the historical perspective as it relates to how U.S. military policy has treated blacks, but it is also imperative to understand the relevancy of DADT's reversal to black LGBTs. Realizing this is essential if one is to appreciate the reasons that black LGBT military personnel and the black community are not likely to view the reversal of DADT in the same way. To begin to grasp the distinctions, it is important to note that on the whole, black LGBTs and even heterosexuals are not as likely to publicly tout the repeal of DADT as an historic event. In addition, blacks—for the most part—do not consider the repeal as a guarantee of major and immediate change in the lives of black LGBT military personnel. The truth is that the effect on black LGBT military personnel will likely be a slow trickle-down handled with extreme caution. This is chiefly because of the looming social issues that still exist following the repeal of DADT, accompanied by ongoing resistance by the black community to lessen its refusal to accept homosexuality and a change in traditional sexual norms. For instance, consider the ever-present possibility and fear of public castigation by fanatical black clergy like Bishop Eddie Long, who has said, "The problem today and the reason society is like it is, is because men are feminized and women are being masculine! You can not say, 'I was born this way.' I don't care what scientists say!"[12] Like Long, other black ministers who refuse to relent on the issue of homosexuality or equal rights for LGBTs have so far not hinted that they will alter their crusade, even though the repeal of DADT was authorized under the leadership of the nation's first black president.

The concern of black active duty LGBTs is legitimate. Their trepidation has persisted since the nation's beginning. The question of who is permitted to serve in the U.S. armed forces fell to the government and needless to say, race has historically been predominant and tops the list of biases related to military policy. And since the choice of who is allowed to serve has typically mirrored the prejudices and treatment of the downtrodden that exist in the larger society, intolerance and prejudicial treatment toward black LGBTs has been significantly greater.

Continuing on with the example of Crispus Attucks, it is difficult to fathom that some of his comrades in arms were not gay or bisexual. It is, in fact, reasonable to propose that throughout U.S. history, LGBTs have taken part in every skirmish and major battle that set this country on a course to its independence. However, it is also true that the eligibility to serve in the U.S. military has in large part been enormously unfair, reflecting contemporaneous societal attitudes. Such regulations obviously gave way to a military fraught with inequitable guidelines, inherent prejudice, and a system in which discriminatory policies were allowed to flourish. For instance, during the Revolutionary War, blacks were not allowed to join the Continental army; early on during the Civil War, black soldiers were forbidden to join the conflict in spite of their eagerness to enter the fight for their freedom. While the Union Army later reversed its position and allowed blacks to serve, they were generally considered incompatible, not fit to fight, and capable only of lowly jobs. Even when permitted to join a segregated U.S. military, black troops were regarded as substandard, they were paid less, and they were treated as inferior to white soldiers. Furthermore, throughout U.S. military history, white officers like Colonel Robert Gould Shaw, who commanded the Fifty-Fourth Massachusetts—a black regiment during the Civil War—and whose experiences were dramatized in the 1989 film *Glory*, was stigmatized and considered second-rate, as were his men. Ironically, from the very beginning, the backstory for black military personnel has been one of proving their fearlessness, worthiness, and above all masculinity. Therefore, it is not surprising that anything that seems to threaten the gains of black U.S. military personnel, such as black LGBTs openly serving, runs counter to traditional black reasoning.

It is hard to fathom now, but when World War II began, blacks were still segregated from whites and made to perform lesser duties that often supported the efforts of white troops. However, during the war, the U.S. Navy—primarily as a result of cost constraints—began testing the integration of enlisted personnel. By the end of the war, in the opinion of high-ranking military personnel, blacks had proven themselves to be valuable fighters. Coincidentally, the experiment also demonstrated that racial integration of the military had no bearing on the combat readiness of military units. In spite of this, the U.S. military would remain racially segregated until President Truman's historic 1948 Executive Order.

When the order was finally executed, it was not at all surprising to Americans that it was met with stiff resistance from political and military obstructionists. These cynics were armed with a Gallup poll that revealed that 63 percent of U.S. adults supported a separation of blacks and whites in the military, while only 26 percent supported integration. According to a 1949 survey of white U.S. Army personnel, some 32 percent wholly opposed racial integration in any form, while a whopping 61 percent opposed integration if whites and blacks would have to share sleeping quarters and mess halls. Years later, in 1993 a report published by the National Defense Research Institute, it was noted that "Many White Americans (especially Southerners) responded with visceral revulsion to the idea of close physical contact with blacks. Many also perceived racial integration as a profound affront to their sense of social order. Blacks, for their part, often harbored deep mistrust of Whites and great sensitivity to any language or actions that might be construed as racial discrimination."[13]

In the early 1980s, the Department of Defense (DOD) established a policy that made it clear that homosexuality was incompatible with serving in the U.S. military. DOD Directive 1332.14, January 28, 1982, Part 1, according to the Government Accounting Office (GAO), accounted for more than 18,000 men and women being discharged after being classified as homosexuals by the U.S. military. Issuance of the policy is blamed for surging occurrences of gay harassment and incidents of violence against gay military personnel. DOD Directive 1332.14 remained in effect until 1993 when, after a prolonged public debate and congressional hearings, the military's ban on gay personnel was overturned. With so many LGBTs being discharged from the U.S. armed forces, the Clinton administration acted swiftly, keeping its promise to bring discrimination on the basis of sexual orientation to an end. However, President Clinton's original proposal was met with intense opposition from the Joint Chiefs of Staff, members of Congress, and a sizeable portion of the U.S. public. The policy was eventually implemented when President Clinton and Senator Sam Nunn (D-GA), chair of the Senate Armed Services Committee, reached a compromise that they called Don't Ask, Don't Tell, Don't Pursue. As part of the agreement, military personnel would not be asked about their sexual orientation and would not be discharged for being gay. Sexual conduct with a member of the same sex would, however, constitute grounds for discharge. Until its repeal, discharges actually increased under DADT, and according to the Service Members Legal Defense Fund, in 1998, there was a 120 percent increase in reported cases of harassment against gay and lesbian military personnel in many locales.[14]

The effectiveness of the Clinton administration's don't ask, don't tell policy for gays in the military received mixed reviews throughout the 18 years that it governed U.S. military policy related to homosexuals. DADT was hotly debated, criticized, and touted by people like former presidential candidate Senator John McCain (R-AZ), who urged that Congress maintain it. Senator McCain's position goes back to the inception of DADT, when it was initially heralded as a livable compromise for gays and lesbians serving in the U.S. military. However, some military observers, including politicians, eventually deemed DADT a complete fiasco and blamed it for rising incidents of harassment and violence against gays, for example, the horrible incident that occurred at Fort Campbell, Kentucky, in 1999. During the episode, Private First Class Barry Winchell was bludgeoned to death with a baseball bat by Private Calvin Glover while Winchell slept. Testimony and witness accounts disclosed a casual culture at the base, one in which Winchell was taunted by Glover and others who called the young private "faggot," "queer," and "homo." Court records also reveal that there was no documentation of an investigation or reprimand by superior officers related to the maltreatment of Winchell. Prosecutors put forth a case that contended Winchell was killed because he was gay. In the aftermath, civilian LGBT organizations and gay rights activists alleged that a pattern of military policy violations and high-level military officers ignoring and even encouraging the harassment had precipitated Winchell's killing. However, the Army Inspector General's report found no evidence of a homophobic culture, and the officers were ultimately cleared. Yet the Winchell murder resulted in First Lady Hilary Rodham Clinton, Vice President Al Gore, and even President Clinton labeling DADT a failure. Al Gore and Bill Bradley, Democratic candidates for the 2000 presidential nomination, vowed that if they were elected, they would work to reverse DADT. Meanwhile, Republican presidential candidates John McCain and George Bush reaffirmed their support for DADT, as did other GOP hopefuls such as Gary Bauer, Alan Keyes, and Steve Forbes, all of whom vowed to completely prohibit homosexuals from serving in the military.[15]

At the start of the new millennium the heated debate over gays openly serving in the military, was an issue that GOP presidential hopefuls had to address. During a debate in 2000 when Republican presidential nominee George Bush was asked about his position on gays in the military, he responded by saying, "I'm a don't ask don't tell man."[16] The soon to be president sounded as if he were auditioning for a Marlboro Man television commercial, a cigarette advertisement that ran from 1950 to 1999 that came to signify the essence of machismo strengthened and fortified Bush's antigay stance. Maybe playing to his base, conservative Republicans and the Religious Right, Bush said precisely what they wanted to hear from the leading GOP presidential candidate.

Both as a presidential candidate and leader of the free world, Bush's stance on issues related to homosexuals were straightforward, consistent, and a matter of record. For example, Bush backed a constitutional amendment banning same-sex marriage, supported DADT, opposed gay adoptions, and opposed a federal law to cover sexual orientation. His Texas brand of straight-shooting made it clear to all where Bush stood on the issue of LGBT equality. If there was any inconsistency at all in Bush's viewpoint on homosexuality, it was seen in his support for DADT, which considered sexual identity a personal matter. However, the thinly veiled caveat that allowed Bush to support DADT while staying true to his base was of course that one's homosexuality had to be concealed. Though under tremendous political pressure to drop the Clinton administration's regulations related to DADT and repeatedly urged by LGBT activists to do so, President Bush consistently refused.

A number of elected officials publicly indicated their opposition to DADT. Among them was former representative Bill Foster (D-IL). Foster made his position crystal clear, saying, "At a time that we are engaged in two wars, DADT has hindered our military readiness and has not contributed to our national security. Secretary of Defense Robert Gates, General Colin Powell and other top military officials all agree that the time has come to change this policy. Every qualified American who wishes to serve in our armed forces, regardless of orientation, should be allowed to come forward to protect and defend our country."[17]

Prior to the repeal of the almost two-decade-old Clinton administration policy that barred gays from openly serving in the military, Illinois LGBT activist and openly gay Deb Miller expressed her feelings about the significance of repealing DADT, saying, "I find it intolerable that an institution discriminates against any group of people. The fact that the government forces individuals to lie in order to serve or defend their country is outrageous. The U.S. is one of a few countries in the world that denies, in fact criminalizes, military service by individuals who are gay or lesbian."[18]

When interviewed in 2010, Miller passionately discussed a concern that had resonated with the entire LGBT community, talking about what the unfairness of U.S. military policies toward LGBTs had come to represent. In 2007, Miller—along with fellow activists and former military officer Jean Albright, U.S. Air Force (Ret.) and Ann Bidwell, U.S. Navy (Ret.)—met with Foster to gain his support for H.R. 1246, the Military Readiness Enhancement Act of 2007. Congressional sponsors were offering H.R. 1246 to amend Title 10 of the United States Code (USC) in order to "Enhance the readiness of the Armed Forces by replacing the current policy concerning homosexuality in the Armed Forces, referred to as 'Don't Ask, Don't Tell,' with a policy of nondiscrimination on the basis of sexual orientation."[19]

Their visit represented a grassroots effort to bring an end to the long and daunting quest to repeal DADT and end discrimination against LGBT personnel in the U.S. military. Albright and Bidwell described for Foster their experiences of not being able to serve as openly gay active duty military personnel. Looking back, Miller expressed astonishment regarding her involvement as an everyday citizen participating in the national effort to repeal DADT, saying:

> I never thought I'd be requesting a personal meeting with my congressional representative to discuss the repeal of DADT. Even now, I could not have imagined that I'd be invited to have dinner with Lieutenant Dan Choi who was discharged under DADT. But, looking back I had become progressively involved in gay rights and have come to believe that my growing involvement was a natural evolution and probably like that of many LGBTQ who understand the importance of the struggle.[20]

However, Miller's background seems to have put her on a course to meet with Foster and champion the rights of members of the lesbian, gay, bisexual, transgender and questioning (LGBTQ) or people who don't exactly fit into one of the other categories, but are still part of the community. She had been a supporter of numerous campaigns for the fair treatment of gays in the military. However, it was the maltreatment that LGBT military personnel were subjected to that profoundly affected Miller, moving her to take action when the opportunity came. Miller explained it this way:

> When I learned that shortly after President Bill Clinton signed what came to be known as Don't Ask, Don't Tell, it struck me as a slick method of eliminating gays and lesbians from the U.S. military. It

seemed no coincidence that almost immediately discharges under DADT increased. As I began to understand the history of discriminatory military policies and anti-gay sentiment post WWII, when the Department of Defense developed a "Homosexual Conduct Policy," it provoked in me a sense of responsibility that I had to do something and to somehow be involved.[21]

Miller went on to say that when she learned about Leonard Matlovich, the first gay service member to take issue with military policy toward homosexuals—and whose headstone reads: "When I was in the military they gave me a medal for killing two men and a discharge for loving one"—then and there she knew she'd advocate for LGBTs and the repeal of DADT. When Miller had an opportunity to do something, she also realized that everyone could have an impact on the repeal of DADT, by letting their elected officials know how they felt. However, in Miller's case, she did not simply write a letter, call, or email the recently elected Foster, who had been seated following a special election to fill the seat of Dennis Hastert (R-IL), who had become Speaker of the House. Instead and at the direct urging of the Service Members Legal Defense Network (SLDN)—a nonpartisan, nonprofit legal services watchdog and policy organization dedicated to bringing about full LGBT equality in the U.S. military and ending all forms of discrimination and harassment of military personnel on the basis of sexual orientation and gender identity—Miller contacted Congressman Foster's office and went there with fellow activists Jean Albright and Ann Bidwell, whose previous military experience bolstered the credibility of their visit.

According to Miller, during the mere 15-minute meeting, Foster was direct in his position and sincere, when saying that he could not publically support or cosponsor H.R. 1246, that is, until after the general election when his tenure as congressman would be extended to a full term. Needless to say, Miller and her comrades were disappointed. However, they were later ecstatic when, following the general election, Foster did as promised and supported the measure to end DADT.

Miller explained her involvement in this activism:

It is this kind of activism, although slow and tedious, that goes a long way on the road toward equality. Besides the repeal of DADT, the meeting with Rep. Foster was significant in the long term to stand against those in society who would dictate to members of the LGBTQ community what is possible or not. For example, whether we can marry, who we love and a host of other issues that ultimately has an enormous bearing on gay youth now and in the future. This kind of power is beyond discriminatory and is totally unacceptable.[22]

Following the September 11, 2001, attacks on the World Trade Center, the Pentagon, and Flight 93 and a ramping up of U.S. military involvement in Iraq and Afghanistan, objections were raised over the 2002 and 2003 DADT-initiated discharges of nine LGBT military linguists. Among them were six LGBTs who were fluent in the vital Arabic language, and who, despite the obvious and crucial need for their expertise, were relieved of duty when their homosexuality was disclosed. The Army's Arabic linguist Lieutenant Dan Choi was one of those discharged.

The timing of the nine discharges, directly on the heels of the nation's most deadly terrorist attacks, proved crucial in advancing the LGBT struggle for fairness. For one, it helped to illustrate how inequitable U.S. military policies toward LGBTs were. Second, it galvanized gay rights activists and members of the LGBT community to unite and begin demanding fair treatment, by challenging the untimely discharges. The discharges would become the catalyst for LGBTs setting their sights on complete reversal of U.S. military policies that were biased against homosexuals. Choi, who is now an LGBT activist, was instrumental in motivating a groundswell of support within the LGBT community and rallying gay rights advocates who strongly denounced DADT and the ill treatment of LGBT military personnel. The ultimate effect was to grow support for the legislation that was in due course introduced in Congress to nullify the restriction of LGBTs openly serving in the U.S. armed forces. This legislation would also bring to an end what was, according to the Government Accounting Office (GAO), an enormously exorbitant endeavor that had, over a six-year period, cost an astronomical $200 million to keep LGBT military personnel in the closet.[23] The high cost of DADT was related to investigating and discharging troops under the Pentagon's policy on gays.

Lieutenant Dan Choi, a Korean American and West Point graduate, had been opposed to DADT since his return from serving in Iraq. While stationed in the Middle East, Choi participated in tribal meeting meetings between the Sunni and Shia Muslims to persuade the Shia not to be ashamed of their identities. Later, Choi would say that he felt like a hypocrite because the U.S. military did not allow him to express his own sexual identity, yet he had encouraged others to not conceal their religious affiliation. Choi's familiarity with sexual identity bias is incredibly similar to what blacks and other minority LGBTs face. What Choi shares with black LGBTs is his exposure to strict religious practices and the taboos associated with homosexuality. Choi's acknowledgement that he feared coming out to his father, a Southern Baptist minister, more than to the U.S. military mirrors the oft-voiced trepidation by black LGBTs and others whose backgrounds include strong religious convictions against homosexuality. Explaining his feelings about coming out, Choi said, "I wasn't afraid of 'don't ask, don't tell' in the military; I was afraid of 'don't ask, don't tell' at home."[24]

Most LGBTs who volunteered for military service just after the September 11, 2001, terrorist attacks are now post-DADT veterans. After patriotically serving, putting their lives on the line and sacrificing in their country's time of need, people like Choi endured the full force of DADT and experienced firsthand the repercussions of unfair military policies. However, in Choi's case, like that of black LGBTs, the ramifications didn't end with the repeal of DADT. Choi and others who share the commonality of religious conviction and the import placed on masculinity and traditional gender roles by family, community, and church are forced to contend with and tolerate the aftermath of DADT into the foreseeable future.

The proliferation of homophobia in the black community correlates to the sacredness of heterosexuality and an expectation of innate virility in black men. These precepts are reinforced and legitimized in day-to-day life by the black family, the Black Church, community, as well as, U.S. military policy that prior to the repeal of DADT supported the ethnic aversion to homosexuality commonplace in black culture. Many heterosexual black U.S. military personnel who are—based on their skills and abilities— able to overcome obstacles stemming from preconceived societal perceptions are hypersensitive about anything that contradicts traditional black sexual norms and masculinity. So as the military brass and political leaders were finally getting down to the nitty-gritty related to the issue of gays openly serving, and some military top leaders like General Powell were choosing to modify their positions, the reality of what repealing DADT would actually mean became an even more contentious issue.

As politicians saw the tide beginning to turn on DADT, people like Senator McCain, who in 2006 said that he would support ending the ban on gays serving openly once the military's top brass told him that they agreed with the change, seemed to renege when advised by the military that it was now on board and prepared to allow gays to serve openly. Seemingly taken by surprise that the tide had turned, McCain appeared to flip-flop in a letter addressed to Senator Carl Levin, chairman of the Committee on Armed Services. McCain said, "I cannot over emphasize the importance of completing the comprehensive review prior to taking any legislative action. Our military is currently engaged in two wars and we need to have a true assessment of the impact of repealing 'Don't Ask Don't Tell' on battlefield effectiveness prior to taking any legislative action. We must remain focused on what is in the best interest of our service men and women and not simply fulfill a campaign promise."[25]

There was also four-star general, George William Casey, Jr., who served as the thirty-sixth chief of staff of the U.S. Army, who appeared to throw a roadblock in the momentum to repeal DADT. Casey publicly stated that there was significant resistance to gays openly serving, and that the repeal of DADT might affect some midcareer personnel who were deemed the backbone of the nation's military. Casey warned that some of the most seasoned military personnel might retire prematurely if DADT were repealed. In a letter related to DADT, Casey wrote, "I remain convinced that it is critically important to get a better understanding of where our Soldiers and Families are on this issue, and what the impacts on readiness and unit cohesion might be, so that I can provide informed military advice to the President and the Congress."[26]

Others opposing DADT's repeal insinuated that homosexuals would run amok with homoerotism and hedonism, and generally wreak havoc on morale and discipline at U.S. military bases around the globe. The issue of homosexuals openly serving in the military and tactics used by antigay activists parallel in a number of ways the tactics related to the protracted effort to prevent racial integration of the military six decades earlier. Even as the United States had joined 25 other countries, including the Israeli army, in allowing gays and lesbians to openly serve, antigay forces collaborated, determinedly opposing the repeal of DADT by using a campaign of fear to egg others on. Such posturing, often expressed as preserving the integrity and image of the U.S. military, implied that the proclivities of homosexuals—if permitted to openly serve—would ultimately lead to the degradation of military personnel and harm the United States' image around the world. This sort of fearmongering presents huge problems related to transitioning to a post-DADT military, but it is especially hard for black LGBTs who are actively serving in the military and who may be considering revealing their sexual identity.

Consider what conservative talk show host and former presidential candidate Pat Buchanan said when arguing against the repeal of DADT and about what homosexuals openly serving in the U.S. military would mean: "You are trying to impose the values of Fire Island on Parris Island. These are 19-year-old Marines. They're very macho guys. Many of them are Christian traditionalists and you got these secular values and you bring open homosexuals into the barracks with these guys—it will be hellish."[27] Buchanan's viewpoint is not unique and is shared by many who wholeheartedly reject gays openly serving in the military. Yet what few civilians realize and what Pat Buchanan fails to mention is that U.S. soldiers—without incident—knowingly fought alongside openly gay NATO soldiers during the Persian Gulf War in 1990. This little-known situation came to be over two decades ago when former Joint Chiefs chairman general John Shalikashvili pointed out that "enforcement of the ban was suspended without problems during the Persian Gulf War, and there were no reports of angry departures."[28] The suspension of U.S. military policy was much needed ammunition for LGBT advocates, who used it to demonstrate that fair and equitable treatment of gay U.S. military forces did not produce the predicted doom forecasted by cynics. It proved an astounding rebuttal of the notion that heterosexuals and homosexuals can't fight and win a war together.

Senator Carl Levin (D-MI), the chairman of the Armed Services Committee who supported ending the ban on gays serving openly, was challenged by persistent opponents like Senator John McCain, the ranking member of the Senate Armed Services Committee, who called the day that the U.S. Senate voted to repeal DADT "a very sad day." McCain added, "I hope that when we pass this legislation that we will understand that we are doing great damage."[29] In late 2010, the Senate blocked legislation to repeal the ban on openly gay personnel serving in the military, while people like Senator Joe Lieberman (I-CT), a leading supporter of the bill to repeal DADT, expressed disappointment that the effort had failed.

Also taking the side of repealing DADT, the nation's top military officer, Admiral Mike Mullen, weighed in, supporting the decision to allow homosexuals to openly serve in the military. He said, "It comes down to integrity: How can we ask citizens of this country to sacrifice time, comfort and even life and limb and not allow them to honestly represent themselves?"[30] Mullen was joined by former defense secretary Robert Gates and top military leaders in support of repealing the ban. General Colin Powell and others who had gone on record in opposition to homosexuals openly serving began to incrementally alter their position as trending suggested growing public acceptance of DADT's repeal. Originally believing that openly serving gays and lesbians would diminish morale and erode discipline, Powell altered his position, saying, "Attitudes and circumstances have changed." Powell added, "Society is always reflected in the military. It's where we get our soldiers from."[31]

In spite of the fact that the repeal of DADT had been years in the making and had undergone an exhaustive analysis by military experts, both anti- and progay organizations contend that there are ramifications yet to be realized. For example, predications have been made that the repeal of

DADT might lead to the defeat of DOMA and the legalization of same-sex marriage nationwide. Others, who compare the repeal of DADT to the 1948 racial desegregation of the U.S. military that ended systematic discrimination against black Americans, say that procedural modifications are still necessary to acclimate and prepare U.S. military personnel for the dramatic changes that the repeal of DADT will ultimately bring.

While it is true that a majority of gay advocates and white LGBT military personnel welcomed the rescission of DADT that brought to an end years of political wrangling over the issue, exactly what the repeal of DADT will mean to black LGBT military personnel and those contemplating military service is still anyone's guess. But if the subdued response from black LGBTs currently serving in the U.S. armed forces is any indication, it may signify the degree of uncertainty that still surrounds the repeal and just how it will play in black culture. It addition, it may be an indication of how, or if, the Black Church will respond any differently than it has in the past to the issue homosexuality and same-sex marriage.

As a heterosexual African American who served in the U.S. Air Force during the early 1970s, just a quarter of a century after President Truman's historic order integrating the military, it is without question mind blowing to witness the official ending of DADT, an unsuccessful and insensitive U.S. military policy toward homosexuals. What is equally amazing is to consider the brief period of time that it took to move toward and effect such a dramatic change in U.S. military policy. To put it into context, less than four decades ago, if an individual who was active in the military had entertained an open discussion about homosexuality, it would have very likely resulted in multiple sessions with a military psychiatrist.

Just how the termination of DADT and gays openly serving ultimately affects U.S. military forces won't be known for some time. However, if the past is any indication, the black community's reaction will be one of extreme caution and distinctly different from the reaction of whites. Among the things that blacks will consider will be their ancestral connection. There will be those who factor in things like inequality, slavery, and a history of systematic bigotry in the civilian and military life of blacks. Besides that, some will take into account the hard-fought struggle to integrate the U.S. military and particularly the compelling religious and ethnic aversion to homosexuality emphasized by the traditional Black Church. These considerations suggest a significantly different way of assessing exactly what the repeal of DADT symbolizes and make plain the stark differences between what it means to whites and blacks.

In a post-DADT era, the reality is that black LGBT military personnel who choose to declare their sexual identity while openly serving run the risk of being exposed to increased discrimination in black society. It also suggests that a possible consequence, while not exclusive to black LGBTs, is much more likely to occur in the homophobic black culture. There are significant societal repercussions for black LGBTs that could emanate from a variety of sources, of which the most obvious is the scorn leveled by black religious leaders, the Black Church, and religious-based community organizations. It is also a possibility that the specter of an increase in HIV/AIDS cases, something that greatly concerns the broader black community, will be an issue that the U.S. military, the black community, and openly gay black LGBTs will grapple with.

Issues like HIV/AIDS may have been exacerbated by people like former congressman Allen West (R-FL), a black man, Tea Party member and former colonel in the U.S. Army. West's controversial statements about gays in the military have infuriated the LGBT community and gay rights advocates. His frank talk and opposition to homosexuality have stoked a heated debate and some say have helped to spread panic about the abolishment of DADT and what it will mean to the black community. In one instance, according to the Tampa Tribune, West said when addressing a question related to the eventual repeal of DADT: "When you take the military and you tell it they must conform to the individual's behavior, then it's just a matter of time until you break down the military." And when someone compared allowing homosexuals to serve openly to abolishing segregated forces in the military, West said, "Let me explain something to you. I can't change my color. People can change their behavior, but I can't change my color."[32] In saying this, West manages to disguise his contempt for homosexuals while cleverly suggesting that members of the LGBT community have a choice when it comes to their sexual identity. West also uses the issue of a racially segregated U.S. military to draw the ire of blacks who rebuke any attempt to link gays openly serving in the military, same-sex marriage, or for that matter anything related to the LGBT campaign for fair treatment to the equality attained as a result of the civil rights movement.

West's insinuation that homosexuals are able to transform themselves into heterosexuals, while ludicrous, is in sync with 2012 fellow Tea Party presidential candidate Michelle Bachman, who once compared homosexuality to "personal bondage, personal despair and personal enslavement."[33] Comments like those from Bachmann, West, and members of the Christian Right provoke the sort of trepidation that is conducive to the growing homophobic culture that exists in the black community, sending black LGBTs into a lifetime of concealing their sexual identity. Going forward, it's likely that it will continue to be the primary reason, even with the repeal of DADT, that the majority of black LGBT military personnel will not dare reveal their sexual identity.

Obviously, the complications and outcomes for black LGBT military personnel post-DADT differ from those of whites. Still, LGBTs from all ethnicities continue to confront challenges due to the fact that the reversal of DADT did not entitle same-sex couples to the benefits afforded to heterosexual couples, for example, health insurance, education, and housing assistance. Unless there is a successful repeal of DOMA, LGBTs of every race and ethnicity will continue to contend with the inequalities that the reversal of DADT failed to address. With near certainty black LGBTs will encounter additional obstacles. Regardless, this in no way negates the mutually shared monumental gain that the overturning of DADT brings to all LGBT military personnel, which is—first and foremost—that it allows them to openly serve without fear of retaliation. Even so, pointing out the differences that remain for black LGBTs is necessary to demonstrate how an ingrained cultural opposition to homosexuality has complicated the issue, making it exceedingly difficult, especially given the powerful forces that they are up against. Frankly, the difficulties confronting black LGBT military personnel are as gargantuan as the homophobic mindset in the black community and equally pervasive. So, for now, it is anyone's guess how it will ultimately play out. Given the unchanging and inflexible position of black ministers and their strong resistance to the fair treatment of black LGBTs a change in the stance toward homosexuality is unlikely. Hopes for a time when blacks dramatically alter their position toward the LGBT community and same-sex unions are similarly remote. To a large degree, the effect on black LGBTs as it relates to the repeal of DADT will largely depend on the response from black ministers. Also, if black LGBT U.S. military personnel are willing, and it's a really big if, to reveal their sexuality identity and thereby compel black ministers to address the issue, it could present an opportunity for meaningful dialogue. Yet it is hard to know how things will turn out. What is known is that just as civilian black gay and bisexual men perpetrate themselves as heterosexuals by living on the DL, so too will black LGBT military personnel continue to do so if the Black Church does not adjust its position. Like their civilian counterparts, LGBT military personnel will continue to respond pragmatically, weighing their options and deciding if they are better off concealing their sexuality rather than facing the all too predictable consequences prompted by disclosing their homosexuality. Given evidence that strongly indicates an unwavering position by the Black Church toward openly gay people serving in the armed forces, it is more likely that black LGBT military personnel will opt for the security that secrecy offers. Chances are that the well-documented scorn and repudiation of the black community, and the wrath of the Black Church, will result in the majority of black LGBT military personnel opting for the continued concealment of their sexual identity.

NOTES

1. Genesis 19:5–8. Holy Bible.

2. Leonard P. Matlovich, "War hero, gay activist," *Philly.com*, June 24, 1988, http://articles.philly.com/1988-06-24/news/26264400_1 _honorable-discharge-gay-rights-homosexuality. Accessed December 5, 2012.

3. *Don't Ask, Don't Tell (DADT) Repeal Implementation, Tier 1 Education, Army G-1*, Version 14, February 24, 2011, http://8tharmy.korea .army.mil/g1_ag/DADT/G1_Tier_1_Tng-v14.pdf. Accessed December 5, 2012.

4. Library of Congress, "Primary documents in American history: 15th amendment to the Constitution," *LOC.gov*, http://www.loc.gov/rr/ program/bib/ourdocs/15thamendment.html. Accessed December 5, 2012.

5. http://www.nbjc.org/dadt. Accessed October 15, 2011.

6. Anthony Stanford. Columnist *Aurora Beacon News*, April 21, 2010.

7. Harry S. Truman Library and Museum, "Desegregation of the armed forces: Chronology," http://www.trumanlibrary.org/whistlestop/ study_collections/desegregation/large/index.php?action=chronology. Accessed December 5, 2012.

8. Harry S. Truman, "Transcript of Executive Order 9981: Desegregation of the armed forces (1948)," www.ourdocuments.gov, http://www .ourdocuments.gov/doc.php?doc=84&page=transcript. Accessed December 5, 2012.

9. http://www.marinecorpstimes.com/. Accessed October 15, 2011.

10. Bob Dylan and Jerry Sears, Song "The Times They Are A-Changin" (New York: M. Witmark, 1964).

11. http://www.reuters.com/article/2009/07/05/us-usa-miltary-gays -idUSTRE5641A920090705. Accessed October 15, 2011.

12. Bishop Eddie Long, Southern Poverty Law Center, *Intelligence* Spring 2007 Issue.

13. http://psychology.ucdavis.edu/rainbow/html/military_history.html, National Defense Research Institute, 1993, 160. Accessed October 15, 2011.

14. http://www.nyrock.com/newz/military.asp. Accessed October 15, 2011.

15. http://psychology.ucdavis.edu/rainbow/html/military_history.html. Accessed October 15, 2011.

16. http://www.nyrock.com/newz/military.asp. Accessed October 15, 2011.

17. Representative Bill Foster (D-IL), April 21, 2010, *Aurora Beacon News*.

18. Anthony Stanford, Columnist *Aurora Beacon News*, April 10, 2011.

19. http://www.opencongress.org/bill/111-s3065/show. Accessed December 15, 2011.

20. Deb Miller, LGBT activist interview with author.

21. Ibid.

22. Ibid.

23. General Accounting Office Info (Source: CNN News Anderson Cooper, January 21, 2011.

24. http://northernstar.info/campus/article_de3677ea-6fb9-11e0-9030-0019bb30f31a.html, April 25, 2011.Accessed December 6, 2012.

25. http://www.mccain.senate.gov/public/index.cfm?FuseAction=Press Office.PressReleases&ContentRecord_id=d5d00574-ce46-10c4-0c80-d916 97758331&Region_id=&Issue_id=f9a5665a-b73f-42fc-91d0-ab93a2876f4c. Accessed October 6, 2012.

26. http://www.mccain.senate.gov/public/index.cfm?FuseAction=Press Office.PressReleases&ContentRecord_id=d5d00574-ce46-10c4-0c80-d916 97758331. Accessed August 25, 2011.

27. Jeff Poor, "Buchanan calls 'don't ask, don't tell' repeal 'trying to impose the values of Fire Island on Parris Island,'" *DailyCaller.com*, December 19, 2010, http://dailycaller.com/2010/12/19/buchanan-calls-dont-ask-dont-tell-repeal-trying-to-impose-the-values-of-fire-island-on-paris-island/#ixzz1VyQ7aDnz. Accessed August 24, 2011.

28. Steve Chapman, "Buried truths about gays in the military: Why it's time to end 'don't ask, don't tell,'" *Reason.com*, February 8, 2010, http://reason.com/archives/2010/02/08/buried-truths-about-gays-in-th.

29. Elyse Siegel, "John McCain DADT repeal reaction: 'Today is a very sad day,'" *HuffingtonPost.com*, December 18, 2010, http://www.huffingtonpost.com/2010/12/18/john-mccain-dadt-repeal-_n_798726.html. Accessed August 22 2011.

30. Six Foot Skinny, "A soldier's plea for gays in the military," *Salon.com*, February 4, 2010, http://www.salon.com/life/feature/2010/02/04/soldier_dont_ask_dont_tell. Accessed August 24, 2011.

31. Clarence Page, "Lifting the ban," *Chicago Tribune*, February 7, 2010, http://articles.chicagotribune.com/2010-02-07/news/1002060239_1

_joint-chiefs-gay-man-or-lesbian-gen-colin-powell. Accessed August 24, 2011.

32. Mark Berman, "Rep. Allen West: Gays will 'break down' military," *OpposingViews.com*, July 25, 2011, http://www.opposingviews .com/i/society/gay-issues/rep-allen-west-gays-will-break-down-military.

33. "Michele Bachmann's Gay Rights Views Take Center Stage," *IBItimes.com*, July 18, 2011, http://www.ibtimes.com/articles/182228/ 20110718/michele-bachmann-gay-rights-michele-bachmann-gay-michele -bachmann-gay-therapy.htm.

SEVEN

LGBTs Today and Tomorrow

Do you not know that the wicked will not inherit the kingdom of God? Do not be deceived: Neither the sexually immoral nor idolaters, nor adulterers nor male prostitutes nor homosexual offenders nor thieves nor the greedy nor drunkards nor slanderers nor swindlers will inherit the kingdom of God.[1]

Just a week after the president of the United States officially rescinded DADT during a televised Republican presidential debate, a gay soldier asked a pertinent question via video from his base in Iraq. Soldier Stephen Hill's question was direct and one that was certainly on the minds of LGBT armed forces members everywhere. The question posed by Hill to any of the nine presidential candidates participating in the debate was stated as follows: "My question is, under one of your presidencies, do you intend to circumvent the progress that's been made for gay and lesbian soldiers in the military?"[2] Rick Santorum, the former Republican Pennsylvania senator took the soldier's question, saying, "I would say any type of sexual activity has absolutely no place in the military."[3] Extending his remarks, Santorum said that the repeal of DADT would be detrimental to the U.S. military, suggesting that abstinence should be practiced by all military personnel. Santorum added that gay and lesbian troops had been given special consideration by the Obama administration, and if he (Santorum) were elected to the presidency, he would bring it to an end. To this, the largely Republican and Tea Party audience cheered enthusiastically.

Santorum's position on DADT and the announcement that he would reinstate the controversial policy if elected president wasn't a shocking revelation. As a matter of fact, Santorum's conservative stance was, on the whole, consistent with that of the other eight GOP presidential candidates with whom he shared the stage that evening. However, what may have shocked viewers tuning in to the debate and embarrassed the GOP was that during the nationally televised debate, the individuals vying for the highest office in the land all stood by while an openly gay U.S. soldier serving his country in wartime, and in an active warzone, was booed and disrespected by a predominantly Republican audience. Not one of the antigay candidates competing for the 2012 Republican nomination, seeking to serve as president of the United States and to represent all the people, moved to admonish the audience for the disrespectful behavior or to distance themselves from Santorum's comment. On the contrary, if anything, they seemed unified in their profound silence and remained so as the young solider was humiliated before his fellow Americans. Before a national audience of potential voters, the rude heckling of the young gay soldier gave many Americans their first glimpse of the treatment unofficially sanctioned at the highest levels of U.S. government toward active duty U.S. military personnel who identify as LGBT. On display for voters in this most public venue came a rare look at the perception of some devout Christian Right and social conservatives toward members of the LGBT community. In this awkward and particularly painful instance, the public saw firsthand the contempt and degradation that homosexuals are made to endure on a daily basis. In this particular case, a young gay solider—with no consideration of the personal sacrifice he was making for his country—was shamed and publicly tormented to show the GOP's solidarity related to the issue of homosexuals openly serving in the U.S. armed forces.

Regrettably, the abhorrent behavior of Republican conservatives and the Christian Right doesn't shock the LGBT community. Gay activists are well acquainted with this sort of mistreatment and are accustomed to those who take advantage of every opportunity to single out LGBTs for public derision. So while the Republican debate gave some Americans their first glimpse of the distasteful treatment of a soldier identifying as LGBT, seasoned LGBT advocates on the front line fighting for fairness and equality have adapted, even learning to use attempts to exploit them to their advantage. In fact, LGBT supporters may have recognized the debate as an opportunity to advance their cause, redirecting the animosity aimed at them to garner support. However, young LGBTs not yet toughened by ridicule are infinitely more susceptible to what they perceive as a never-ending barrage of insults, bullying, and exclusion. They are often made to feel that they have no choice but to endure the abuse. In some cases, out of desperation and despair, they are unable to withstand the oppression, and over time, they withdraw by choosing to live in isolation. In more extreme cases, an inability to cope drives some to commit suicide. In spite of the monumental gains made by gay activists for fair treatment and equality for LGBTs, the unrelenting and callous persecution of homosexuals is extremely difficult for young LGBTs.

In its 2008 study "Suicide Risk and Prevention for Lesbian Gay, Bisexual, and Transgender Youth," the Suicide Prevention Resource Center (SPRC) points out that "LGB youth as a group experience more suicidal behavior than other youth. A variety of studies indicate that LGB youth are nearly one and a half to three times more likely to have reported suicidal ideation than non-LGB youth. Research from several sources also revealed that LGB youth are nearly one and a half to seven times more likely than non-LGB youth to have reported attempting suicide."[4] The study raises the issue of how great an effect prejudice against young LGBTs has and how their humiliation is directly associated with risk factors linked to suicide, mental health issues, and heterosexism.

Many Americans saw the humiliation of the gay solider as an embarrassing and even unpatriotic incident, but the reality is that members of the LGBT community have come to expect and deal with stigma and discrimination on a daily basis. Over the past decade, proponents and opponents of the gay rights movement have become skilled at deploying a variety of strategies and using technologies like social media to advance their agendas. Following the Republican debate during which Hill was publicly demeaned, national networks, cable news outlets, and social networking sites were abuzz with millions of people outraged by Hill's treatment and demanding an apology from the GOP. GOProud, a gay Tea Party organization, issued a statement saying, "That brave gay soldier is doing something Rick Santorum has never done—put his life on the line to defend our freedoms and our way of life . . ."[5] Whether one supported or opposed LGBT equality, the incident came to symbolize the daunting challenges facing young LGBTs. In addition, it provided Americans with an uncensored example of how homosexuals are too often treated and how they are viewed by socially conservative Republicans and evangelicals.

The ridicule and mocking that Hill endured is no different than that endured by people who choose to live their lives as openly gay. When the former CEO of the Chicago Public Schools, Ron Huberman, took on the herculean task of heading the nation's third largest school district, the appointment was seen by some as the most challenging endeavor of his storied career. However, in 2009, when Huberman—a former Chicago police officer—came out to the public, he became an instant inspiration to LGBT youth throughout Chicago who were struggling to cope with their homosexuality and to live among those who despised them because of their sexual identity. Huberman, who came out to his parents at age 15, talked about it in an interview, saying, "It's always difficult for kids. It was difficult for my parents at first. But they've become very accepting and very supportive."[6]

Huberman's experience as a young homosexual is like that of many young LGBTs, who ultimately face the difficult decision of whether to disclose their sexual identity to family and friends. For some, it is as Huberman says, the toughest part about coming out. Mental health professionals agree that it is an exceedingly difficult choice for a child. Still, many young LGBTs, particularly minorities, face not only the challenge about whether to come out, but a host of challenging circumstances mostly beyond their control. These situations, usually ethnically linked, are generally unavoidable. For example, from the start, young black LGBTs are coerced into adhering to strict sexual norms as defined by the black experience, enforced by the black community, and supported by the Black Church. Not only must they handle the individual issues of their homosexuality, but they must also grapple with the inevitability of the entire black community, their families, and church rejecting them. It is true that LGBTs of all races, to some extent, suffer as a result of the actions of Christian evangelicals, radical clinicians, socially conservative politicians, and religious zealots who insist that being a homosexual is a matter of choice that with proper treatment, prayer, and counseling can be cured. However, in the case of young black LGBTs, not only must they deal with the black community's opposition to homosexuality, but also with the strong resistance to homosexuality bolstered by homophobic black ministers who use the pulpit to proclaim distain for homosexuals and to rake members of the LGBT community over the coals.

A year before Huberman became CEO of the Chicago Public Schools, school officials were considering a "gay-friendly" high school like the first one in the nation, which was opened in New York City in 2003 and named for slain San Francisco supervisor Harvey Milk. Chicago's proposal for a gay-friendly high school evolved out of the everyday realities of gay students and what was seen as necessary to deal with the increasing abusive treatment and harassment of LGBT students. The aftereffects of the persistent persecution leveled against LGBT students were seen in increased skipping of classes, poor grades, and ultimately an upsurge in dropout rates. Early on, the proposal received broad support, including the backing of then Chicago Public School chief executive officer (CEO) Arne Duncan, who would later become President Obama's secretary of education.

The unrelenting provocation of LGBT students—which was substantiated in a national study conducted by the Gay, Lesbian and Straight Education Network (GLSEN)—generated stunning results, bringing attention to the widespread persecution of young homosexuals. Touted as the most comprehensive nationwide report related to LGBT students, the GLSEN report yielded findings that gave insight into the everyday lives and drudgery of young LGBT students. CNN reported that "The national study, which the group says is the most comprehensive report ever on the experiences of lesbian, gay, bisexual and transgender students nationwide, found that 86.2 percent of those students reported being verbally harassed, 44.1 percent physically harassed and 22.1 percent physically assaulted at school in the past year because of their sexual orientation."[7] The study's conclusions, while alarming to the general public, did not surprise veteran gay rights activists. LGBT advocates cited as the cause the mean spirited no-holds-barred strategies used by antigay activists and religious extremists to obstruct equality for LGBTs and same-sex marriage, and to demean homosexuals. Seen as the chief contributing factor to the increasing harassment of LGBT students, some gay activists voiced concern that the tactics employed by the Religious Right were purposely intended to incite mistreatment and hostility toward young LGBTs.

Social conservatives, evangelicals, and homophobic black clergy routinely give a picture that homosexuality is the main reason for the destruction of family values and family structure. Gay antagonists are quick to mention the spread of HIV/AIDS and to use it as an indictment of the entire LGBT community. When, HIV/AIDS is used by black religious leaders to support their contention about members of the LGBT community, the HIV/AIDS issue is an especially potent strategy because of the related alarming scientific data.

In the end, political pressure from a variety of antigay forces and LGBT equality obstructionists successfully labeled the Chicago proposal to open an all-gay school a misuse of public funds. Leading the opposition were people like the Reverend James Meeks, who had also been the only black state legislator to antagonize the LGBT community by casting a vote against an Illinois LGBT nondiscrimination bill. Meeks and other antigay stalwarts were eventually instrumental pulling the proposal from consideration. Rick Garcia, the former political director for the gay rights group Equality Illinois, seemed to make a valid point—which other gay rights advocates agreed with—when he said, "If we're going to have a separate high school, let's put the bullies in the high school, not gay kids."[8] Garcia's viewpoint on the issue of separate schools for young LGBTs can also be seen at the New York Harvey Milk School, which opened its doors in 2003. The school, seen by some as a practical educational alternative for young gays and lesbians, has from the time its doors opened been plagued by controversy. For example, the school's detractors continue to charge that the city is using taxpayer dollars to subsidize homosexuality. After the school opened, an evangelical group and socially conservative Democratic state senator Ruben Diaz, Sr., a Pentecostal minister from the Bronx brought a suit asking that the $3.2 million in public funds used to finance the school be revoked. The school's detractors asserted that the experimental school was a waste of public money. This attitude is not isolated and was the subject of a 2005 New York News and Features piece by John Colapinto that acknowledged, "Even some gay rights advocates call the Harvey Milk High School a decisive step backward in homosexuals' quest for equality and acceptance—a 'uniquely bad idea,' as one liberal critic puts it . . ."[9]

The fact that some educators, parents, gay activists, and LGBT youth consider the separation of heterosexual and LGBT students a new social norm and viable solution does not play well with committed critics of segregation. These cynics are joined by gay and human rights advocates who believe that the model bears a strong likeness to the defunct segregated school system that was a staple of the South prior to the civil rights movement. Moreover, they consider it wrong and even dangerous to entertain the idea of separating homosexuals and heterosexuals. They argue very effectively and with considerable corroboration that the already intense prejudice and hatred toward LGBT pupils would most likely increase and homophobic attitudes flourish if a divided heterosexual and homosexual public educational system were to be implemented. Some predict that adopting this as a solution would eventually create a homophobic public school system and one within which LGBT students would be singled out and made to suffer as a result of institutionally approved isolation. They also assert that in the long run, it could result in a deficiency in LGBT student's ability to socialize with others.

Pointing out that the high school experience is already difficult enough for many students, opponents of the separate school plan cite the effect on young LGBTs as they grow older and are confronted with issues related to self-esteem and an inability to fit into broader society. In this scenario, critics aptly point out that eventually, homosexuals and heterosexuals will have no choice but to interact with one another. It is a powerful argument that has ultimately caused some who originally backed the proposal to rethink their position and seek alternative solutions. Opponents of the strategy strongly believe that efforts to adapt the nation's public educational system, offering the option of separate schools for LGBT and heterosexual students, will result in major disadvantages for both homosexual and heterosexual students. They stress that the consequences would be disastrous for the country's entire public educational system, pointing out that chief among the drawbacks is the singling out of LGBT students. They also maintain that educational professionals who support a segregated system that uses public funds would be contributing to the demise of the public educational system. Finally, predicting an alarming outcome, some say that separating students in such a manner could result in blaming the spread of HIV/AIDS or other sexually transmitted infections (STIs) on either group, making them social outcasts. The segregation issue is difficult for many to consider because of its potential to foster discrimination.

There are, of course, those who take a completely opposite view and advocate gay-friendly high schools that are totally separate places of learning exclusively for lesbian, gay, bisexual, and transgender students. They argue persuasively the merits of the model and maintain that the separation of heterosexual and homosexual youth in the public educational system will help to resolve the ever more difficult problem of LGBT students being targeted by heterosexual students, who they contend premeditate ways to socially ostracize gays. Insisting that the struggles of LGBT students in the public school system signify the apparent failure of the public educational system to accommodate LGBTs, which they assert is patently unfair, these prosegregation activists continue to rally in support of a complete separation of LGBT and heterosexual students. They convincingly declare that not only is the idea of an alternative system worthy of consideration, but also one whose time has come. They also offer a powerful line of reasoning that is especially potent given violence against LGBT students, which has become more commonplace throughout the nation's public school systems. This, along with horrific reports of bullycide, defined as "the act or an instance of killing oneself intentionally as a result of bullying, is helping to garner support for those who back segregated pupil school systems."[10]

Black LGBT youth who are victimized by an unsympathetic community often can't depend on family members for support. In many cases, the denouncement and exploitation they experience is encouraged by their community, family, and house of worship. To further support the separation of heterosexual and homosexual students, backers emphasis the surging harassment by pointing out violent incidents like the 2008 murder of a

California eight grader, Lawrence King. Because King's physical appearance was different than that of the other boys, and he identified as gay, and wore nail polish and makeup to school he was shot in the head by a fellow classmate in front of a classroom full of students. Following the tragedy, the National Gay and Lesbian Task Force responded to the tragic incident by issuing a forceful statement which said, in part, "Our hearts go out to Lawrence's family and to all young lesbian, gay, bisexual and transgender kids who are right now, right this minute being bullied and beaten in school while adults look the other way."[11] Supporters of changing the public educational system are working to find ways to help LGBT students. One way they are strengthening their position is by identifying poor scholastic performance and high dropout rates, saying that the personal lives of some of these young people are already in a state of flux due to the pressures they face as LGBTs. They warn that repeated victimization and rejection at the hands of heterosexual peers is sometimes more than young LGBTs are able to handle, and as a result, their lives can easily spiral out of control. Without question, both sides make a persuasive case that merits a closer look by educational officials who are seeking a balanced solution.

Young LGBTs must tolerate the outlandish theories propagated by people like the husband of 2012 presidential candidate Michelle Bachmann, Marcus, who declared that Christian therapy to reorient homosexuals would cure homosexuality, as if it were some variant strain of sexuality. Ideas like this are not at all helpful in encouraging fair treatment for members of the LGBT community. The fact that the spouse of a presidential candidate would have the audacity to make this sort of statement makes an already difficult existence for young LGBTs even tougher. This sort of declaration tends to exacerbate the difficulties faced by these young people and contributes to misconceptions about homosexuality that are already rampant in U.S. society. They are also apt to encourage bias and maltreatment of members of the LGBT community by inferring that if only they exercised control over their sexuality, they could avoid being portrayed as abnormal. This belief already prevalent in the black community is given credence when echoed by political leaders and members of the black clergy.

In another instance, Chicago's cardinal Francis George, a longtime and outspoken critic of the gay community whose views related to same-sex couples and unions are considered contentious and incendiary made a comment during a December 2011 Fox newscast that infuriated the LGBT community. During the interview, when George was asked for his opinion regarding comments made by a Chicago pastor who had expressed concerns that Chicago's 2012 gay pride parade would conflict with morning Mass and possibly cause disruption, George supported the pastor's viewpoint, saying, "He's telling us that they won't be able to have church services on Sunday if that's the case. You know, you don't want the gay liberation movement to morph into something like the Ku Klux Klan, demonstrating in the streets against Catholicism." George continued, "So I think if that's what's happening, and I don't know that it is, but I would respect the local pastor's, you know position on that."[12] Here again, demonization of the LGBT community in George's analogy is in the long run very harmful and especially so as it relates to impressionable young LGBTs. Taken literally and coming from the hierarchy of the Catholic Church, George's inflammatory comparison of LGBTs to one of the most ominous hate groups in American history is particularly divisive rhetoric. For black LGBTs, George's statement contributes to the complexity of their struggle by casting them alongside the villainous perpetrators who terrorized generations of blacks and other minorities. Moreover, George's insinuation is beyond the pale and ammunition for antigay provocateurs to connect homosexuals, the Ku Klux Klan, and the civil rights movement.

In the case of minority LGBT youth dealing not only with issues related to their sexuality, but also with a powerful cultural resistance by their race to accept nonconformity to traditional sexual standards, their lives are apt to be considerably more difficult. This is true for blacks and Hispanics whose cultural sensitivities related to homosexuality and masculinity provide severely limited choices for young LGBTs struggling to find their way. For them, the effect of coming out and revealing their true sexual identity is infinitely more risky and even dangerous. It has significantly increased potential to bring about insurmountable life-changing events. For black LGBTs, the likelihood of an extreme and dire outcome is considerably higher and includes the distinct possibility of a negative reaction emanating from what may be the only sources of support available to them. Well aware of this, some black LGBTs decide early on to escape the ridicule by posing as heterosexuals. However, because disguising homosexuality is viewed as the ultimate deception, blacks who do so run the risk of increasing the anger of the black community and Black Church if they are discovered. Yet in the end, the result can be a life that is equally difficult for blacks who decide to live openly as homosexuals.

Social exile and the impact of the stigma of identifying as a black LGBT is impossible to overstate and is directly tied to risk factors for depression and suicide. It is known that discrimination has a strong association with mental illness, and that heterosexism may lead to isolation and family rejection. The problems play out in urban America, where social pressures on black gay youth are overwhelming and are frequently worsened by cultural taboos that continue to thrive and threaten the black LGBT population. Such homophobic ideas also threaten the Black Church, the cornerstone of the black community. When black ministers accept these notions and encourage churchgoers to rebuke black Christian LGBTs, who they know are among the most active members of the black religious experience, it speaks to the intensity of the struggle within the Black Church and the level of hypocrisy that engulfs it.

Proof of substantial and persistent animosity toward black LGBTs was highlighted in a report by the National Black Justice Coalition (NBJC) and Freedom to Marry, which stated that "Among African-American youth, 55% believed that homosexuality is always wrong, compared to 36% of Latino youth and 35% of White youth. Forty-eight percent of all Black male youth and 29% of Black female youth surveyed agreed that homosexuality is always wrong. 10% more males than females opposed the legalization of marriage equality (50% v 39%)."[13]

However, there is a possibility that the outcome of the study may have been influenced by what, according to the Pew Research Center, could be evidence of disproportionate media coverage related to faith-based initiatives. According to a Pew study, one was 50 percent more likely to find faith-based issues on the front page of national newspapers in 2001 during the Bush administration than in 2009 under the Obama administration. The Pew Forum statistics support the fact that blacks are the only ethnic group to have become less supportive of gay rights, possibly as a result of increased preaching against homosexuality by black ministers, during the Bush presidency and in connection with faith-based funding competition. Therefore, it is reasonable to consider that the Black Church and some black religious leaders who routinely denounce homosexuality and speak out against same-sex marriage may have used their pulpits and power to manipulate the thinking of black churchgoing heterosexuals during the Bush era. If true, they may have helped to drive the belief that being a homosexual is wrong and a matter of personal choice. If so, black clergy continue to reinforce the ethnic belief that homosexuality is abhorrent, a sign of weakness and flawed character, and an affront to God.

Black ministers who promote this belief can see the result that their unsympathetic preaching and admonition of homosexuality is having on black LGBT youth who are besieged on numerous fronts. In addition, black clerics who play a part in the public admonishment of LGBTs are helping buttress the prevailing destructive viewpoint that is prevalent among blacks as it relates to homosexuality and marriage equality. It is this mentality that continues to drive young gay and bisexual black men to choose to live clandestinely on the DL instead of considering coming out and living as openly gay. Invariably, it also results in making the black community's already prejudicial posture toward black LGBTs even worse by reinforcing long-held beliefs about homosexuality and same-sex unions. The phenomenon encompasses generations and impacts young black LGBTs adversely and in a number of ways. Most notably, it affects their emotional stability and confidence, and it erodes the black family structure.

The case is strong that throughout inner-city neighborhoods, black LGBTs must regularly deal with issues related to their sexualiry in ways that transcend those of other cultures. Concerns like the DOMA, gay rights, and equality for LGBTs are trumped by the more personal and immediate concern of gauging the affect that their sexual identity will have on the way they are perceived by their community, church, and family. The thing that is so very different for black LGBTs relates to the consequences of revealing their sexual identity and the severity of the response related to doing so. It is no exaggeration to say that most are acutely aware of what disclosing their homosexuality will likely mean to their day-to-day existence. Saddled with the difficulty of navigating and surviving in what is described as an innately homophobic culture, the decision of whether to come out can realistically be a matter of survival. The seriousness of the choice is something that young black LGBTs must quickly understand, especially when the question of one's sexuality is subject of speculation. Gossip or the assumption that a young black man or woman is homosexual has the potential to dramatically affect the community's perception of the individual. So for young black LGBTs, options are limited and time sensitive, and often come down to concealing true sexual identity to avoid an across-the-board social rejection. Most already know that the homophobia so prevalent in their community is deeply ingrained in the black experience. They realize that distain for homosexuals is widely supported by black religious organizations and prominent black ministers who are held in high esteem. Black LGBTs also know that a decision to live openly as a homosexual will not likely be viewed in a positive way by peers, friends, family, and fellow churchgoers; rather, doing so has the potential to destroy their lives.

Young black LGBTs figure out rather quickly that the outcome of revealing their sexual identity will be exceedingly different and more traumatic than it is for white LGBTs. This is not to say that white LGBTs who come out don't face negative repercussions, some similar to that of blacks. However, it is generally the case that when whites come out, they do not elicit reactions nearly as severe or pervasive as that of black LGBTs. There are, of course, consequences that are shared by LGBTs of all ethnicities. However, by in large, the hardships and aftereffects suffered by blacks and whites are not the same. For instance, it is far more likely in black culture that family members, friends, and fellow churchgoers will be aligned with those who partake in the abusive ridicule and rejection of LGBTs. Sadly, this is more likely to occur for black LGBTs who openly exhibit what are thought to be inappropriate effeminate or masculine traits. Black LGBTs exhibiting these traits seem to provoke the most unsympathetic and repugnant reaction from the black community, and are more likely to endure an incessant spewing of ridicule and distasteful treatment that over time intensifies their trepidation and affects their ability to socially assimilate. When confronted with similar treatment by their faith community, black LGBTs feel unwelcome in the Black Church and sometimes feel browbeaten by black clergy who say that homosexuality offends God.

Indeed, young black LGBTs are cautioned to properly adhere to traditional sexual norms. Young black boys are constantly reminded of appropriate behavior and the demeanor that they should maintain. If there is any indication of nonconformity from acceptable sexual behavior, it will be countered by stern cautioning that is reinforced by peers, teachers, and community and religious leaders. Typically, those who ascribe to these beliefs are acting out of a sense of obligation to the community. Unfortunately, little thought is given to how hurtful it is to a young gay person struggling with the implications of his homosexuality and is told to straighten up and stop acting like a sissy. Instead, first and foremost comes an effort to "fix" the young LGBT who is exhibiting what is deemed inappropriate behavior or comportment that does not measure up to the customary standard of black sexuality. Young black boys are especially susceptible to harsh criticism if they exhibit effeminate behavior or mannerisms that are perceived as weak and repulsive. Regularly, young black males who fit this description realize that a public display of femininity will not be tolerated. Continuation of the behavior will embarrass the community and be frowned upon by many in the black community. Therefore, most adapt and learn to disguise their effeminate tendencies. They begin the desperate and sometimes lifelong effort to escape the humiliation and community shunning.

Yet some dare to live openly gay and still others, specifically some black male bisexuals, make the conscious decision to fake heterosexuality by duping unsuspecting women into believing that they are entering heterosexual relationships. In some cases, they carry out this charade for years, even marrying and having children. Some are never discovered, spending a lifetime in sham relationships. More often, though, they are eventually exposed as they either succumb to guilt or HIV/AIDS. One way or another, ultimately, their true sexual identity often comes to light. Those who continue feigning heterosexuality by living on the DL are frequently reminded that any person doing so is considered a pariah and reviled by the black community. If they are discovered, they are often outed by the black community. Irrespective of the consequences, these choices are the realities that young black LGBTs begin to contemplate early in life as they consider their severely limited options.

When a black homosexual seriously deliberates coming out, it brings ever closer the awareness and immediacy of the inevitable certainties that go along with facing a black community whose inflexible aversion toward homosexuality is brutal and unforgiving. Bearing in mind the negative and inescapable reality, black LGBTs often choose as a matter of practicality to conceal their sexual identity to avoid being considered outcasts.

While it is generally thought that this sort of thing occurs only in urban areas, the truth is that it also happens in suburbia, where a growing number of minorities now reside. The sometimes confused and extremely vulnerable, young minority LGBTs must often contend with the daunting struggles related to their sexuality, as well as their desperate fight to fit in. Their relatively limited choices and the hardship posed by their double minority status—race and homosexuality—can literally come down to choosing the path that seems safest and the least problematic. It is not surprising that concealment of sexual identity is the path taken by many black LGBTs who opt for a sanctuary where their homosexuality is less likely to be at issue. Then there are those who chose to live openly LGBT, and who get an early start in preparing themselves for the repercussions associated with such a bold and rare decision. It is true that this could describe LGBTs from every race and ethnicity. However, blacks and Hispanics who choose to live openly as homosexuals, or gay men who exhibit unrestrained effeminate tendencies, run an almost certain risk of being singled out by an unsympathetic minority culture in which the proclivity to treat them harshly is deeply engrained. The possibility of this occurring is dramatically increased when provoked by religious leaders who say little to dissuade the maltreatment of LGBTs.

In black culture, where heterosexuals are encouraged to show no mercy, to verbally abuse, and to treat homosexuals as miscreants, some black ministers egg on this behavior by preaching against homosexuality and demonizing LGBTs by implying that they are an insult to God. Religious extremists like Bishop Eddie Long, whose notorious damnation of homosexuals incites hostility toward members of the black LGBT community, are common in the Black Church. Unfortunately, this is the stuff of everyday life in black inner-city neighborhoods, where a young black boy who is unable to conceal his effeminate demeanor becomes the target of vicious scorn from schoolmates and contemporaries who for inexplicable reasons treat the youngster heartlessly.

Frankly, there isn't much that a young black LGBT can do when subjected to adverse treatment by the black community. Since there is no way to really prepare for the wrath and unfathomable onslaught of mocking that being a black gay person can bring, the odds of being victimized are quite high. Typically, young black LGBTs are cornered by the realities of their sexual identity, as well as their social and economic predicaments. It is rare that these young people can pick up and move to another community where perceptions are less severe. Therefore, by the time they have reached adolescence, they've already experienced severe lambasting from most segments of black culture. By then, there is a high probability that they will view their persecution as inescapable. In spite of this, some hope and believe that instead of castigating black homosexuals, eventually the black community and church will join their struggle for fairness and support their fight for equality.

They base their hope on the premise that striving for LGBT parity is no different from the renowned struggle for equal rights waged during the 1960s. However, the hitch is that younger black LGBTs not born during the civil rights era don't identify with the racial inequalities that existed over a half century ago. For many of them, Jim Crow, lynching, and the hard-fought battle by blacks to attain the civil liberties enjoyed today is what appears in history books. Now synonymous to folklore, the glue that once held the black community together is fast becoming a relic of the past. In yet another perplexing irony exclusive to the black ethos are millennials, generation X and Y gay activists who are working to achieve fairness for black LGBTs, yet who are caught up in a dispute with older black LGBTs who oppose the methods used to achieve parity. These sensitivities are heightened when black LGBTs compare their fight for equality to the revered civil rights struggle or flagrantly exhibit effeminate tendencies.

Moreover, there are crucial issues that the black LGBT community must effectively deal with if it is to achieve fairness. For one, equality will not come until black religious leaders lessen their resistance to homosexuality. For this to happen, it could very well come down to black LGBTs speaking out forcefully about the risky sexual practices of black gay and bisexual men whose promiscuity, unprotected sex, and life on the DL are a major cause of the negative perception held by the black community and church. This could be achieved in part by using the momentum gained by celebrities like CNN anchor Don Lemon, whose coming out offered an opportunity for others in the black LGBT community to discuss the legitimate fears of black heterosexuals. Also topping the list of things to overcome is the notion, which is now substantiated by scientific fact, that black homosexual behavior is responsible for the growth of HIV/AIDS, which is wreaking havoc and decimating black communities and families. While this direct association does not justify the mistreatment and ostracizing of black LGBTs, there is no denying that HIV/AIDS is frequently cited as one of the reasons that black LGBTs are widely rejected in black culture. The belief that they are spreading the deadly illness is supported by data from the CDC, which estimates that by 2015, nationwide, people 50 and older will make up more than half of those infected with HIV/AIDS. The CDC statistic suggests that older black LGBTs are not following the advice of the CDC related to safe sex and intravenous drug use, and that younger black LGBTs are also not likely to do so. In cities like Chicago, these statistics give weight to the alarming numbers related to the CDC's 2015 estimates and are used by antigay activists to make their point. For example, a survey conducted by the Chicago Department of Health showed that "... Nearly 70 percent of men and 58 percent of women living with HIV infection are older than 40, and almost a third are older than 50."[14] Some are exposed to the disease via intravenous drug use. Others acquire HIV/AIDS through unsafe sexual practices. Data like these help substantiate the case being made by antigay hardliners, among them black ministers, who say that the very idea of homosexuality and the LGBT "lifestyle" or "orientation" is wrong and destructive. It is also extremely effective in compelling the black community's disapproval of homosexuality and fortifies opposition against equality for homosexuals and the legalization of same-sex unions.

As a black minister and attorney, Juan Thomas has a unique viewpoint regarding the black experience and religious perspective as it relates to the acceptance of homosexuality. Thomas believes that the word of God should comfort the convicted and convict the comfortable. He feels that the Black Church ought to be a comfortable place to have uncomfortable conversations about the issue of homosexuality and how the Black Church has dealt with it. Thomas asserted his feelings regarding the issue of homosexuality, saying,

Sadly, most of our Black Churches are not able to create a space where gay and straight brothers and sisters can have an authentic and mutually respectful interchange. When I pastored a small church in the United Church of Christ, which is one of the most progressive and liberal Christian dominations, I soon discovered that the overwhelming majority of African-American churches are not "Open and Affirming," by that I mean to accepting homosexual relationships. In fact, one of my female parishioners asked me if I would approve of her "dating" another woman in the church and then asked me to keep it quiet for fear of retribution from her church family. Too many Black clergy quote the familiar Old Testament scriptures when condemning homosexuality, while conveniently ignoring the real life impact that it has on members of their congregations. The Minister of Music is gay, but we don't talk about it; the deacon's son was gay and died due to complications of HIV/AIDS but we don't talk about it; the youth pastor is gay, but is advised by the elders of the church if he ever wants to be a Senior Pastor, he needs to marry a woman; the Senior Pastor lives a double lifestyle, but we pretend not to know about it. These anecdotes are not fiction, but authentic examples that I personally witnessed during my time as minister of a Black Church, and sadly they are not isolated examples.

I once heard a colleague in the ministry state that her passion was to have Christians live and be their authentic selves. We are called to worship in "spirit and in truth." So, perhaps we ought to live our lives in spirit and in truth. The Black Church and Black community at-large continues to condemn homosexuality with narrow and traditional theological precepts. It is as if, they do not want to, or simply refuse to acknowledge the biological, psychological, and sociological realities of a lifestyle that we were told was sinful by the Black Church. As a result, some Black ministers have great difficulty engaging in an open and honest interchange with its parishioners about how homosexuality affects the black community. In fact, the Black Church demonstrates a profound inability when dealing with most LGBT issues.

In the bible, John shares a conversation between Jesus and a man named Nicodemus, where he asks Jesus, how can a person be born again? As believers of Jesus Christ who embrace the teachings of Jesus, we should remember Jesus' response to Nicodemus that night: *"That God so loved the World that he gave is only begotten son that whosoever believes in him should not perish, but have everlasting life."* We are called to remind our brothers and sisters that *whosoever* is inclusive and doesn't exclude anyone based upon their race, gender, or sexual preference. Let us, therefore, create a comfortable space.[15]

The wise and insightful observations of Thomas are indicative of what black LGBTs see as a monumental issue in dealing with their sexual identity and inability to obtain respect and fairness from the Black Church and community. Here Corey Highsmith, a 30-something openly gay black gay man, gives an account of the challenges and horrific treatment that he experienced when growing up as a black homosexual in Arkansas. Taunted and vilified by friends, members of his congregation, and even relatives, Highsmith's understanding of the issue offers rare insight into the angst and trepidation that black homosexuals must contend with while trying to traverse the long and treacherous circumstances related to being black and gay. Highsmith's courageous decision to live as an openly gay black man is an inspiration to young black LGBTs who are considering coming out. In his very personal point of view, Highsmith conveys his experience growing up as a young black gay in the Black Church. Highsmith's perspective is one that many black LGBTs will relate to.

It literally sent chills down my spine when as a little boy I'd hear the phrase while sitting in church that, "God made Adam and Eve, not Adam and Steve." I would think to myself, is the pastor really going there again? I'd hold my head down sensing that people were looking at me as the preacher railed on from the pulpit. Yes, I was just a child, but his words made me want to crawl beneath the pew and weep. Yet, even as a young boy a power was working within me to help me through it all. Sometimes, I'd rationalize the situation by simply remembering that God had made all of us, and other times, I'd find humor in what had been an intentional attempt to disparage people like me.

On those occasions when the preacher would shout, proselytizing his interpretation of a particular biblical versus related to homosexuality for example, "If you lay down in the bed with another man, you are going straight to hell." Or reference something to entice churchgoers to go along like, "God made a man to be with a woman," I'd think to myself how can this man, or anyone tell me that I am going to hell for being the person that I am? Truth is that deep down, I was toiling with the acceptance my sexuality. But, throughout my personal struggle, I always knew that only God had power over me. However, as a defenseless child the scornful preaching was hurtful, and I'd pray to God asking, that he please take away the gay.

It seemed that I had known the pain of being called a sissy for as long as I could remember. Sissy, was a crushing word and maybe the first word, that as a child, I somehow knew was intended to single me out and to rebuke me. The mocking would escalate and soon words like punk, little girl and fag, would bring similar sadness. Yet the sting of it was devastating when it came from friends and family. As I got older, I imagined the things that my mother must have heard, the things that people said about me being a sissy, a punk or gay, or as some put it, "having sugar in my tank." I knew that it was difficult for her to bear and her silence not mentioning it was, I believe, her way of coping and doing all she could to insulate me from what she must have known was tearing her fragile child apart. Still, and even now, I am not sure if my mother realized the magnitude of what I had to deal with day-to-day. For example, in school, on the playground and in church my childhood was one of torment and humiliation. Inevitable, maybe, but eventually my anger turned toward God, as I began ask, why despite my prayers to be like the other boys, God had forsaken me? My young mind rationalized that since it was the one thing that I had consistently prayed for, that God had abandoned me. Ironically, my bitterness evolved because I so believed in God.

For a long time I have been sadden by the acts of mainly Christians, some members of the black community who say that LGBTs have a choice in their sexuality. I realize that this idea is mostly rooted in a cultural hatred toward homosexuality that has been passed down from generation to generation. However, the truth is that the only real choice that exists is to see this for the nonsense that it is, and to reject the illogical aversion toward LGBTs that is commonplace in black culture. First of all, it is a preposterous notion that a heterosexual would claim to know what it feels like to be gay. Frankly, I am blown away by opinionated heterosexuals, who put their two cent in, but have no idea what it is like to have to defend or conceal their sexuality. However, if given the chance I'd ask them if homosexuals had a choice, why in the world would they choose to be gay and to suffer mistreatment, or to endure, the pain and scorn for a lifetime? Who in their right mind would prefer ridicule and rejection over a normal existence? But, since I already know that they have no idea of what it is like to have friends, church members and relatives who shun and treat you like a leper, it would be almost certainly a complete waste of my time to pose the question.

Yet, for me the real irony is that very person that molested me when I was a child was a black guy who was a couple of years older than me. It started when I was about seven years old. He'd say things like, "I'll whoop a faggot's ass if he tries to hit on me." However, the very first opportunity he had to make a move on me he did, making me do things that I didn't want to do. It has been my experience that the most homophobic black men are the ones that an openly gay black man must be most concerned about. They so very often epitomize the "Down Low Brother," and typically demonstrate hostility toward gays because they themselves desire other men. This is most likely their way of dealing with their own insecurities, a deflection of their true sexuality occurs when they bash others in order to feel better about themselves. The truth is that they are at war with themselves, fighting desperately not to face the reality of their homosexuality.

A friend who happens to be white and heterosexual expressed gratitude for my friendship saying that I was his first black friend and that our friendship had changed his life. I rejoiced in the fact that my sexuality had never been an issue and saw his open mindedness as refreshing, and so unlike that of some blacks who had not given me a fair chance. For me, it spoke volumes about black culture and how blacks have cast aside the fundamental lesson of the civil-rights movement, which is to judge others by the "content of their character." How regrettable it is that the yearning and long struggle of black folks to attain equality has taken on a pragmatic event and forgotten by many.

I know that some blacks refuse to even discuss the issue of homosexuality, and if they do, they mostly harp on the biases, criticizing LGBTs based on what has been passed down through past generations. Most, give barely a thought to how their actions might contribute to deteriorating a gay child's self-esteem, or the power of their harsh and biting words do to drive a young person into seclusion. Young black LGBTs who are engaged in a fight for equality don't discount that the majority of blacks believe when they stand against homosexuality and same-sex marriage that it is a righteous stance and a cultural necessity. Yet, this way of thinking makes it exceedingly hard for young black LGBTs who are trying to deal with their sexuality to find hope that eventually things will change and that retribution by members of their own race will end.

Increasingly tired of being judged, mistreated and used as scapegoats by black ministers, these young black LGBTs are leaving the traditional Black church in droves. This is happening because they are not finding the love, guidance, fellowship and sanctuary that they desperately need. I remember, in my late teens, at home one summer from college and attending the Baptist church that I had belonged to as a child being an unbearable experience. However, when I began attending a predominately white church the experience and acceptance by the congregation was totally different. It was nothing like the church of my childhood where when an associate pastor had confided in the church Pastor regarding his personal struggle with being gay and having feelings for men. Before long, the details of his confidential discussion were known to many members of the congregation and talked about among rumormongering churchgoers who whispered about the personal struggles of the young associate pastor. I was incensed by it and remember feeling a sense of personal betrayal and pondering what the larger implications of not being able to confide in your minister were. What I ultimately concluded was that for members of the black LGBTs community that as tremendously important as it may seem, the interim solution may be to find a place of worship where exposure to negativity that so many black congregations are predisposed as a consequence of their upbringing is minimized. In my case, it is a predominantly white church, and of course, I regret that it is not a traditional Black church. Oh, but how I appreciate being a part of a healthier and spiritually rich experience.[16]

Highsmith's experiences growing up gay and the torment he suffered in a traditional Black Church, while disgraceful, are commonplace. Indications that the sway of the Black Church and its stance against homosexuality have spread to other traditionally black institutions was evidenced in 2011 when Robert Champion, a 26-year-old Florida A&M University student and drum major who was said to be gay, was severely hazed and beaten to death.[17]

Salimah Turner is a social worker and volunteer for Youth Outlook, an organization that does outreach to help young LGBTs who live in the suburbs of Chicago. On the front line for a number of years, Turner has considerable experience in counseling LGBT youth and shepherding them through the difficulties associated with their sexuality and coming out. She is also intensely aware of issues that are unique to young black LGBTs. Turner recognizes the stark and sometimes subtle acts of discrimination that black LGBTs must deal with, versus those of other ethnic groups. As an African American, Turner also relates to the limited options available to an overwhelming majority of black LGBT youth and the consequences that seem to follow when their sexual identity is revealed. Turner's insight is helpful to LGBTs trying to navigate the obstacles and prejudices that prevent the black community from budging on matters related to homosexuality. She also understands the potential problems facing young black LGBTs who desperately want to find their place in black culture.

For example, when black LGBT youth who are frequently psychologically maimed by their treatment seek guidance or are faced with the effect that their coming out brings, they routinely present with a piling on of other social problems. They are often dealing with a myriad of issues like educational and health disparities as well as growing up poor and in an environment plagued by violence. Very often, topping the list of hindrances that must be addressed prior to tackling issues related to sexual identity and coming out is the matter of their survival. For black LGBTs, it is crucial that they are prepared for the intolerant homophobic black culture that awaits them. It is a peculiar mix of homophobia, classism, and intraracism that has the potential to, and often does, bring about a dreadful outcome. One regrettable result is seen in the CDC's statistics that reflect a rapidly increasing rate of HIV/AIDS infections among black LGBTs, which is significantly higher than that of any other ethnic group. Another corollary is the mounting occurrence of suicide and homelessness among black LGBT youth, which is greater than in the general population and rising exponentially for LGBT youth of color.

Turner shares what she believes are the reasons that it is more difficult for black LGBT youth to come out, explaining that "There is more difficulty associated with black LGBT youth coming out given the negative stigma associated with identifying as LGBT. These young people having witnessed throughout their young lives the visceral response toward homosexuality in the black community very often see themselves as having no way out. They seem to instinctively understand that within black culture the worst thing that one can be is gay."[18] Turner's candid assessment of the severe circumstances confronting black LGBTs, and all young people who identify as LGBT, is supported by groups like the Gay, Lesbian and Straight Education Network (GLSEN), which backs efforts like the National Day of Silence, a day in which students nationwide take a vow of silence to bring attention to anti-LGBT name-calling, bullying, and harassment in their schools. The annual effort helps bring attention to the problem and fight against antigay verbal assault and bullying.

Black LGBTs struggle with coming out because they realize that doing so will intensify their already tumultuous relationships and more often choose to conceal their sexual identity. Some see sexual anonymity as less problematic, that is, and a way to avoid the complications that coming out presents. For example, concealment offers some an escape from the epidemic of mistreatment plaguing the U.S. school systems. Media coverage, like CNN's 2011 special report "Bullying: It Stops Here," goes a long way to help increase awareness of the issue that has led to a crisis in U.S. schools and that continues to have an incredibly negative effect on young

LGBTs. In some cases, the aftermath has been tragic, with young LGBTs taking their lives when they are unable to cope with the vicious verbal and physical abuse. For black LGBTs, the intimidation and resulting anguish can seem impossible to escape and is amplified in places where one would not expect to find hostility. It occurs in places nearly impossible to avoid like, school, home, and even church, where escape from the spiteful contempt seems a reasonable expectation. The reality is that perpetuation of the aggression toward black LGBT is encouraged by the entire community.

Unfortunately, it is also a fact that efforts to stop antigay behavior in the black community have had a minimal effect, especially in aiding young black boys who exhibit effeminate mannerisms. These youngsters are susceptible to relentless ridicule and are made to suffer at the hands of practically every sector of their communities. It is a scenario that can have catastrophic results, as was seen in the heartbreaking case of one youngster, Carl Joseph Walker Hoover. The 11-year-old boy hung himself with an extension cord in 2009 after being taunted by schoolmates. Walker's mother said that her son's tormentors were worse than the breast cancer that she had survived.[19] According to Dan Olweus of the National School Safety Center, "American schools harbor approximately 2.1 million bullies and 2.7 million of their victims."[20] Harassment of LGBT students occurs about 26 times a day, or once every 14 minutes.[21]

While there is a heightened awareness of LGBTs issues and more resources are available as compared to previous years, still efforts to educate has not eradicated, or produced a significant change in, the deep-seated loathing that exists toward homosexuals within the black community. In fact, the problems of black LGBTs are increased twofold because of the enduring belief that they must choose between their racial and sexual identity. Some black LGBTs believe that it is, if not easier, then certainly more practical to embrace their ethnicity and keep their sexuality concealed. For gay and bisexual black males, who often feel inordinate pressure to be "manly-men," this appears to be particularly true and in keeping with ethnic standards of what a black man must be. They realize that choosing to deviate from traditional black norms will almost certainly result in being seen in the eyes of the black community as less than a man. As for black lesbians and transgenders, they are likely to encounter the triple threat of racism, sexism, and a homophobic black community.

In black culture, the condemnatory acts against black LGBTs that start at an exceptionally young age and are reinforced throughout adolescence are glimpsed in the hardship suffered by people like Highsmith. When black ministers disparage homosexuals, believing it is their obligation to tell black Christian LGBTs that they are sinners in the eyes of God and bound for hell for not following traditional sexual customs, they are adding to the problem. Black religious leaders who mock homosexuals—telling their congregations that LGBTs are the root of the black community's problems and are accelerating the deterioration of the black family structure—are increasing the divide between black LGBTs and black heterosexuals. Their divisive tactics warp the perception of black LGBTs in the minds of churchgoers and contribute to the continuation of ignorance and bias in the black community.

According to Turner and other LGBT advocates, when black clergy use a stringent interpretation of biblical reference to homosexuality, it can be tremendously harmful to young black LGBTs. Their radical theological fixations expand homophobic attitudes and contribute enormously to the disillusionment of black LGBTs by creating yet another obstacle in their effort to adjust in society. Considering this, it's no surprise that many feel dejected, despondent, and even believe that they have no one to turn to. However, advocates like Turner hasten to add that these homophobic black ministers do not represent the stance of all black clergy. According to Turner, fanatical homophobic black ministers should not be seen as epitomizing the entire Black Church. Turner points out that some black churches welcome openly gay parishioners and affirm the acceptance of all persons regardless of sexual identity. One example is Chicago's Trinity United Church of Christ, where Reverend Jeremiah Wright, former pastor to President Barack Obama, serves as pastor emeritus. Trinity is one of the few black megachurches with a gay-friendly ministry. Trinity stands out when homophobic attitudes are so deeply rooted in the black religious experience and the Black Church has woefully failed to meet the spiritual needs of black LGBTs.

The fact that it is not unusual to hear ministers from traditional black churches condemning same-sex partnerships from their pulpits speaks volumes about the progress made so far. The routinely cited biblical scripture and warnings that those who identify as LGBT are an "abomination" and will burn in hell for their "lifestyles" is a clear indication of the lack of progress made by the Black Church to deal with the issue. Given the awesome power of the Black Church and the role that it plays in black culture, such proclamations—especially in the eyes of impressionable young black LGBTs—are without a doubt psychologically damaging. In their pliable young minds, the church becomes an extension of the larger community in which they are already subjected to rejection and scorn. Ultimately, some view the church as a hostile environment that encourages fear and acts of reprisal. If these young people dare to reveal their sexual identity, the punishment will be more direct. Those who have endured the contemptuous and damning assertions coming from the mouths of their own pastors and who are already predisposed to depression are also prone to becoming more conflicted about their sexuality. Some constantly worry about how they will be viewed by fellow church-goers, peers, and members of their communities. Because they are LGBT, nearly every aspect of their lives is affected and complicated by the decision of whether to come out. Further muddling the matter is the reality of being cast off by friends and family, and degraded by their spiritual leader.

Already saddled with tremendous pressure, some of these young people must face the definitive insult—rejection by their families. As it would be for any other homosexual, familial relationships are essential for young black LGBTs. Families are looked to for acceptance, support, nurturing, and love. They are also where young LGBTs will ultimately learn to deal with a society in which hate and discrimination will be their reality. However, when the rejection comes from the family, the young black LGBT is at a significant disadvantage. There is the real potential that it will adversely impact their self-perception and ability to assimilate. Furthermore, it walls them off from the public, leaving some to anticipate obstacles and insults, real and imagined, and in time, causing them to insulate themselves from the threat of emotional pain. Before long, this can have an insidious domino effect on their relationships. These are some of the things that prompt black LGBT youth to conclude that coming out is not in their best interest. The fear of damaging the few relationships that they have managed to cultivate is far too risky.

However, this by no means suggests that all African American LGBT youth fear rejection and endure negative responses from family members —there are those who, despite the black community's bias, are encouraged to be themselves and are able to thrive with the phenomenal support of family, friends, community, and church. Yet in the overwhelming majority of cases, an opposite situation exists, one that is so diametrically opposed that even a discussion related to homosexuality is considered taboo and entirely off limits, unless its purpose is to demean members of the LGBT community.

In African American families where LGBTs are barely tolerated and frequently made to feel different, some family members will go so far as to refuse to acknowledge the sexual identity of their gay relative, even when the person has publicly come out. Sometimes, LGBTs are excluded from family events and decision making, and are generally treated unfairly. It is this kind of behavior that continues to produce unhealthy relationships and tear families apart. Given the difficulty of finding a way through these complex relationships and the host of issues they breed, it should not come as a shock that black LGBT youth are confused and resistant to disclosing their sexual identity. Considering what they have witnessed, their pragmatic reaction and rationale is logical, especially considering the pros and cons of what disclosure of their homosexuality could mean. In explaining the rationality of their decision, they may, for example, reason that they have little to gain by coming out. For example, they realize that bringing gay friends or a partner to family functions or broaching the subject of homosexuality is entirely off limits.

Soundly among the middle class, blacks and Hispanics reside in great numbers in suburban America. They also represent a significant portion of the expanding impoverished suburban population. Of course, among them are LGBT minorities who are challenged by their surroundings and the struggle to fit in on several fronts that are complicated by race. What makes the suburban minority LGBT's experience different from that of minority LGBT youth residing in inner cities is that racial and sexual identity biases are likely to occur simultaneously in the suburbs. Furthermore, black LGBTs who reside in suburban communities, in addition to dealing with the day-to-day problems related to race, are sometimes rejected by white suburban LGBTs. Black LGBTs who attend suburban schools, while more likely than they would have been in the past to encounter heterosexual blacks, are not normally accepted by them. Add to that the absence of traditional black institutions in suburbia and incidents of discrimination toward LGBT youth of color, and the complexity of their predicament is apparent.

Another example of the intricacy of black homosexuality can be seen in the performance of a black gay man playing a straight character. The late African American actor and Academy Award nominee Howard Rollins, Jr., star of stage and screen, is said to have been gay and died of AIDS-related lymphoma. Still, Rollins played very macho characters in movies, including *Ragtime* and *A Soldier's Story* as well as the television series *In the Heat of the Night*, all without any obvious conflict.[22] However, the issue of acceptance goes only so far and is subject to drastic change when black masculinity is blatantly threatened. Anything that directly contradicts the perception of masochism and the might of the black male, such as a black male ballet performer, or someone like the multitalented RuPaul, would almost certainly be viewed by the black community as unacceptable.

Taking the importance of masculinity in black culture a step further, what would the response be if a traditional black ethnic play were cast without regard to color? For example, if Edwin DuBose Heyward's *Porgy and Bess* were performed by a talented all-white cast. My guess is that it would probably garner a fair amount of media attention, but I doubt that the performance would provoke racial discord. On the other hand, if a production of Charles Fuller's Pulitzer Prize–winning production *A Soldiers' Play*, which depicts black men in very powerful and masculine roles, were cast with an all-black openly gay cast, chances are good that it would be viewed as extremely provocative and would almost certainly rouse a robust outcry from the black community. Fortunately, the race of performers generally does not affect the audience's appreciation of the performance. However, whenever LGBTs of any race go along with stereotypical portrayals, they are helping to perpetuate a stereotype that feeds biases and adversity.

Keyon Gaskin is a black performance artist who believes that human beings categorize their past experiences to define the world in which they live, and that this aspect of human behavior is necessary and essential to survival. Gaskin says that what is most regrettable is that those past experiences are also used to hinder the human connection. Gaskin, who is a professional dancer, believes that he is frequently perceived as homosexual and has seen how deterrents based on past experience affect homosexuals of every race and in a variety of ways. Still, he prefers to focus on how his race and perceived sexual orientation affect the way his art, and primarily his solo performances, are received by audiences.

Gaskin illuminates the issue, saying:

For example a person's character is an amalgamation of their whole experience, mind, biology and physical attributes. Yet some physical attributes, due to their association with certain societal and historical factors, hold more weight within our society when it comes to determining the content of one's character. As a person of color, being judged based on your race is an unavoidable and consistent occurrence. In my experience and from my knowledge of historical perspectives, black men are one of the most scrutinized and devalued demographics on the planet. People are constantly making assumptions regarding my intent, both in my personal life and performance and mostly based on my ethnicity and gender. I've noticed a similar occurrence with regard to what some perceive is my sexual orientation. Though the reactions to my supposed sexuality are not nearly as frequent or overt as to my race, it is another factor that comes into play when people are attempting to define my character, or analyze my work. In feedback that I've received, it seems that people's perceptions of me as a black gay man, wholly impacts the way they perceive my work.[23]

As a contemporary movement artist, Gaskin deals with universal themes that do not adhere to strict narrative. As a result, he is afforded creative freedom, which allows the audience to construct, or imagine, what they will. Gaskin talks about this saying:

My general hope is to affect people emotionally and cerebrally. However there are occasions when this hope is thwarted because of the viewer's predisposed perception of my race or sexual orientation. I have been told that sometimes people feel sympathy rather than empathy for my characters. It was a friend and supporter of my work who said, "How hard it must be being black and gay in America." The piece she was referring to, addressed the oppressive nature of power structures and effort was intended to comment on the impact of tyrannical forces on all of humanity, not just black gay men.[24]

Gaskin's referral to tyrannical forces appears to cast a wide net. What is known is that again and again, black LGBTs name the Black Church as an unyielding power that often gets in the way of equality for homosexuals. Still, Gaskin is not offended by ideas that are gleaned from his work. Gaskin believes that race and perceived sexual orientation are factors that impact his creative process, but he does not suggest that his plight is any more arduous than the plights of other artists who are bound by their identity, demographics, and circumstance. However, Gaskin does believe that as a performer, public opinion of black men and homosexuality requires a particularly unique struggle when it comes to relating to audiences. Summing it up, Gaskin says, "People are multi-dimensional beings and it is a travesty that anyone should be primarily defined and judged by a singular facet of their being."[25]

What's clear is that black clergy and civic leaders who continue to oppose the comparisons made by LGBTs in their fight for equality to that of the civil rights movement are conveniently omitting the contributions of people like the late Bayard Rustin, an openly gay civil rights leader who worked closely with Dr. Martin Luther King, Jr. Because of his effeminate traits, Rustin's impact on the civil rights movement is almost entirely absent from the storied history of the civil rights struggle. Sadly, Rustin's omission is acceptable to the black community due to its rejection of homosexuality and the prominent role that the Black Church played at the height of the civil rights era.

The ongoing tradition of gay bashing and rebuke of homosexuality continues in the Black Church and every facet of black culture. Several months after CNN anchor Don Lemon's heroic coming out, and on the heels of the momentum it reaped for the black LGBT community, Lemon's colleague, black political commentator Roland Martin, was suspended by CNN. Martin's suspension was related to tweeting statements that were characterized by CNN as "regrettable and offensive."[26]

Martin issued a statement, saying, "Based on several tweets I made on my Twitter feed on Super Bowl Sunday yesterday, I have been accused by members of the LGBT community of being supportive of violence against gays and lesbians and bullying. That is furthest from the truth, and I sincerely regret any offense my words have caused."[27] However, innocuous comments may seem and in some cases, not intended to ridicule, they help to increase tension between the black LGBT and heterosexual communities.

As far as the battle being waged over same-sex marriage goes, advocates and antagonists saw another dramatic twist when a federal appeals court overturned California's Proposition 8. The court's February 7, 2012, decision declared the 2008 ban on same-sex marriage unconstitutional. In the 2–1 ruling, the U.S. Ninth Circuit Court of Appeals suggested that California's prohibition on same-sex marriage served no purpose other than to "lessen the status and human dignity of gays and lesbians."[28]

Reaction to the court's decision by social conservatives and the Religious Right was swift as they vowed to protect DOMA, signaling that the fight over same-sex wedlock is far from over. Yet even as Washington joined the six states and the District of Columbia that already recognized same-sex marriage, intolerance and bias suffered by black LGBTs is certain to continue.

In 2012, a day after North Carolina voted to ban same-sex marriage, President Barack Obama completed his long evolution on the issue and made history, becoming the first sitting U.S. president to support same-sex marriage. Still, many religious African Americans, Latinos, and older voters remain steadfast in their opposition to same-sex marriage. In 2012, according to the Human Rights Campaign, there were 30 states with constitutional amendments or statutes banning same-sex marriage.[29]

Ultimately, the issue of same-sex marriage seems headed for the nation's highest court. As 2012 drew to a close, the U.S. Supreme Court announced that it would take up the matter of *Hollingsworth vs. Perry*, a case that could decide the issue of same-sex marriage once and for all. Sadly, this momentous announcement offers little hope to black LGBTs who know that in black culture, the Black Church reigns supreme.

NOTES

1. Corinthians 6:9–10 (NIV).

2. Steve Benen, "Republican debate audience boos U.S. soldier," *WashingtonMonthly.com*, September 23, 2011, http://www.washington monthly.com/political-animal/2011_09/republican_debate_audience_boo 032384.php.

3. Sam Stein, "Rick Santorum: DADT repeal has been 'detrimental' for gay soldiers," *HuffingtonPost.com*, September 23, 2011, http://www .huffingtonpost.com/2011/09/23/santorum-dadt-repeal-detrimental_n_977 715.html.

4. Suicide Prevention Resource Center, *Suicide Risk and Prevention for Lesbian, Gay, Bisexual, and Transgender Youth* (Newton, MA: Education Development Center, Inc., 2008).

5. Michael Muskal, "GOProud, a gay-rights group, condemns Santorum's debate comments," *LATimes.com*, September 23, 2011, http://articles.latimes.com/2011/sep/23/news/la-pn-rick-santorum-dadt -debate20110923.

6. Fran Spielman, February 1, 2009, *Chicago Sun-Times*.

7. Mallory Simon, "Chicago may get 'gay-friendly' high school," *CNN.com*, October 13, 2008, http://articles.cnn.com/2008-10-13/us/gay .friendly.school_1_gay-and-lesbian-students-transgender-students-sexual -orientation?_s=PM:USa.

8. Associated Press, "Plan for gay-friendly high school in Chicago halted," *FoxNews.com*, November 19, 2008, www.foxnews.com/story/ 0,2933,454507,00.html.

9. John Colapinto, "The Harvey Milk School has no right to exist: Discuss," *NYMag.com*, May 21, 2005, http://nymag.com/nymetro/news/ features/10970/.

10. "Bullycide," *Dictionary.com*, http://dictionary.reference.com/ browse/bullycide.

11. John Cloud, "Prosecuting the gay teen murder," *Time.com*, February 18, 2008, http://www.time.com/time/nation/article/0,8599,171421 4,00.html.

12. Cynthia Dizikes, *Chicago Tribune*, December 23, 2011.

13. www.nbjc.org/news/marriage_report.pdf+nbjc.org/news/ marriage&cd=1&hl=en&ct=clnk&gl=us. Accessed February 10, 2012,

14. Andrea K. Walker, *Chicago Tribune*, October 14, 2011.

15. Juan Thomas, interview with author, December 22, 2011.

16. Cory Highsmith, interview with author, November 17, 2011.

17. Denise Marie Balona, *Chicago Tribune*, January 11, 2012.

18. Salimah Turner, interview with author, November 18, 2011.

19. ABC News, "Carl Joseph Walker-Hoover commits suicide over anti-gay taunts," *HuffingtonPost.com*, May 15, 2009, http://www .huffingtonpost.com/2009/04/14/carl-joseph-walker-hoover_n_186911.html.

20. http://www.makebeatsnotbeatdowns.org/facts_new.html.

21. http://www.nmha.org/index.cfm?objectid=CA866DCF-1372-4D20 -C8EB26EEB30B9982.

22. "Howard Rollins," *FamousWhy.com*, http://people.famouswhy .com/howard_rollins/.

23. Keyon Gaskin, interview with author, January 11, 2012.

24. Interview with Keyon Gaskin.

25. Interview with Keyon Gaskin.

26. Dylan Stableford, "CNN suspends Roland Martin over 'offensive' Super Bowl tweets," *Yahoo.com*, February 8, 2012, http://news.yahoo .com/blogs/cutline/cnn-suspends-roland-martin-over-offensive-super-bowl -195422269.html. Accessed February 8, 2012.

27. http://www.dfw.com/2012/02/08/573552/cnn-suspends-roland -martin-over.html. Accessed December 4, 2012.

28. Maura Dolan and Carol J. Williams, *Chicago Tribune*, February 8, 2012.

29. K. Hennessy, *Chicago Tribune*, May 10, 2012.

APPENDIXES

Presidential Documents

Appendix 1: Executive Order 13198 of January 29, 2001

AGENCY RESPONSIBILITIES WITH RESPECT TO FAITH-BASED AND COMMUNITY INITIATIVES

By the authority vested in me as President by the Constitution and the laws of the United States of America, and in order to help the Federal Government coordinate a national effort to expand opportunities for faith-based and other community organizations and to strengthen their capacity to better meet social needs in America's communities, it is hereby ordered as follows:

Section 1. *Establishment of Executive Department Centers for Faith-Based and Community Initiatives.* (a) The Attorney General, the Secretary of Education, the Secretary of Labor, the Secretary of Health and Human Services, and the Secretary of Housing and Urban Development shall each establish within their respective departments a Center for Faith-Based and Community Initiatives (Center).

(b) Each executive department Center shall be supervised by a Director, appointed by the department head in consultation with the White House Office of Faith-Based and Community Initiatives (White House OFBCI).

(c) Each department shall provide its Center with appropriate staff, administrative support, and other resources to meet its responsibilities under this order.

(d) Each department's Center shall begin operations no later than 45 days from the date of this order.

Sec. 2. *Purpose of Executive Department Centers for Faith-Based and Community Initiatives.* The purpose of the executive department Centers will be to coordinate department efforts to eliminate regulatory, contracting, and other programmatic obstacles to the participation of faith-based and other community organizations in the provision of social services.

Sec. 3. *Responsibilities of Executive Department Centers for Faith-Based and Community Initiatives.* Each Center shall, to the extent permitted by law: (a) conduct, in coordination with the White House OFBCI, a department-wide audit to identify all existing barriers to the participation of faith-based and other community organizations in the delivery of social services by the department, including but not limited to regulations, rules, orders, procurement, and other internal policies and practices, and outreach activities that either facially discriminate against or otherwise discourage or disadvantage the participation of faith-based and other community organizations in Federal programs;

(b) coordinate a comprehensive departmental effort to incorporate faith-based and other community organizations in department programs and initiatives to the greatest extent possible;

(c) propose initiatives to remove barriers identified pursuant to section 3(a) of this order, including but not limited to reform of regulations, procurement, and other internal policies and practices, and outreach activities;

(d) propose the development of innovative pilot and demonstration programs to increase the participation of faith-based and other community organizations in Federal as well as State and local initiatives; and

(e) develop and coordinate department outreach efforts to disseminate information more effectively to faith-based and other community organizations with respect to programming changes, contracting opportunities, and other department initiatives, including but not limited to Web and Internet resources.

Sec. 4. *Additional Responsibilities of the Department of Health and Human Services and the Department of Labor Centers.* In addition to those responsibilities described in section 3 of this order, the Department of Health and Human Services and the Department of Labor Centers shall, to the extent permitted by law: (a) conduct a comprehensive review of policies and practices affecting existing funding streams governed by so-called "Charitable Choice" legislation to assess the department's compliance with the requirements of Charitable Choice; and (b) promote and ensure compliance with existing Charitable Choice legislation by the department, as well as its partners in State and local government, and their contractors.

Sec. 5. *Reporting Requirements.* (a) Report. Not later than 180 days after the date of this order and annually thereafter, each of the five executive department Centers described in section 1 of this order shall prepare and submit a report to the White House OFBCI.

(b) Contents. The report shall include a description of the department's efforts in carrying out its responsibilities under this order, including but not limited to:

   (1) a comprehensive analysis of the barriers to the full participation of faith-based and other community organizations in the delivery of social services identified pursuant to section 3(a) of this order and the proposed strategies to eliminate those barriers; and

   (2) a summary of the technical assistance and other information that will be available to faith-based and other community organizations regarding the program activities of the department and the preparation of applications or proposals for grants, cooperative agreements, contracts, and procurement.

(c) Performance Indicators. The first report, filed 180 days after the date of this order, shall include annual performance indicators and measurable objectives for department action. Each report filed thereafter shall measure the department's performance against the objectives set forth in the initial report.

Sec. 6. *Responsibilities of All Executive Departments and Agencies.* All executive departments and agencies (agencies) shall: (a) designate an agency employee to serve as the liaison and point of contact with the White House OFBCI; and

(b) cooperate with the White House OFBCI and provide such information, support, and assistance to the White House OFBCI as it may request, to the extent permitted by law.

Sec. 7. *Administration and Judicial Review.* (a) The agencies' actions directed by this Executive Order shall be carried out subject to the availability of appropriations and to the extent permitted by law.

(b) This order does not create any right or benefit, substantive or procedural, enforceable at law or equity against the United States, its agencies or instrumentalities, its officers or employees, or any other person.

THE WHITE HOUSE,
January 29, 2001.

Source: Federal Register 66:21 (January 31, 2001).

Appendix 2: Executive Order 13199 of January 29, 2001

ESTABLISHMENT OF WHITE HOUSE OFFICE OF FAITH-BASED AND COMMUNITY INITIATIVES

By the authority vested in me as President of the United States by the Constitution and the laws of the United States of America, and in order to help the Federal Government coordinate a national effort to expand opportunities for faith-based and other community organizations and to strengthen their capacity to better meet social needs in America's communities, it is hereby ordered as follows:

Section 1. *Policy.* Faith-based and other community organizations are indispensable in meeting the needs of poor Americans and distressed neighborhoods. Government cannot be replaced by such organizations, but it can and should welcome them as partners. The paramount goal is compassionate results, and private and charitable community groups, including religious ones, should have the fullest opportunity permitted by law to compete on a level playing field, so long as they achieve valid public purposes, such as curbing crime, conquering addiction, strengthening families and neighborhoods, and overcoming poverty. This delivery of social services must be results oriented and should value the bedrock principles of pluralism, nondiscrimination, evenhandedness, and neutrality.

Sec. 2. *Establishment.* There is established a White House Office of Faith-Based and Community Initiatives (White House OFBCI) within the Executive Office of the President that will have lead responsibility in the executive branch to establish policies, priorities, and objectives for the Federal Government's comprehensive effort to enlist, equip, enable, empower, and expand the work of faith-based and other community organizations to the extent permitted by law.

Sec. 3. *Functions.* The principal functions of the White House OFBCI are, to the extent permitted by law: (a) to develop, lead, and coordinate the Administration's policy agenda affecting faith-based and other community programs and initiatives, expand the role of such efforts in communities, and increase their capacity through executive action, legislation, Federal and private funding, and regulatory relief;

(b) to ensure that Administration and Federal Government policy decisions and programs are consistent with the President's stated goals with respect to faith-based and other community initiatives;

(c) to help integrate the President's policy agenda affecting faith-based and other community organizations across the Federal Government;

(d) to coordinate public education activities designed to mobilize public support for faith-based and community nonprofit initiatives through volunteerism, special projects, demonstration pilots, and public-private partnerships;

(e) to encourage private charitable giving to support faith-based and community initiatives;

(f) to bring concerns, ideas, and policy options to the President for assisting, strengthening, and replicating successful faith-based and other community programs;

(g) to provide policy and legal education to State, local, and community policymakers and public officials seeking ways to empower faith-based and other community organizations and to improve the opportunities, capacity, and expertise of such groups;

(h) to develop and implement strategic initiatives under the President's agenda to strengthen the institutions of civil society and America's families and communities;

(i) to showcase and herald innovative grassroots nonprofit organizations and civic initiatives;

(j) to eliminate unnecessary legislative, regulatory, and other bureaucratic barriers that impede effective faith-based and other community efforts to solve social problems;

(k) to monitor implementation of the President's agenda affecting faith-based and other community organizations; and

(l) to ensure that the efforts of faith-based and other community organizations meet high standards of excellence and accountability.

Sec. 4. *Administration.* (a) The White House OFBCI may function through established or ad hoc committees, task forces, or interagency groups.

(b) The White House OFBCI shall have a staff to be headed by the Assistant to the President for Faith-Based and Community Initiatives. The White House OFBCI shall have such staff and other assistance, to the extent permitted by law, as may be necessary to carry out the provisions of this order. The White House OFBCI operations shall begin no later than 30 days from the date of this order.

(c) The White House OFBCI shall coordinate with the liaison and point of contact designated by each executive department and agency with respect to this initiative.

(d) All executive departments and agencies (agencies) shall cooperate with the White House OFBCI and provide such information, support, and assistance to the White House OFBCI as it may request, to the extent permitted by law.

(e) The agencies' actions directed by this Executive Order shall be carried out subject to the availability of appropriations and to the extent permitted by law.

Sec. 5. *Judicial Review.* This order does not create any right or benefit, substantive or procedural, enforceable at law or equity by a party against the United States, its agencies or instrumentalities, its officers or employees, or any other person.

THE WHITE HOUSE,
January 29, 2001.

Source: Federal Register 66:21 (January 31, 2001).

Appendix 3: Executive Order 13279 of December 16, 2002

EQUAL PROTECTION OF THE LAWS FOR FAITH-BASED AND COMMUNITY ORGANIZATIONS

By the authority vested in me as President by the Constitution and the laws of the United States of America, including section 121(a) of title 40, United States Code, and section 301 of title 3, United States Code, and in order to guide Federal agencies in formulating and developing policies with implications for faith-based organizations and other community organizations, to ensure equal protection of the laws for faith-based and community organizations, to further the national effort to expand opportunities for, and strengthen the capacity of, faith-based and other community organizations so that they may better meet social needs in America's communities, and to ensure the economical and efficient administration and completion of Government contracts, it is hereby ordered as follows:

Section 1. *Definitions.* For purposes of this order:

(a) "Federal financial assistance" means assistance that non-Federal entities receive or administer in the form of grants, contracts, loans, loan guarantees, property, cooperative agreements, food commodities, direct appropriations, or other assistance, but does not include a tax credit, deduction, or exemption.

(b) "Social service program" means a program that is administered by the Federal Government, or by a State or local government using Federal financial assistance, and that provides services directed at reducing poverty, improving opportunities for low-income children, revitalizing low-income communities, empowering low-income families and low-income individuals to become self-sufficient, or otherwise helping people in need. Such programs include, but are not limited to, the following:

(i) child care services, protective services for children and adults, services for children and adults in foster care, adoption services, services related to the management and maintenance of the home, day care services for adults, and services to meet the special needs of children, older individuals, and individuals with disabilities (including physical, mental, or emotional disabilities);

(ii) transportation services;

(iii) job training and related services, and employment services;

(iv) information, referral, and counseling services;

(v) the preparation and delivery of meals and services related to soup kitchens or food banks;

(vi) health support services;

(vii) literacy and mentoring programs;

(viii) services for the prevention and treatment of juvenile delinquency and substance abuse, services for the prevention of crime and the provision of assistance to the victims and the families of criminal offenders, and services related to intervention in, and prevention of, domestic violence; and

(ix) services related to the provision of assistance for housing under Federal law.

(c) "Policies that have implications for faith-based and community organizations" refers to all policies, programs, and regulations, including official guidance and internal agency procedures, that have significant effects on faith-based organizations participating in or seeking to participate in social service programs supported with Federal financial assistance.

(d) "Agency" means a department or agency in the executive branch.

(e) "Specified agency heads" mean the Attorney General, the Secretaries of Agriculture, Education, Health and Human Services, Housing and Urban Development, and Labor, and the Administrator of the Agency for International Development.

Sec. 2. *Fundamental Principles and Policymaking Criteria.*
In formulating and implementing policies that have implications for faith-based and community organizations, agencies that administer social service programs supported with Federal financial assistance shall, to the extent permitted by law, be guided by the following fundamental principles:

(a) Federal financial assistance for social service programs should be distributed in the most effective and efficient manner possible;

(b) The Nation's social service capacity will benefit if all eligible organizations, including faith-based and other community organizations, are able to compete on an equal footing for Federal financial assistance used to support social service programs;

(c) No organization should be discriminated against on the basis of religion or religious belief in the administration or distribution of Federal financial assistance under social service programs;

(d) All organizations that receive Federal financial assistance under social services programs should be prohibited from discriminating against beneficiaries or potential beneficiaries of the social services programs on the basis of religion or religious belief. Accordingly, organizations, in providing services supported in whole or in part with Federal financial assistance, and in their outreach activities related to such services, should not be allowed to discriminate against current or prospective program beneficiaries on the basis of religion, a religious belief, a refusal to hold a religious belief, or a refusal to actively participate in a religious practice;

(e) The Federal Government must implement Federal programs in accordance with the Establishment Clause and the Free Exercise Clause of the First Amendment to the Constitution. Therefore, organizations that engage in inherently religious activities, such as worship, religious instruction, and proselytization, must offer those services separately in time or location from any programs or services supported with direct Federal financial assistance, and participation in any such inherently religious activities must be voluntary for the beneficiaries of the social service program supported with such Federal financial assistance; and

(f) Consistent with the Free Exercise Clause and the Free Speech Clause of the Constitution, faith-based organizations should be eligible to compete for Federal financial assistance used to support social service programs and to participate fully in the social service programs supported with Federal financial assistance without impairing their independence, autonomy, expression, or religious character. Accordingly, a faith-based organization that applies for or participates in a social service program supported with Federal financial assistance may retain its independence and may continue to carry out its mission, including the definition, development, practice, and expression of its religious beliefs, provided that it does not use direct Federal financial assistance to support any inherently religious activities, such as worship, religious instruction, or proselytization. Among other things, faith-based organizations that receive Federal financial assistance may use their facilities to provide social services supported with Federal financial assistance, without removing or altering religious art, icons, scriptures, or other symbols from these facilities. In addition, a faith-based organization that applies for or participates in a social service program supported with Federal financial assistance may retain religious terms in its organization's name, select its board members on a religious basis, and include religious references in its organization's mission statements and other chartering or governing documents.

Sec. 3. *Agency Implementation.*

(a) Specified agency heads shall, in coordination with the White House Office of Faith-Based and Community Initiatives (White House OFBCI), review and evaluate existing policies that have implications for faith-based and community organizations in order to assess the consistency of such policies with the fundamental principles and policymaking criteria articulated in section 2 of this order.

(b) Specified agency heads shall ensure that all policies that have implications for faith-based and community organizations are consistent with the fundamental principles and policymaking criteria articulated in section 2 of this order. Therefore, specified agency heads shall, to the extent permitted by law:

(i) amend all such existing policies of their respective agencies to ensure that they are consistent with the fundamental principles and policymaking criteria articulated in section 2 of this order;

(ii) where appropriate, implement new policies for their respective agencies that are consistent with and necessary to further the fundamental principles and policymaking criteria set forth in section 2 of this order; and

(iii) implement new policies that are necessary to ensure that their respective agencies collect data regarding the participation of faith-based and community organizations in social service programs that receive Federal financial assistance.

(c) Within 90 days after the date of this order, each specified agency head shall report to the President, through the Director of the White House OFBCI, the actions it proposes to undertake to accomplish the activities set forth in sections 3(a) and (b) of this order.

Sec. 4. *Amendment of Executive Order 11246.*
Pursuant to section 121(a) of title 40, United States Code, and section 301 of title 3, United States Code, and in order to further the strong Federal interest in ensuring that the cost and progress of Federal procurement contracts are not adversely affected by an artificial restriction of the labor pool caused by the unwarranted exclusion of faith-based organizations from such contracts, section 204 of Executive Order 11246 of September 24, 1965, as amended, is hereby further amended to read as follows:
"SEC. 204 (a) The Secretary of Labor may, when the Secretary deems that special circumstances in the national interest so require, exempt a contracting agency from the requirement of including any or all of the provisions of Section 202 of this Order in any specific contract, subcontract, or purchase order.

(b) The Secretary of Labor may, by rule or regulation, exempt certain classes of contracts, subcontracts, or purchase orders (1) whenever work is to be or has been performed outside the United States and no recruitment of workers within the limits of the United States is involved; (2) for standard commercial supplies or raw materials; (3) involving less than specified amounts of money or specified numbers of workers; or (4) to the extent that they involve subcontracts below a specified tier.

(c) Section 202 of this Order shall not apply to a Government contractor or subcontractor that is a religious corporation, association, educational institution, or society, with respect to the employment of individuals of a particular religion to perform work connected with the carrying on by such corporation, association, educational institution, or society of its activities. Such contractors and subcontractors are not exempted or excused from complying with the other requirements contained in this Order.

(d) The Secretary of Labor may also provide, by rule, regulation, or order, for the exemption of facilities of a contractor that are in all respects separate and distinct from activities of the contractor related to the performance of the contract: provided, that such an exemption will not interfere with or impede the effectuation of the purposes of this Order: and provided further, that in the absence of such an exemption all facilities shall be covered by the provisions of this Order."

Sec. 5. *General Provisions.*

(a) This order supplements but does not supersede the requirements contained in Executive Orders 13198 and 13199 of January 29, 2001.

(b) The agencies shall coordinate with the White House OFBCI concerning the implementation of this order.

(c) Nothing in this order shall be construed to require an agency to take any action that would impair the conduct of foreign affairs or the national security.

Sec. 6. *Responsibilities of Executive Departments and Agencies.* All executive departments and agencies (agencies) shall:

(a) designate an agency employee to serve as the liaison and point of contact with the White House OFBCI; and

(b) cooperate with the White House OFBCI and provide such information, support, and assistance to the White House OFBCI as it may request, to the extent permitted by law.

Sec. 7. *Judicial Review.*

This order is intended only to improve the internal management of the executive branch, and it is not intended to, and does not, create any right or benefit, substantive or procedural, enforceable at law or in equity by a party against the United States, its agencies, or entities, its officers, employees or agents, or any person.

THE WHITE HOUSE,
December 12, 2002.

Source: Federal Register 67:241 (December 16, 2002).

Appendix 4: Executive Order 13280 of December 16, 2002

RESPONSIBILITIES OF THE DEPARTMENT OF AGRICULTURE AND THE AGENCY FOR INTERNATIONAL DEVELOPMENT WITH RESPECT TO FAITH-BASED AND COMMUNITY INITIATIVES

By the authority vested in me as President by the Constitution and the laws of the United States of America, and in order to help the Federal Government coordinate a national effort to expand opportunities for faith-based and other community organizations and to strengthen their capacity to better meet social needs in America's communities, it is hereby ordered as follows:

Section 1. *Establishment of Centers for Faith-Based and Community Initiatives at the Department of Agriculture and the Agency for International Development.* (a) The Secretary of Agriculture and the Administrator of the Agency for International Development shall each establish within their respective agencies a Center for Faith-Based and Community Initiatives (Center).

(b) Each of these Centers shall be supervised by a Director, appointed by the agency head in consultation with the White House Office of Faith-Based and Community Initiatives (White House OFBCI).

(c) Each agency shall provide its Center with appropriate staff, administrative support, and other resources to meet its responsibilities under this order.

(d) Each Center shall begin operations no later than 45 days from the date of this order.

Sec. 2. *Purpose of Executive Branch Centers for Faith-Based and Community Initiatives.* The purpose of the agency Centers will be to coordinate agency efforts to eliminate regulatory, contracting, and other programmatic obstacles to the participation of faith-based and other community organizations in the provision of social services.

Sec. 3. *Responsibilities of the Centers for Faith-Based and Community Initiatives.* Each Center shall, to the extent permitted by law:

(a) conduct, in coordination with the White House OFBCI, an agency-wide audit to identify all existing barriers to the participation of faith-based and other community organizations in the delivery of social services by the agency, including but not limited to regulations, rules, orders, procurement, and other internal policies and practices, and outreach activities that either facially discriminate against or otherwise discourage or disadvantage the participation of faith-based and other community organizations in Federal programs;

(b) coordinate a comprehensive agency effort to incorporate faith-based and other community organizations in agency programs and initiatives to the greatest extent possible;

(c) propose initiatives to remove barriers identified pursuant to section 3(a) of this order, including but not limited to reform of regulations, procurement, and other internal policies and practices, and outreach activities;

(d) propose the development of innovative pilot and demonstration programs to increase the participation of faith- based and other community organizations in Federal as well as State and local initiatives; and

(e) develop and coordinate agency outreach efforts to disseminate information more effectively to faith-based and other community organizations with respect to programming changes, contracting opportunities, and other agency initiatives, including but not limited to Web and Internet resources.

Sec. 4. *Reporting Requirements.*

(a) Report. Not later than 180 days from the date of this order and annually thereafter, each of the two Centers described in section 1 of this order shall prepare and submit a report to the White House OFBCI.

(b) Contents. The report shall include a description of the agency's efforts in carrying out its responsibilities under this order, including but not limited to:

(i) a comprehensive analysis of the barriers to the full participation of faith-based and other community organizations in the delivery of social services identified pursuant to section 3(a) of this order and the proposed strategies to eliminate those barriers; and

(ii) a summary of the technical assistance and other information that will be available to faith-based and other community organizations regarding the program activities of the agency and the preparation of applications or proposals for grants, cooperative agreements, contracts, and procurement.

(c) Performance Indicators. The first report, filed 180 days after the date of this order, shall include annual performance indicators and measurable objectives for agency action. Each report filed thereafter shall measure the agency's performance against the objectives set forth in the initial report.

Sec. 5. *Responsibilities of the Secretary of Agriculture and the Administrator of the Agency for International Development.* The Secretary and the Administrator shall:

(a) designate an employee within their respective agencies to serve as the liaison and point of contact with the White House OFBCI; and

(b) cooperate with the White House OFBCI and provide such information, support, and assistance to the White House OFBCI as it may request, to the extent permitted by law.

Sec. 6. *Administration and Judicial Review.* (a) The agency actions directed by this executive order shall be carried out subject to the availability of appropriations and to the extent permitted by law.

(b) This order is not intended to, and does not, create any right or benefit, substantive or procedural, enforceable at law or equity by a party against the United States, its agencies, or entities, its officers, employees or agents, or any other person.

THE WHITE HOUSE,
December 12, 2002.

Source: Federal Register 67:241 (December 16, 2002).

Index

About the Author

Anthony Stanford is a freelance writer and journalist in the Chicago, Illinois, area. Among his many published works are cutting-edge *Chicago Tribune* perspectives on politics, race, and religion, including articles such as "Race as a Burning Issue" and "On a Day of Rebirth, Grieving a Loss of Faith." Stanford writes a column for the Sun-Times Media Group.